D1481420

'As leaders of people, we are rightfully committed to looking for the good, finding the right fit, and developing people's potential. [But] in this book, MacRae reminds us that we ignore the "dark side" at our own peril. *Dark Social* gives us a glimpse behind the curtain, provides evidence-based insights as to why people act as they do, and further deepens that learning with well-reported case studies. In an era where so much time is spent both working and socializing in a virtual context, much can be learned from the research and insight delivered in this book.'

Roberta Sawatzky, Professor, Okanagan School of Business

'The world has faced many shocks in the past decades … and so it's more important than ever to understand the brain, the mind and our behaviour – how we can deploy both analytical thinking and social and emotional skills to optimise brain performance. In *Dark Social,* Ian MacRae effectively exposes these vital issues.'

Harris A. Eyre MD PhD and William Hynes DPhil,
co-leaders of the Neuroscience-inspired Policy Initiative of the
Organisation for Economic Co-operation and Development

'A captivating compendium of all that is light and dark about the human personality, and an essential guide to the angels and demons lurking within 21st-century workplaces and virtual environments. Like the *Divine Comedy*, MacRae guides us through the tiered levels of treachery as mankind's mind melds with machines – from fake news to online bullying – yet leads us to a brighter conclusion: just as our virtual lives can lead to Machiavellian ends, so too can they offer a substrate for wellbeing, growth, and benevolence. MacRae masterfully shines a light into the darkest crevices of our virtual world to produce a work that is destined to become lighthouse for all who aspire to mindfully navigate our brave new, often dimly-lit, virtual world.'

Jessica Carson, Director of Innovation,
American Psychological Association

'In *Dark Social*, Ian MacRae offers a wonderfully nuanced exploration of our behaviour in person and in cyberspace. He convincingly demonstrates the many shades of grey in all personality traits, and their potential for good and ill, and offers eminently practical strategies to bring out the best in ourselves and others. I discovered countless insights for my own life and I would heartily recommend this book to anyone who wishes to improve their working relationships and clean up their online persona.'

David Robson, science writer and author of
The Intelligence Trap

'If you've ever wondered about the psychological cost of our culture of constant connection, this book is for you. With a focus on the workplace, MacRae covers all aspects of what "always being on" means for people, organizations and, ultimately, human society.'

Damita Pressl, news anchor and journalist,
Kronen Zeitung

dark social

understanding the darker side of work, personality and social media

Ian MacRae

BLOOMSBURY BUSINESS
LONDON • OXFORD • NEW YORK • NEW DELHI • SYDNEY

BLOOMSBURY BUSINESS
Bloomsbury Publishing Plc
50 Bedford Square, London, WC1B 3DP, UK
29 Earlsfort Terrace, Dublin 2, Ireland

BLOOMSBURY, BLOOMSBURY BUSINESS and the Diana logo are trademarks of
Bloomsbury Publishing Plc

First published in Great Britain 2021

Copyright © Ian MacRae, 2021

Ian MacRae has asserted his right under the Copyright, Designs and Patents Act, 1988, to be identified as
Author of this work

For legal purposes the Acknowledgements on p. 10 constitute an extension of this copyright page

All rights reserved. No part of this publication may be reproduced or transmitted in any form or by
any means, electronic or mechanical, including photocopying, recording, or any information storage or
retrieval system, without prior permission in writing from the publishers

Bloomsbury Publishing Plc does not have any control over, or responsibility for, any third-party websites
referred to or in this book. All internet addresses given in this book were correct at the time of going to
press. The author and publisher regret any inconvenience caused if addresses have changed or sites have
ceased to exist, but can accept no responsibility for any such changes

A catalogue record for this book is available from the British Library

Library of Congress Cataloguing-in-Publication data has been applied for

ISBN   978-1-4729-8312-1; eBook   978-1-4729-8313-8

2 4 6 8 10 9 7 5 3 1

Typeset by Deanta Global Publishing Services, Chennai, India
Printed and bound in Great Britain by CPI Group (UK) Ltd, Croydon CR0 4YY

MIX
Paper from
responsible sources
FSC
www.fsc.org   FSC® C020471

To find out more about our authors and books visit www.bloomsbury.com
and sign up for our newsletters

For Brendan and Elizabeth MacRae

Contents

A note on case studies   9
Acknowledgements   10
Foreword by Michelle Carvill   11

SECTION ONE THE DARK SIDE OF PERSONALITY
AND BEHAVIOUR ONLINE   15

1   The dark side of personality – in cyberspace   17
2   Bad apples or bad barrels?   22
3   How big are the barrels? The effect of
    filter bubbles   31
4   Who builds the barrels? How social media
    shapes behaviour   38
5   Maybe they're born with it, maybe they've
    developed a personality disorder   50

SECTION TWO THE CONTINUUM OF PERSONALITY
AND OPTIMALITY   63

6   The dark side of brightness   65
7   The bright side of darkness   74
8   Teams, personality clashes and conflict   89
9   The 'true self' online and offline   103
10 How leaders succeed   116
11 How leaders fail   127

SECTION THREE PERSONALITY STYLES
AND WORK   139

12   Cluster A – The eccentric personality styles   141
13   Cluster B – The assertive personality styles   152
14   Cluster C – The anxious personality styles   168
15   Personality styles and dysfunction at work   177
16   Identifying personality disorders at work   188

SECTION FOUR TOXIC ORGANIZATIONS
AND SYSTEMS   199

17   The social (media) context   201
18   The rapid spread of toxic ideas   209
19   Toxic digital leadership   221
20   Automated amplification of toxicity   231
21   Colluding followers   238
22   Online conspiracy theories, fear and isolation   249
23   Toxic leadership – an applied example   258

Afterword   268
References   271
Index   282

A note on case studies

To protect individual privacy in the case studies in this book, some identifying facts and noncritical clinical information has been altered.

The case studies are based on real people, many of whom have not been identified by name. These are real examples from interviews with contacts and colleagues. The behaviours, approaches and work context is explained, but in some cases the identity of the topic of the case study is not provided. In these, some minor details may have been changed to protect the identity of the person. For example, their name may not be used, their exact job title may not be given, or their general roles and responsibilities may be explained without the specific organization they work for being mentioned. In other cases, some details may be changed to protect the identity of the topic or the people who were interviewed.

Acknowledgements

I would like to express my profound thanks to everyone who contributed to this book, shared their stories and provided case studies. While I would normally name every person who contributed, this book covers many issues that are sensitive, personal or confidential, so to protect the identities of everyone who contributed, the names will not be printed here.

Thank you so much to everyone who provided insight, your experience and your stories to this book. The personal context and knowledge from so many people of different backgrounds and experiences really helps to illustrate how important these topics are, and the impact (positive or negative) that people can make on others' lives, careers and mental health. Thank you so much for contributing to this book.

Foreword

It's fair to say that social media technologies are now firmly embedded as natural channels of communication across the world. Regardless of whether you're using popular platforms such as Facebook, Instagram, Twitter, WeChat, YouTube or LinkedIn (and the range of others) for personal or business use – daily, weekly, (perhaps even hourly) – it's highly likely that your children, grandchildren, colleagues, clients, customers, employees, prospective customers, prospective employers and even investors are engaged to a greater or lesser degree with these far-reaching and totally pervasive connected technologies. And of course, there's a range of dedicated internal-facing social media channels. Whether it's a popular one such as WhatsApp, Telegram or Slack, or a bespoke social intranet, connected technologies are a key component of our existence.

Social media technologies have democratized global connectivity, giving everyone a 'voice'. Whether that's the voice of incensed or enthused teenagers to drive a global message on climate change, aggrieved customers demanding better service levels, under-represented or silenced individuals sharing their story, or world leaders using the channels to influence and campaign, social media provides a world stage for individuals, organizations, governments and world leaders to connect, communicate, build communities, serve, share, learn, advise, rant, educate, raise awareness, raise funds – and let's not forget, to advertise and target messages directly into the hands of those chosen to influence. Love them or hate them … the opportunities of such mass connectivity are vast.

Over the past couple of decades, as these platforms have evolved to become a natural thread in the fabric of everyday life, we've seen a lot of news stories about both the positive and negative aspects of social media. The platforms have been put to good use in a variety of ways, from building evidence in major crimes, galvanizing collective support for meaningful campaigns, to bringing communities together to effect change, to name but a few. But of course, as with anything we shine a light on for bringing good into the world, there is of course a darker, 'shadow' side. Fake news, cyber-attacks, manipulated algorithms, conspiracy theories, toxic leadership... I could go on.

As a marketer, excited from the inception of these platforms by the genuine human-to-human connectivity afforded, when I've consulted, trained, mentored and written about social media, my focus has always amplified the importance of genuinely 'being social'. We are who we are, and whether we're in a room, a meeting, an office or online, our personality and traits will inevitably play a key part in our social engagement with others. Realistically, the technologies are simply enablers of human connectivity. Therefore, what we do with the channels, the content we share, the way we respond, the communities we join, the messages we buy into, are really but a reflection of who we are.

What Ian has brought to light so clearly with *Dark Social* is that virtual social environments are not separate from in-person social environments. And with that social environment comes all the fascinating complexities and differences in personality, traits and disorders we remarkable humans occupy.

Given our growing reliance upon connected social technologies, particularly in the workplace (which became ever more evident over the initial 18 months of the global COVID-19 pandemic), it's never been more important for organizations and individuals, particularly those charged with engaging others into the workplace, to fully understand how the dynamics of social media technologies and personality are inextricably linked.

Our behaviours are our behaviours, people do not have different personalities or a different sense of self whether online or offline – but of course, social technologies provide a far-reaching stage on which to play, connect, influence and exist. This gives opportunity for those personalities and behaviours (not all of them positive) to become magnified and amplified online.

Personally, for me, whilst there is so much to take from this book, I admire and respect how Ian has masterfully married the psychology and sociology of who we are as individuals and what this means for the way we behave in digital environments – the influences, the challenges, the human endeavour. The insight contained herein poses some serious considerations for the workplace and leadership – whilst all the time considering the impact of far-reaching connected technologies and why we need to be mindful of their opportunity to amplify and magnify behaviour.

Humans are social animals, and as Ian outlines at one point, social animals are wired for social contact. What *Dark Social* brings is an intellectual, practical and smart understanding of what it means for technology and humans to have that 'social contact' – how our psychology engages with the technology and how the technology impacts our psychology.

In my view, understanding our 'connected' behaviours is an important next stage in the evolution of social technologies. Bravo to Ian for stepping onto this important next stage – and to the reader, I have no doubt you'll take as much important insight from *Dark Social* as I did.

Michelle Carvill
Author and founder of Carvill Creative

The Dark Side of Personality and Behaviour Online

I

The dark side of personality – in cyberspace

People are social animals. From their earliest experiences, human development is shaped by social experiences. People learn who they are in the context of who they are around other people and how others interact with them. While there are innate, inborn psychological traits and characteristics, they interact with the environment. That environment is inherently social.

Social relationships have been moving online for more people, and more often. While this trend has emerged relatively quickly over the 21st century, 2020 was the year that flipped a switch. The international COVID crisis meant that people all over the world had to keep physical distance from their friends, their family, their colleagues and even from strangers to slow the spread of the virus.

The obvious solution was to take whatever tools and resources we had available to move social interaction online wherever possible. The tools were available, and digital communication tools have existed for a long time but were only ever the default for a relatively small minority of people.

All of a sudden the issues that had been simmering away in the background, like the role of social media on social interaction, fragmenting opinion, fake news and filter bubbles became even more relevant. Understanding how to motivate and engage people, and monitor their performance when they weren't in the same room, became critical. Keeping teams working, people collaborating and connected when they didn't occupy a shared physical space was essential.

> Filter bubble: A situation where a person or group of people only encounters information that tends to be consistent with their current beliefs (Carvill & MacRae, 2020).

Yet much of the research about how digital communication tools affect our social relationships, our communication and even our sense of our selves is in its infancy. What are the consequences of our social interactions being dominated by online spaces?

There are certainly advantages to being connected, but no tools or technology are free of costs or consequences. The tools we use to communicate and develop a sense of ourselves, of other people and of social relationships colour everything they touch. There are opportunities to this, but there is also a dark side.

That's why the title of this book is *Dark Social*. 'Dark Social' has been used as a marketing term to refer to all of the 'dark' areas of social media that we can't assess with basic metrics, like page views, clicks or 'engagements'. It's all of the communication that happens outside of the heavily monitored social media spaces like Facebook or Twitter; it's the information that advertisers and market researchers have trouble accessing.

In this book, I'd like to extend the idea of 'Dark Social' a bit further. It's all of the psychological processes that happen that may not be immediately visible or measurable. It's the conscious and unconscious psychological factors at play online, acting in concert with the invisible algorithms working to shape behaviour. For all of the people using social technologies publicly online – we can see what they are saying and sharing, but not necessarily what they are thinking. In some ways, there's a large unconscious part of the Internet. There are algorithms working away behind the scenes, although their activities are not necessarily observable to anyone. They pick and choose and filter content, send notifications and even interact with different people, in different ways, depending on the person's behaviour.

There are feedback systems that happen largely out of sight, affecting which people are connected, and which are not, who is shown what content, and whose content is shown to others. Every person who uses the Internet provides input which governs what they see – although the underlying process is largely invisible to any single user.

In some ways, 'Dark Social' could be seen as Jungian 'shadow psychology'. These are all of the invisible processes that go on under the surface, but we can't easily access. But 'Dark Social' also refers to what personality psychologists often refer to as the 'dark side', meaning personality disorders: the destructive and malicious behaviours that come out, and the dark side of what can be positive traits. This book will go into depth on the dark and light sides of different personality traits and styles, especially in Chapters 7, 8 and 12–14. Many of the other chapters will explore related elements of personality psychology, looking at different types of personalities that can be effective, or optimal, for certain circumstances, especially in the context of work and social relationships, but then become 'dark' or destructive in others.

It introduces aspects of online environments and digital social relationships in the context of how they can affect people individually, but also the larger forces that influence individuals and groups. Because so much of social interaction happens online, and social interaction is such a fundamental part of who we are and how we relate to others, it's impossible now to look at social interaction or communication without looking at the role of different forms of communication, in particular, online.

Key themes

There are three key themes that will be revisited and explained throughout this book.

1. **Online behaviour is an extension of offline characteristics.** People's reactions are influenced by different environments (including online environments), but the underlying psychological processes are remarkably similar. Online behaviour is an extension of behaviour in general: it is not fundamentally different in online spaces than it is in physical spaces.

2. **People can improve**. Understanding the internal forces (such as personality) as well as the external forces (such as the social environment) can help people change their behaviour and improve themselves and have a positive influence on others around them.

3. **Work can get better.** The social environment has a profound impact on people, their work, their productivity and their wellbeing. By actively trying to improve these environments work can be better *for* people and bring out the best *from* people.

Many of the issues discussed in this book *seem* new, but are new manifestations of problems, concerns and anxieties that people have had for decades, centuries or even longer. Worries about fake news and propaganda are centuries old. One persistent worry about social media and digital technology is the concerns that are raised about privacy. This is a timeless problem. When the Austrian empire introduced house numbers as a mandatory part of their census-collecting in the 19th century, there was an outcry against the government's invasion of privacy: people worried it would make it easier for the government to enforce new taxes and conscription (Rady, 2020). That's not to say concerns about new technologies are unfounded, but we will be much more equipped to deal with them when we understand them in both psychological and historical contexts.

Discussions of concepts like social media bubbles, fake news, misinformation and conspiracy theories are not new. We understand a great deal about how they form, why they exist and even how to counter them. While the pace of technological and social change can seem overwhelming, understanding and situating some of these issues within past research, psychology and history can make it seem more manageable and comprehensible.

SECTIONS OUTLINE

To do this, the chapters are grouped together in general themes.

The first section (Chapters 1–5) lays out key psychological principles, especially in relation to individual differences of personality and personality disorders. They outline some key psychological findings, then explain how those principles help us understand people's personality and behaviour in cyberspace as well as in the physical world.

The second section (Chapters 6–11) moves towards individual differences, especially personality psychology and the focus on workplace psychology. This helps to narrow down the focus to understanding personality and personality disorders specifically in the workplace and virtual workplace settings.

The third section (Chapters 12–16) delves much more deeply into different disordered personality styles, to look at very specific patterns of behaviour and how they can be adaptive or dysfunctional at work in general, in specific types of work, and how they look in online environments.

Finally, section four (Chapters 17–23) focuses more on the larger-scale trends and the destructive tendencies that spread so easily online. From the impact of fear and isolation, from amplification by bots, emotional contagion and the rapid spread of conspiracy theories, section four explains some of the psychological processes behind these trends.

The book moves from individual level factors and development, then 'zooms out' to team, group and then organizational level factors, eventually looking at the broader environment, technology and trends that affect everyone. The case studies throughout bring together many of the points from different chapters to illustrate how the different concepts look in the real world of people's lives and the workplace.

2

Bad apples or bad barrels?

The perennial questions about the dark side of personality and dark and destructive behaviour are: where does it come from? Whose fault is it? In any group or organization when something goes wrong, the first instinct is usually to look for scapegoats. Whenever one person or a group of people get caught for unethical, illegal or destructive behaviour, the organization tends to default on individual blame and responsibility. A few people get fired and the actions are explained away as just the work of a few bad apples who were working alone and who do not represent the group or the organization.

Obviously, the 'bad apple' explanation is rarely the whole story. The majority of this book will explain the unique characteristics of personality disorders and how they can be extraordinarily adaptive in some environments but incredibly destructive in others. However it is necessary to look at how toxic environments, relationships and companies can induce the most psychologically healthy and even the most normal of workers into unethical behaviour.

How could violence or even murder in institutions like the police or armed forces occur solely because of a few bad apples? This chapter looks at how some institutional elements can contribute to a toxic environment, and then uses a specific example from the US Armed Forces prisoner torture in Abu Ghraib. Perhaps when bad behaviour within a company or institution is exceptionally rare and uncharacteristic it could be the responsibility of a few bad apples. Yet often these large and catastrophic errors or inability to identify the bad apples is symptomatic of a bigger problem within a group or an organization. Letting bad behaviour carry on without oversight or consequence to the offenders is a systematic problem – a symptom of bad barrels, not just bad apples.

GENETICS V. ENVIRONMENT

While personality disorders are still a rapidly developing area of psychological research, we do know a great deal about the brain structures and functions involved in personality disorder, and we know some of the main causes of personality disorder and dysfunction and how to spot it early in people's lives and careers (see Chapter 5). Are people born rotten? Not exactly, but some people are born with a much higher *risk* of being corrupted by bad barrels.

We also know that a significant amount of the variance in personality disorders is heritable. Between about 55–75 per cent of the variation is caused by genetic predispositions (Treadway, 2015), but a genetic disposition is not a guarantee (as will be discussed in greater detail in Chapter 5). Certain situations, risk factors and stressors can trigger or exacerbate destructive behaviour.

However, individual differences in personality should not be used as absolution from bad, or even illegal, behaviour. We will return to this discussion in later chapters, but this chapter focuses on the situational and environmental factors that can cause people to behave badly. This is particularly important in the workplace, where companies and employers define the culture, attitudes and behaviours that are desirable and necessary within the working environment.

There are two landmark studies in psychology that help to highlight the social and environmental factors that explain why otherwise normal, psychologically healthy people do destructive things.

1. The Milgram experiment – obedience to authority
In the 1960s Stanley Milgram was interested in the reasons given by Nazis for their genocide during World War II. During the Nuremberg Trials, many of the Nazi war criminals defended themselves with some variation of 'I was just following orders'. Milgram's research tested the validity of that assertion: 'Could it be that Eichmann and his million accomplices in the Holocaust were just following orders? Could we call them all accomplices?' (Milgram, 1974).

Milgram's landmark study was set up to test the degree to which participants would follow orders from an authority figure. Participants, however, were not told of the real purpose of the study. Instead, they were told they were participating in a 'scientific study about learning a memory'. The experimenter (and authority figure) was in charge of the study. Two participants would enter the experiment: one actual participant who knew nothing about the real purpose of the experiment was asked to be the teacher, and another person who was a confederate of the researcher and actor would play the role of the learner.

Key people in Milgram's experiment

Experimenter – in charge of the experiment and the study, the main authority figure.

Teacher – the participant responsible for punishing the learner with electric shocks.

Learner – an actor and confederate who will receive electric shocks as punishment after making errors.

The setup of the experiment was designed to impress upon the teacher the importance and authority of their surroundings, as well as the potential severity of the electric shock punishment. This experiment was set up in the 1960s, so this was not a modern, slick setting of clean white surfaces and backlit electronics. The participant was positioned in front of a large and imposing shock generator with a distinctive 'line of 30 switches, ranging from 15 volts to 450 volts' with labels ranging from 'SLIGHT SHOCK at 15 volts' to 'DANGER – EXTREME SHOCK at 375 volts'. Beyond 420 volts it just displayed 'x x x'.

The teacher is the research participant who is genuinely unaware of the purpose of the experiment, while the learner is an actor who will pretend to receive the shocks of varying severity. The learner will not come to any physical harm during the experiment, but the teacher will believe they are inflicting electric shocks on the learner.

As the learner makes more mistakes, the levels of the shock increase and Milgram (1979) describes the varying levels of discomfort:

75 volts – the learner grunts in discomfort.
120 volts – the learner complains verbally.

150 volts – the learner demands to be released from the experiment.
285 volts – the learner's response can only be described as an 'agonizing scream'.
315 volts – the learner falls silent and unresponsive.

In Milgram's initial experiments, 100 per cent of participants continued the experiment up to 300 volts, and 65 per cent continued to administer the shocks up to the maximum of 450 volts. Milgram notes in *Obedience to Authority* (1974) that it's difficult to convey the intensity of the experiment and the emotions it inflicts on participants without seeing it first-hand. 'For the subject, the situation is not a game; conflict is intense and obvious' (p. 4). There's an intense conflict between the influence of orders from an authority figure and the intense discomfort that results from inflicting pain on another person. And there was little nuance or complexity in the orders. When participants expressed their desire to stop, the experimenter would respond with each of the four prompts:

1. Please continue.
2. The experiment requires that you continue.
3. It is absolutely essential that you continue.
4. You have no other choice, you *must* go on.

If and when participants protested against their participation a fifth time, the experiment would be terminated. Yet, despite the intense pain and possible death they believed they could be causing to the learner, the majority of people completed the experiment, and even the remaining 35 per cent participated well up to a level that could have caused extreme pain.

There's a few lessons from this that are worth taking forward to the next chapters:

1. Given the right circumstances and the right (or wrong) authority figure, most people will do destructive things when they are following orders.
2. Bad behaviour can be the result of external, environmental forces.
3. Although we can explain the external pressures that lead to destructive behaviours, factors like obedience to authority does not absolve people of responsibility for their actions.

It's also worth noting that this experiment, like the next one that we will discuss, was one of the landmark experiments that led to changes in the ethical requirements on human research.

2. The Stanford prison experiment – perceived power

The second landmark study is Philip Zimbardo's infamous Stanford prison experiment in 1971. Zimbardo was studying the effects of power and perceptions of power on potentially bad behaviour. Unlike Milgram's study, Zimbardo's research removed the influence of an authority figure. Instead of obeying an authority figure, Zimbardo set up a mock prison in a Stanford University basement where participants were randomly assigned to the role of either prison guards or prisoners.

The experiment tested a group of 24 young, psychologically healthy and stable college students. The participants took a series of psychological tests which determined they had no underlying physical or psychological health issues. They had no history of psychological disorders, and the screening did not identify any personality disorders or other factors that would indicate they were likely to behave abnormally.

The students were then split up into roles and shifts, and the experiment simulated an extreme power imbalance and psychological experience of captivity and power from the very start. After the initial screening and consent, students who were assigned to the prisoner role were taken from their homes in the simulated arrest by the guards, followed by detention in the makeshift prison.

The guards were provided matching uniforms and equipment and assigned the task of managing, disciplining and monitoring the prisoners. The guards were given little advice on managing the prisoners, there was minimal oversight governing their behaviour, and they had no experience or training in managing a prison. Within days the guards had become aggressive and authoritarian captors, inflicting harsh physical and psychological abuse on the innocent prisoners. Within only a few days, the prison became what Zimbardo (2007) describes as a 'descent into Hell' (p. 39).

One of the most surprising and concerning findings from the research is that the normal and psychologically healthy prison guards very quickly developed elaborate and oppressive techniques to manage and punish the prisoners. But their techniques were incredibly disproportionate and abusive, even though there were no psychological indicators to suggest these young men were uniquely predisposed to violence, aggression or cruelty.

The Stanford prison experiment is one of the prime examples of how a 'bad barrel' like the simulated prison environment can descend extremely quickly into bad behaviour of individuals. Another lesson from the study is the role of authority, and Zimbardo later described how he acted as both the researcher and the prison warden in the experiment. That conflict of roles and responsibilities meant that his personal investment in the study led him to temporarily ignore the suffering of the prisoners in the interest of continuing the study.

Writing retrospectively, Zimbardo emphasizes his own complicity in allowing the abusive behaviour of the guards in the study to go unchecked and unpunished. He explains, in detail, that lack of oversight was one of the major components of the 'bad barrel' understanding of destructive behaviour. Zimbardo said that in his dual role, as researcher and prison warden, he too got caught up in the details of the experiment; he protected and persisted with the experiment because of his own investiture in its continuation. However, he acknowledges in hindsight that it should have been shut down much earlier.

Zimbardo, however, has been one of the strongest advocates of learning from the experience and has been an ongoing advocate for ethical oversight and controls in psychological research. For anyone interested in the story, Zimbardo's book *The Lucifer Effect* (2007) is well worth a read, and a film adaptation of the study came out in 2015, which is instructive.

THE STANFORD PRISON EXPERIMENT RECREATED: THE NIGHTMARE AT ABU GHRAIB

In 2004, the conditions in the original Stanford prison experiment were recreated in a profoundly more dangerous, more threatening and more consequential environment. The photos of American soldiers torturing Iraqi prisoners in Abu Ghraib prison are firmly fixed in much of the world's collective memory (Follath et al., 2006), and are likely some of the most enduring images that will characterize the US's second war in Iraq.

In Abu Ghraib, military prison guards had no training as prison guards; they worked 12-hour shifts with few or no breaks, seven days a week. Prison guards who were normally physically athletic had no time to exercise and did not take regular meals. Guards reported constant fear of prisoners, of Iraqi guards and constant fear of external attack that created mounting exhaustion with little supervision, training or oversight.

Philip Zimbardo served as one of the expert witnesses for the defence of US soldiers who were pictured celebrating the torture of prisoners in Abu Ghraib. He investigated and testified on behalf of members of the US Armed Forces, who were perpetrators of the depraved and sadistic torture. One of the important points in his defence case was that while people are ultimately accountable for their actions, in the situation at Abu Ghraib, like in the Stanford prison experiment, there were systematic factors that created a culture and environment likely to lead to abuse and there was no control or oversight to prevent abuse from happening.

Zimbardo testified that lack of oversight and insufficient training, combined with an environment characterized by severe threats, will create an environment in which most normal, healthy and psychologically balanced people are likely to act destructively. In the case of Abu Ghraib, where a group of soldiers humiliated and tortured Iraqi prisoners, there is obviously no excuse, no escaping the personal accountability of bad behaviour. Yet the responsibility for the atrocities must be shared with the leadership who allowed that environment to develop and fester and failed to provide proper oversight to prevent the abuse from happening.

The example from an Iraqi prison is an extreme one, but it is a useful reminder that systemic factors and environmental influences can lead to abuses of power in 21st-century organizations. Abuse of power may not take the same form as it does for members of the Armed Forces in a military prison, but abuse of power certainly does exist in different forms today.

Bringing Milgram online

Stanley Milgram and Philip Zimbardo's experiments in the 1960s and 1970s may seem to be like old studies from a period of history and psychological research that we have moved far away from. Perhaps people were different back then, would new generations of young people still have the same levels of obedience to authority now, in the 21st century, as they did in the 20th century? What about the different environment? So much of people's lives and communications are mediated by computers and smartphones, perhaps that has fundamentally changed how people interact with, and are influenced by, authority and power?

Or, perhaps not. Milgram's experiment has been replicated in different places and in different ways in the 21st century. The research generally demonstrates that psychologists find similar results now as Milgram observed in the 1960s. Although it is extremely unlikely the Milgram study would be allowed to be replicated in countries like the US or UK today, it was repeated in Poland in 2015 (Dolinksi et al., 2017). In the Polish study, 90 per cent of participants proceeded to deliver all levels of simulated shock.

A French documentary experiment disguised as a game show replicated the Milgram experiment in 2010 (Greenwood, 2018). The idea was to investigate the potential authoritative effects that TV could have on people, suggesting that reality TV generally relied on increasing levels of cruelty and humiliation to attract audiences (Beardsley, 2010). This research found similar results again to Milgram's original study. In this experiment, 80 per cent of participants continued to simulate electric shocks even when they could see it was causing the other person extreme pain.

It's also not too hard to imagine different ways to set up the experiment where people would be willing to deliver the shock. What about setting up a game show or reality TV show where people could deliver electric shocks to people with opposing political viewpoints? Perhaps setting up a livestream channel where the shocks were framed as a prank or hazing that got out of hand. Changing the authority of the experimenter and the parameters of the environment offer all sorts of ways that the same potentially harmful behaviours could appear online today.

Virtually torturing people

Another take on the Milgram experiment was investigated in 2006, when Mel Slater and colleagues at University College London used a virtual character as the recipient of electric shocks instead of a real person. The purpose of this study was not to test obedience to authority, but whether participants would have similar psychological reactions when they knew the person they were being asked to harm was neither a real person nor experiencing any physical pain. Their findings showed (unsurprisingly) that the majority (85 per cent) of participants complied with the instructions to administer shocks to the virtual 'person'. However 15 per cent did withdraw, which is consistent with the results from the Polish and French replications. One of the important findings of this study was that people showed intense discomfort even in response to a crudely simulated virtual person. These results would indicate that the same psychological factors and consequences are at play whether or not people are online or offline, and whether or not their behaviour affects real people.

The findings were significant because Slater and his colleagues showed that people respond in remarkably similar ways to virtual characters as to real people. There are psychological consequences for the torturer, harasser, cyberbully or troll, as well as to the victim. This has been demonstrated consistently in many different studies of simulated social interaction (e.g. Cheetham et al., 2009; Gonzales-Franco et al., 2018). It also confirms that most people will acquiesce to authority figures and torture a virtual character, even though it causes them significant distress to participate.

Advances in both computing and brain-scanning technology means the Milgram experiments can be revisited with computer simulations. In 2009 a group of researchers decided to repeat the Milgram study to examine the effects of delivering electric shocks to a virtual character while observing the brain activity of participants. The results showed that patterns in brain activity were consistent with emotional discomfort but not with empathy. In other words, people found it unpleasant to deliver shocks to a virtual character but were not necessarily empathizing with the character in the same way they would with another person.

This is a developing field, but there are profound implications for how we interact with each other online, and even in how we interact with non-human characters that now serve important functions in many people's lives (Siri, Alexa, Google Home). This leads into some interesting discussions for subsequent sections. In the next chapters we'll look at different social environments online and the impact they can have on people's behaviour.

3

How big are the barrels? The effect of filter bubbles

The environment and the people in it can have powerful effects on human behaviour. This is true in digital spaces as well as in the physical world. This means we need to look at digital spaces like social media platforms as social environments. They still have social and environmental cues that are designed to encourage, reinforce and elicit certain types of behaviours. In fact, they are designed to draw on as much data as possible to elicit or encourage certain behaviours. Their main objective is to capture and keep your attention, and there are consequences of that.

It is important to look at these platforms as social environments that are designed to take advantage of core psychological processes like motivation, attention, reward-seeking, reinforcement and interpersonal relations. Social media platforms capitalize on people's need to be recognized, to belong and to attain social validation. They also make use of attentional and emotional processes: fear, anger and outrage as well as other emotional processes can be used to capture and keep users' attention.

That's not necessarily to say they are inherently *good* or *bad,* but they are products of their design and certainly have positive and negative consequences. When someone spends a significant portion of time on personal social media platforms like Twitter, Instagram and Facebook or on professional social media platforms like LinkedIn, Slack and Teams, those platforms will exert an influence on shaping that person's social world and their views of themselves and other people.

A major advantage of instant access to seemingly limitless amounts of information and social connection is that it potentially broadens access and saves time. Tasks that used to take days in a library can be accomplished in hours or minutes. People can connect all around the world for meetings, discussions, recreation, conferences or any other purpose without having to travel to physical spaces.

WHAT ARE FILTER BUBBLES?

The reality of this ease of access to, and dissemination of, information generally seems to be useful and positive. The opportunity to connect with people anywhere in the world carries the same potential risk of connecting with others as it always has: It's just as easy for those with positive intentions to connect with others as it is for those with more destructive objectives to find targets. Now it's even easier to develop and distribute reams of information, whether the intention behind it is benevolent or malicious. The audience and its appetite is wider and more ravenous.

One of the impressive aspects about information technology over the previous decades is that it has proved remarkably effective at filtering out information. From the overwhelming amount of information, combined with the even more boundless amounts of propaganda, spam, pornography, bot activity and general detritus of the Internet, it is possible to find exactly what you are looking for with only a few clicks and keywords. Search engines have an astounding ability to filter out overwhelming amounts of content to help us identify the precise content we want. However, there is always a dark side of getting exactly what we ask for and that, paradoxically, is 'getting what we ask for'.

Filter bubbles occur when a person or 'a group are only exposed to a very narrow view of information and opinion'. Search engines and social media platforms do this automatically. They filter out all the content they think you probably *don't* want to see, based on your previous activity. Friends or family members you do not interact with frequently online are de-prioritized. News stories and adverts that are not related to your interests rarely or never appear. This has the potential to create 'echo chambers' (Iyengar & Hahn, 2009). Products, services or content that the algorithm thinks you will be interested in are pushed to the front of the queue. Try searching online for baby clothes or holidays and see what adverts follow you around the Internet afterwards.

Filter bubbles are not new

The research into filter bubbles is not new, it actually goes back at least 70 years. Some of the earliest available research looked into religious and political biases of newspapers, particularly in Europe (Müller et al., 2020). Historically, newspapers in some European countries would be polarized and tailored to Catholic or Protestant readership (Borgesius et al., 2016). US elections are often used as an example of political polarization and a fragmented media dominated by filter bubbles, but examination of this goes back to Lazarsfeld and colleagues' book, *The People's Choice* (1944), which is credited as one of the first rigorous social scientific studies on the media's influence of voting intentions.

People have a tendency to look for information they agree with, and social media algorithms have a tendency to show people content similar to previous content they have seen. However, some research also indicates that popularity, social endorsements and recommendations have a greater effect on prioritizing content than political or ideological affiliation (Messing & Westwood, 2012). Anything that is popular enough can burst through bubbles. This tends to be true for most people, except for those on the fringes and extremes. A study by Flaxman and colleagues analysed the online behaviour of 1.2 million Americans. Of the 50,000 who regularly read online news, respondents did have a moderate preference towards news sources that aligned with their political beliefs, but the vast majority consumed a fairly balanced diet of news media and information.

There was a small amount of bias that did exist, but the effect was modest. The vast majority of people tend to be slightly insulated in a bubble, but generally fairly well exposed to different points of view. It's at the extremes that bubbles tend to become more insulated. However, the more socially isolated people are, and the more information people consume digitally, the easier it is to fall down that rabbit hole.

How bubbles are created

Not all filter bubbles are imposed on people; there is a general tendency for people to select information that fits within their own worldview (known as confirmation bias). There's two main, interdependent effects that lead to filter bubbles (Borgesius et al., 2016):

Self-selecting personalization is when people choose content that aligns with their own worldview. Confirmation bias is in play here. For example, people with a strong political ideology are more likely to read sources and stories that tell them what they want to hear or frame issues in a way that aligns with their interpretation. People getting drawn into conspiracy theories search for more information that is congruent with what they already believe or what they want to believe.

Pre-selected personalization is when the information is filtered based on someone else's decisions or an algorithm that chooses content for the person. A newspaper editor is an example of pre-selected personalization: choosing what content readers see. Online personalization algorithms take personalization to a new level though, showing each person a unique set of content specifically tailored to them based on their previous activity. This happens 'without the user's deliberate choice, input, knowledge or consent'.

These two mechanisms for creating bubbles interact too: self-selecting personalization triggers pre-selected personalization. As an example, if you have been searching for 'Flat Earth' conspiracy theories, your social media accounts will be more likely to show you related pages and adverts. YouTube will start recommending conspiracy theory videos and, if you trigger the right keywords, Amazon will be quick to start advertising the tinfoil you might need to make your own hat. Their algorithm knows what people with similar interests are looking for online.

Self-selecting and pre-selected personalization have already been around, but the use of personalization algorithms combined with the availability of data has made this more widespread in recent years. And it's popular because it is useful. Try out search engines like DuckDuckGo that preserve your privacy and limit personalization, and you'll find that while they are good, there is a reason that personalization has been so successful: it's useful. One of the biggest problems is the degree to which algorithms will uncritically offer this personalization (the next chapter explains how people get led from slightly biased but relatively mainstream content into extremely radical or bizarre content very quickly by social media algorithms). Where pre-selected personalization happened in a very limited way with newspapers, TV channels and magazines, it never came close to the level of personalization built into social media platforms. People would choose newspapers, magazines or information sources that broadly fitted into their worldview, but that content was still produced in a way that generated the same content for all subscribers or consumers of that product.

Now everyone gets a unique, personalized appearance. Do you spend more time lingering on the most extreme political content on your feed? Spend a lot of time looking for violent content? Then expect to get a lot more of the same, combined with *even more* extreme content. You don't even have to click on something, your social media algorithms know what you have been looking at.

In this way, people can become more fragmented, falling down rabbit holes that are completely separated from social interaction, untethered from the normal buffers we have of sharing and processing information with people in our direct social bubble (this is discussed in much more detail in Chapter 22 in the context of COVID-19, conspiracy theories and social isolation).

ISSUES RELATED TO SOCIAL MEDIA BUBBLES

There are a range of issues, opportunities and risks associated with filter bubbles in social media, but the key concerns fall into five general areas (Borgesius et al., 2016).

1. **Polarization.** The obvious problem with segmenting and fragmenting groups of people, then personalizing content based on people's preferences and biases, is that it has the potential to push people further apart. People start to have fewer shared experiences because online they are not having similar experiences. They may see different content, advertisements, information sources and be recommended different jobs, social connections and products. The research so far shows this polarization has a modest effect in the centre and has most pronounced effects on the fringes, but it does have the potential to pull people further away from the centre.

2. **New gatekeepers and influencers.** The traditional gatekeepers of information and opinion were people like press barons, public

censors or state regulators. There are always legitimate concerns
with who are the gatekeepers of information and what their
motives are. Now there are new gatekeepers that are content
providers, like app stores, social media platforms and search
engines whose algorithms are the major influencers. They can
bestow favour (and views) and then just as quickly take them
away. For example, estimates suggest Facebook recommended
far-right conspiracy theorist Alex Jones to users around 15
billion times before removing him from the platform in 2018
(see Chapter 12).

3. **Limiting autonomy.** Filter bubbles have the potential to either
increase or diminish personal autonomy and independence.
There is the potential for people to access a seemingly limitless
amount of content online, giving people more choice than they
could ever want in a lifetime. But to make decision-making
easier, algorithms filter out most of the content to provide a
narrow window for each person. What people choose is heavily
influenced by what is presented, so it creates a self-perpetuating
feedback loop. Pre-selected personalization reduces personal
autonomy when people's options online are limited to a very
specific range that has been chosen for them.

4. **Lack of transparency.** One of the major criticisms of
pre-selection filter bubbles is that there is little transparency
about how the algorithms work. They change often, and what
we learn about the algorithm is a limited view from people
reverse-engineering and observing the effects. We know people
are being influenced, and we have some sense of how, but the
full picture is not available.

5. **Social sorting.** Social sorting, or market segmentation, has
always been a part of business activity. It helps to identify groups
and target specific communications to those groups. There are
many legitimate and ethical ways to do this, but problems
arise when the practices are discriminatory or disadvantage
certain groups (e.g. targeting job advertisements at a particular
demographic group). Recent research has found social media
algorithms can introduce significant racial bias into targeted
marketing, even when that is not the advertiser's intention.

Filter bubbles certainly have an effect on people's information ecosystems and can play a key role in membership of groups. For people who are anxious and lonely, any opportunity for group membership, even some of the more toxic groups online, may seem appealing. Just like cults use the acceptance of false information and indoctrination, online cults like QAnon (more on this topic in Chapter 21) use the acceptance of fake news and false information as an important signifier of group membership. In these cases, the content of the fake news becomes less important than the group membership.

Filter bubbles also provide fantastic opportunities for marketing. Social media companies are essentially media and marketing companies, so market segmentation is a natural consequence. The ability to segment users into different categories, use social links and divide people into groups based on what types of products or information they would be willing to 'buy' is a natural consequence of the platform. The question then, if we are revisiting the bad apples v. bad barrels issue in the context of social media, is: Who builds the barrels?

4

Who builds the barrels? How social media shapes behaviour

Any environment elicits certain behaviours. Some of this comes from internal cues, and some from external cues. For many people, those internal cues, like experiences, memories, goals, values and their personalities, shape how they behave in an environment. How does a person act at a party full of their friends or a room full of strangers? In an unfamiliar part of town or on a wilderness holiday? People develop and use mental representations about how they think they should act, and how they want to act, in different environments.

No environment is completely neutral, but some environments are very specifically designed to get people to behave in a certain way. Supermarkets, for example, are very deliberately designed to make people walk in certain directions, take certain paths, put certain products in sightlines, and encourage people to act (and purchase) in very deliberate ways. More businesses are trying to become 'experiences' where, instead of just selling you a product, they provide all of the external cues to hint at specifically how you're intended to think, feel and behave in particular times and circumstances. It's an art as much as a science, and certainly a lucrative business for companies that get it right.

Social media companies are even more deliberately designed; they are social environments that elicit certain behaviours. They are social environments free from any constants of physical space. This means the way that the platforms are designed can have a significant impact on the way people think and act on those platforms. Many people may not be aware that social media platforms are continuously providing them with different signals, cues and consequences, but information that is processed unconsciously can still have a significant impact.

In Chapter 2 we discussed the bad apples v. bad barrels argument about behaviour. Creating an institutional setting that encourages or allows violent or destructive behaviours is relatively easy to set up, and it's not very difficult to get normal, psychologically healthy adults to demonstrate the capacity to do incredibly harmful things to other people. And, as we saw in Chapter 2, even an experienced psychologist can mistakenly set up a harmful environment through a combination of misguided priorities and negligence.

Now, social media is much more immersive and a place for much more naturalistic behaviour than in an experimental setting like a university laboratory or virtual reality testing room. For many people, social media has been a core part of their social environment for years, or even decades. The now defunct MSN Messenger started in 1999 and MySpace started in 2003 and was the dominant platform until being overtaken by Facebook in 2008. But Facebook has been around since 2004, YouTube and Reddit since 2005 and Twitter since 2006. The 2010s brought a host of new platforms from streaming service Twitch (2011), Instagram (2012) and TikTok (2016).

Social media is not just a diversion; many people spend a significant amount of time looking for information, having discussions, exploring ideas and developing a sense of themselves and their relationships with other people and their social environment on social media. The average Internet user spends over two hours on social media per day, and 18–24 year olds spend over three hours per day on social media. More time spent on social media means greater social pressures emerging for those users.

Social interactions are fundamental to human development, and although the nature and structure of communication online may be slightly different, they are fundamentally social platforms. All humans have an innate social capacity, and social relationships influence the development of the individual neurochemistry, along with the way people think and feel and make sense of the world (Magnavita & Anchin, 2014).

How do people learn behaviours?

Although learning is a complex and dynamic process, there are some common processes underlying how people develop behaviours. In some instances, it's actually easier to describe how these operate on social media than in the real world, because much of social media is structured as algorithms and computer programs, coding human interaction as basic building blocks with clear structures and defined parameters; the original behaviourists would have been absolutely fascinated by it.

There are three key psychological theories that are worth mentioning. Each of these has profound roles in how people can be shaped by social media:

1. Classical conditioning

Ivan Pavlov was a Russian physiologist who was researching salivation in dogs in the 1890s. He was looking to measure the quantity of dogs' salivation in response to food. He would attach tubes to the dogs to collect their saliva and present them with food. Pavlov initially predicted that the food would trigger the salivation response, but as the research progressed, he noticed that the dogs would start salivating when they picked up on other cues. The approach of a lab assistant's footsteps was enough to trigger the salivation. His discovery of classical conditioning was accidental, but it was an important advance in understanding the psychology of learning.

Animals (including humans) quickly learn to associate two things when they are often presented together. Salivation is a natural and automatic response to food in dogs; other stimuli can be conditioned to elicit a response to that food. Then later, Pavlov tried other cues, like a ticking metronome and ringing a bell to signal mealtime to the dogs. Both worked to trigger salivation and demonstrated that the response could be connected to unrelated signals (neutral stimuli).

Classical conditioning on social media
Social media uses classical conditioning to train your mind to make associations with previously neutral stimuli in ways you probably don't think about. The best example is probably notifications. Notifications on a PC, laptop or smartphone send a symbol to alert

you of an event. The symbol can be presented in a variety of subtle but meaningful ways. A unique tone or sound, a specific pattern of a tiny notification light on a phone, or even a specific pattern of vibration would seem meaningless to the uninformed observer. But the user has learned that one light means a message, a certain pattern of vibrations means an email and a certain tone indicates a notification from a particular person or application.

This can be positive or negative. Maybe you have learned to associate a particular tone, light or message with a like. Without even opening your phone, you know someone, somewhere, has given you a bit of positive reinforcement and it triggers the production of the pleasure-inducing chemical in your brain, dopamine. That's classical conditioning. The stimulus triggers a feeling of excitement, happiness or pleasure just from the notification, before even checking what it says.

Classical conditioning can also work in the same way with negative emotions. For example, a Slack message notification received from a supervisor or manager. Without knowing the content of the message, this is a neutral stimulus. But after repeated associations, this can be learned to be generally either a positive or a negative. If the message then usually conveys criticism, anger or even unpredictability, anxiety may be a common response to the notification even before seeing the content of the message. In this way, anxiety can become the conditioned response.

2. Operant conditioning

Classical conditioning is a basic learning process, but it certainly does not explain the depth and complexity of learning processes. Another theory of learning is B.F. Skinner's behaviourist approach, which was developed in the 1930s. This is another relatively straightforward theory but is a powerful psychological process.

Operant conditioning teaches an individual to associate a particular behaviour with a specific outcome. In the classic example of his work, he would put a pigeon in a box with a food-delivery system. Then, by encouraging specific behaviours bit by bit, he could get the pigeon to complete complex tasks. By this same process he eventually could teach pigeons to reproduce complex tasks like playing ping pong. If he were alive today, he would probably have a great YouTube channel.

Anyone who has trained a dog knows how operant conditioning works. With a few treats, it's relatively easy to teach a dog simple behaviours like sitting, lying down or jumping. With a bit more effort and operant conditioning, dogs can learn incredibly complex behaviours like guiding blind people, detecting various chemicals or completing obstacle courses.

The critics of operant conditioning would say that people are a bit more complex than just responding to rewards and punishments, which is true. However operant conditioning does still play a strong role in learning and provides an excellent explanation of how social media platforms exert psychological influence.

'Likes', 'endorsements', 'shares', 'kudos' are all points systems that use the principle of operant conditioning to influence behaviour on social media platforms (Muench, 2014).

Operant conditioning on social media

It is not hard to see how operant conditioning works on social media platforms. Indeed, the most popular social media platforms are primarily built around operant conditioning. The reinforcement provided on social media platforms are typically some variation of likes, endorsements or upvotes. Some platforms like Facebook and Instagram try to focus on positive reinforcement by only providing positive interaction buttons, whereas other platforms like YouTube and Reddit allow the user to provide negative endorsements in the form of dislikes or downvotes. But of course, for any social media platform, no interaction or no response tends to be interpreted by users as a negative response.

The consequence of operant conditioning on social media, depending on the context, may or may not be a problem. People tend to repeat the behaviour they get rewarded for, and people's brains interpret likes or social endorsements as extremely pleasurable, just as they would during an in-person social interaction or when getting another type of reward.

3. Social learning

Although classical and operant conditioning are both powerful psychological mechanisms of learning, they still do not explain the full range of behaviour. In 1977 Albert Bandura explained that, although classical and operant conditioning were important, he had two key additions. First, stuff happens (mediating processes) in between the stimulus and the response. In other words, people are not simple computational machines with just inputs and outputs. People think, consider, ponder, reflect on things, and different people with different experiences react in different ways. Second, people can learn behaviours without reinforcement. People can pick up on things without being explicitly told what to do or induced into behaviour. People can learn just from watching others.

People test out behaviours all the time that they have never been taught or rewarded for. People are social creatures and learn by imitating and testing out the behaviours of other people around them. What is the first thing most people do when they are in an unfamiliar country, location or setting? If you have no reference point for the appropriate or expected behaviour, most people look around them and try to imitate what other people are doing.

This is another important influence on how people behave on social media. People look around the platform and see how other people are behaving, or what they are posting. Most platforms have their own distinct social rules. And subgroups within social media platforms also have their own variations on those rules.

That is why it's so important to model desirable behaviour on company social channels like Slack. Desirable behaviour does not automatically emerge naturalistically, people observe what the standards or norms are for behaviour and then seek to emulate it. Then, naturally, people tend to get rewarded when their behaviour matches the social norms (initiating operant conditioning).

Social learning on social media
Many people are relatively familiar with one or a few social media platforms. Perhaps they already have a profile, a network of connections and a general knowledge of who they are talking to, what they want to talk about and how to go about doing it.

But what about someone who is completely new to social media? Or completely new to a platform? A good example of this would be a young graduate who has experience using a range of different social media platforms for communication. Assume they understand the cultural rules and norms for using social media with friends and/or family. They already know how they should interact and how they want to interact with others on platforms they are familiar with like Snapchat, Instagram and WhatsApp.

However, what happens when they enter a new social media environment? For example, moving into their first job and signing up to channels on the company's Slack. They may have never used the software, have no experience on that social network and have little or no experience using social media in a workplace context. The first thing many people will do is look around and explore the platform and the channels. They look to see what other people are posting, what others are saying, how colleagues are talking with each other (formally v. informally, regularly v. infrequently, courteously v. abruptly). Then, they may try and post about similar topics and communicate in a similar way. That's why it's so important for managers and leaders to take an active role in shaping digital communications (MacRae, 2020a) as we will discuss in Chapter 17.

Generally, people can learn from their environment even when they have no prior experience in that environment. It is not always a matter of stimulus and response, action and consequence; people can learn and experiment with behaviours without operant or classical conditioning. Although, once they start to test out behaviours, the other learning mechanisms start kicking in, they start getting likes and positive responses, and there are even companies that are linking corporate compensation and bonus packages to operant conditioning on social media.

Reinforcement schedules

Another psychological concept that is useful to understand in this chapter is reinforcement schedules. Reinforcement schedules are a component of operant conditioning which is used to impact behaviour. Workplaces use different reinforcement schedules in pay, perks and

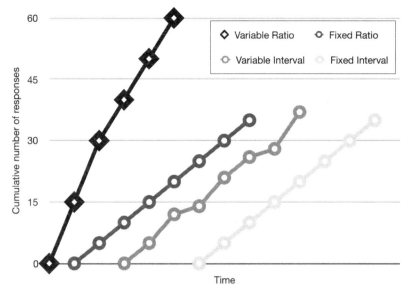

FIGURE 4.1 Reinforcement schedules

benefits packages. Casinos finesse their games to get people to stay and play as long as possible. Social media companies use reinforcement schedules to encourage people to stay online and to return to their platforms (Muench, 2014).

Different schedules of delivering rewards have varying effects on behavioural change. A fixed interval reward schedule, like a monthly salary, is the least effective reinforcement schedule. Whereas a variable ratio schedule, where rewards are provided after an unknown number of responses, tend to be the most effective. Slot machines, which use a variable ratio schedule, are extremely effective at getting people hooked.

Reinforcement schedules act on the dopamine circuits, the reward mechanisms of the brain. Dopamine also tends to be more oriented towards the anticipation of events than the result. Expectation of a reward floods the brain with dopamine, even more so than receiving the reward. The expectation generated by a social media notification actually generates more brain activity than the content of the message.

Reinforcement schedules

Variable ratio – reinforcement is delivered at an unpredictable number of interactions (e.g. after response 1, 2, 6, 13)

> **Fixed ratio** – reinforcement is delivered after a predictable number of interactions (e.g. every 5th correct answer)
>
> **Variable interval** – reinforcement given at unpredictable times (e.g. after 3, 12, 14, 30 minutes)
>
> **Fixed interval** – reinforcement given at fixed time periods (e.g. every 5 minutes, 10 hours, 30 minutes).

Online examples

Let's look at two examples of how this plays out on social media.

1. Facebook tests out a variable-response reinforcement schedule

Think of Facebook as a digital Skinner box. B.F. Skinner put his pigeons in a box to ensure that the only stimuli the pigeons received were the objects or rewards that were designed to elicit or reinforce certain types of behaviour. Social media platforms can affect behaviour in similar ways. People spend time experimenting, trying different behaviours and then certain behaviours are reinforced with likes. This is carefully structured to maximize people's interactions and time online. It is not quite the real-time or naturalistic environment that it can appear to be. Facebook notifications do not happen in real time. Notifications work on their own reinforcement schedule, designed to attract and hold your attention for as much time as possible (Ravenscraft, 2019). Notifications on Facebook are not a simple timeline of events; they are based on carefully crafted algorithms designed to capture, keep and then recapture users' attention.

A Facebook notification is not the same as an interaction with a friend, and the way notifications are presented may even serve to deliberately distort social interaction. Facebook notifications are the perfect example of operant conditioning. Whatever notification you receive from Facebook, whether it's a ping, a beep, a light flash or a buzz of vibration, a certain emotion has been conditioned and it comes with a response (open the app!). One of the engineers who developed Facebook said that each Facebook like induces 'bright dings of pseudo-pleasure' (Lewis, 2017).

Facebook is a perfect example of technology that uses the psychology of reinforcement schedules to keep people returning to the platform, checking notifications and generating content in the hopes of getting rewarded with likes, comments and more notifications. It is a continuous feedback loop that takes up about 40 minutes per day (about 10 days/ year) of the average US adult's time. It's deliberately designed to become addictive, and there is an ongoing debate about whether social media platforms have a benign or malignant impact on people's lives.

There are concerns about the way Facebook and other platforms compete for people's attention. Netflix CEO Reed Hastings said they weren't concerned with their competitors, but their biggest competitor was 'sleep' (Hern, 2017). So there's the potential problem of media and social media companies to monopolize every possible moment of people's time, seeing even basic biological functions as competition for attention.

The other serious concern is when a sophisticated communications system that is integrated firmly into many people's real-world social networks can easily be hijacked by bad actors. The algorithms are fairly straightforward and particularly easy to manipulate once you understand their basic principles. And they are a mass communication tool that has been hijacked for various purposes, like trying to influence elections which we discuss throughout Section 4.

1. Trying to cut back on Facebook?
Facebook is a bit like an ex-partner who never realized that the relationship ended. It jumps at every possible sign of interest and tries to draw you back in. The more you interact with Facebook, the more interested the algorithm thinks you are, and the more updates, notifications and interactions it will push to your phone. To limit this, reduce your interaction. Use the Web version of Facebook instead of the mobile app. Better yet, turn notifications off and only sign in when you choose, instead of when Facebook asks you to come back (dozens of times daily).

2. YouTube's 'recommended videos' pushes people to extremist content
Earlier, this chapter discussed how operant conditioning can gradually change behaviour, often by increasing the intensity or the frequency of previous behaviours. It can easily be used to train a pigeon to spin in circles, play ping pong, and there was even a project during World War II where pigeons were trained as a guidance system to potentially be used in missiles. Operant conditioning is extremely effective.

Most people have had some experiences of falling down rabbit holes somewhere online. Perhaps it's delving deep into Wikipedia links, exploring connections between topics or discovering some obscure online community. Almost any interest, hobby or pastime now has astounding levels of discussion, information and content online. If you're breeding racing pigeons, building model trains or casting your own metal, there's probably a thriving community online.

While every harmless fringe interest is likely to have a community online, this is also true for the less harmless groups. Internet communities and social media are thriving recruiting grounds for radicals of every stripe. And while falling deep into a rabbit hole of content from the model train community or the knitted sock puppet community may be a bit eccentric, it is ultimately harmless.

YouTube's 'recommended content' feature is an algorithm that has been described as 'a petri dish of divisive, conspiratorial and sometimes hateful content', and a tool that 'drives people to the Internet's darkest corners' (Roose, 2019).

Using YouTube's autoplay feature means that watching mainstream political content eventually steers people towards extremist content. People watching videos of Donald Trump automatically get steered towards white supremacy rants and Holocaust denial. People watching videos of Hillary Clinton eventually get steered towards left-wing conspiracies about secret government organizations and conspiracy theories about the US government being behind the 9/11 World Trade Center attacks (Friedersdorf, 2018).

This effect is noticeable in almost any topic. People watching videos about vegetarianism end up getting steered towards veganism. Others who watch videos about jogging will eventually end up seeing content about ultra-marathons. This is called the long-tail effect: more people move away from the most generic, middle-range content and gravitate towards more specific-niche content. The wider the range of options, the more people tend to move in different directions instead of gravitating towards the centre.

The long tail of extremism is a phenomenon that has been opened up by the sheer volume and range of content available online. Most people, when given the option, tend to go down rabbit holes of particular interests. They veer off the trodden path often into more specific and more obscure sub-topics. And on one hand that's great – no matter how unique or obscure someone's interests, there is probably a community of like-minded individuals who are eager to talk about it. But that's a double-edged sword, with dangerous consequences.

THE ENVIRONMENT, LEARNING AND DEVELOPMENT

Environments elicit behaviours. Any digital environment is very specifically designed in a way that shapes, teaches and reinforces certain behaviours. Social media platforms are, by their very nature, social. A significant part of the process is social learning, where people imitate the behaviour of others on the platform and test out different approaches to see what gets them the desired result.

However, a great deal more goes on behind the scenes. Most social media platforms have little interest in what their users are talking about or how they go about communicating. Social media platforms want the greatest amount of users on their platform for the longest amount of time because social media platforms are essentially advertising platforms. The old aphorism 'if you're not the customer, you're the product' holds true.

Yet not everyone uses the Internet in the same way. Not everyone has the same interests or is attracted towards the same thing. Individual differences mean people use the tools and resources at hand in different ways. But how do these individual differences emerge? In the next chapter, we will look at personality, personality disorders and how these systems of thinking, feeling and behaving emerge and develop.

5

Maybe they're born with it, maybe they've developed a personality disorder

Although psychology has come a long way in understanding personality and personality disorder, we still have a lot more to learn about how it develops, its specific causes and how to prevent the development of personality disorders or mitigate their effects.

Since personality and personality disorders crystallize (stabilize) in a person's mid-20s and in most cases any major change is remarkably rare for the rest of a person's life, the indications are that personality does not change *under normal circumstances* (Livesley, 2003). However, there is some recent evidence that suggests some change can be achieved over much longer periods of time, and some personality disorder symptoms can change (but rarely disappear) over a period of 12–18 years. Unfortunately there are no magic bullets, miracle cures or instant overnight changes (Beck et al., 2016).

Personality is much less stable, however, in children than in adults. During childhood development, early experiences and relationships, especially from caregivers, create an important foundation for how people understand the world, how they relate to others and how they understand social relations (or in some cases, fail to learn about social relations).

In this chapter we'll look at some of the causes and risk factors for personality disorders and help to explain how they develop. At the end of this chapter we use a case study from a well-known public figure (former President Donald Trump) to explain how personality disorders can develop in childhood, which become patterns of thinking and behaving that persist through adult life.

FIGURE 5.1 The continuum of personality styles and disorders

PERSONALITY DISORDERS V. PERSONALITY STYLES

Throughout this book, there will be two terms that are used often: *personality disorders* and *personality styles*. There are key differences, but they are part of the same spectrum. Personality disorder is the clinical term used to describe specific disorders as they would be diagnosed by a psychiatrist. These tend to correspond to significant problems the individual experiences in functioning in day-to-day life.

Whereas personality styles represent similar patterns of thinking, acting and behaving to the personality disorders, but not at the extreme levels of dysfunction, and often would not occur at the severity that would require medical treatment. Figure 5.1 shows how they are describing patterns of thought and behaviour along a spectrum, but at different levels of intensity. This point will be revisited and explained in much greater detail in subsequent chapters.

NATURE

We know that there are genetic markers and predispositions that contribute to the development of personality disorders. From twin studies, genetic studies and neuroscience, we are starting to understand some of the genetic and neurological components of personality disorders.

However, there is still a lot more to learn about the specific genetic and neurological causes of personality disorders. Although we know that there is a strong genetic component to most personality disorders (estimates for the genetic contribution are in Table 5.1). Estimates vary, but depending on the specific personality disorder are generally estimated to be 50 per cent or more (Torgersen et al., 2000; Ma et al., 2016).

TABLE 5.1 Heritability estimates of DSM personality disorders

Cluster	Personality Disorder	Heritability Estimate	Corresponding Personality Style
Cluster A (see	Paranoid	50–66 per cent	Wary
Chapter 12)	Schizoid	26–29 per cent	Solitary
	Schizotypal	61 per cent	Unconventional
Cluster B (see	Antisocial	50–80 per cent	Aggressive
Chapter 13)	Borderline	69 per cent	Impulsive
	Histrionic	63 per cent	Dramatic
	Narcissistic	77 per cent	Confident
Cluster C (see	Avoidant	28 per cent	Sensitive
Chapter 14)	Dependent	28–66 per cent	Selfless
	Obsessive-compulsive	27–77 per cent	Perfectionistic

Note: We'll be talking about these in much greater detail in subsequent chapters and sections.

NURTURE

While psychologists and neuroscientists are still learning about the specific genetic and neurological components of personality disorder, we do understand some of the environmental mechanisms that contribute to personality disorder.

Some people have a natural predisposition to certain personality disorders, and when a certain set of genetic or brain structures ends up in the wrong environment, those people may be much more likely to develop personality disorders as a result. It's the same with many physical illnesses or disorders. For example, some people may be genetically much more at risk of getting diabetes. But for two people, with similar lifestyle factors like obesity and diet, one person may be more likely than the other to develop diabetes because genetically, they are more at risk.

There are five major childhood developmental factors that significantly contribute to the development of personality disorders.

1. Family dysfunction
A key part of healthy childhood development is for children to learn that they can develop caring, reciprocal social bonds with other people. If this does not happen early, it can become a lifelong challenge.

One of the most important things children learn to help them eventually adapt to wider society is that the rules at home reflect the wider rules of society. So once children learn how to relate to their primary caregiver and immediate family, that understanding can then be applied to friends, peers, teachers and widening groups of people as the person gets older and their social circle expands.

When children learn about reciprocity, kindness to others, learning to share, listening and having respect for other people in their family environment, they tend to take those lessons with them out into the world. When children learn that their parent(s) or caregivers are a source of affection, trust, comfort and security (both physically and emotionally), they tend to apply that rule more generally to people in their life, assuming that other people will treat them with kindness, fairness and respect, and see relationships with other people as a source of security and strength.

However, children may also develop insecure attachment with parents or caregivers, perceiving that person as inconsistent, distant or even a source of fear or anxiety. If children learn that a family dynamic is dominated by anxiety, humiliation, rejection or other negative emotions, as the child gets older they tend to generalize that experience to people in general. Then, other people may be seen as threats, rivals, or even just as resources to be exploited (the case study in this chapter will explain this in more detail).

Some specific factors have been linked to the development of personality disorders, although it is important to note that these factors do not *guarantee* the development of personality disorders, but they do make children more vulnerable to the development of personality disorders.

Family breakdown can be a risk for family dysfunction (Livesley, 2003), particularly in instances like the breakdown of a marriage or a family where the adults develop particularly hostile behaviour, or become neglectful or combative. When children's social relationships are dominated by hostility between warring factions, where social relationships are always a matter of 'picking sides' and different parents or sides of the family can be pitted against each other, children are much more at risk of developing personality disorders like borderline PD, where social relationships tend to be intense and unstable later in life.

2. *Invalidating environments*

Invalidating environments, from a psychological perspective, means circumstances where a child's emotions, thoughts and feelings are ignored, denied or directly contradicted. This can often happen in dysfunctional family environments, but may occur in a variety of different circumstances.

Part of childhood development is learning to understand oneself and one's own emotions. Very young children and babies actually have a limited capacity to understand which emotions should connect with particular experiences or events. That's why they look to their primary caregivers for cues about how to react to certain events.

When in unfamiliar circumstances, or confronted with new stimuli, they look to their caregivers to see how they should react. If they see a new or a strange face, they look to their caregiver to see if they should react with excitement, curiosity or fear. When encountering a new animal, say, a dog, they will look to their primary caregiver to see whether they should approach it with interest, caution or fear. Parents can quite easily pass on their phobias, insecurities or fears (e.g. fear of dogs, spiders, mice, etc.) because young children are exceptionally good at picking up on cues from their caregivers.

This tends to be a good survival mechanism; young children with little knowledge of their environment or the potential threats they could face pick up on social cues (both consciously and subconsciously) from their parents about their environment. Generally, it's an adaptive feature of development, but it can also serve to pass on phobias, neuroses, dysfunction and maladaptive psychological traits from parents to children.

The other problem that can come from invalidating environments in childhood development is when parents pass on misinformation to their children through social cues, or are unresponsive. For example, some caregivers can be described as *unresponsive*. These caregivers are not at all responsive to the emotions or reactions of their children. If a child is nervous or scared, and the parent completely ignores them, and this is an ongoing pattern, then the child 'learns' that other people are not a source of comfort or affection, and that other people cannot be relied upon during a difficult time. Conversely, part of healthy childhood development is learning that other people (especially close connections) provide comfort, emotional warmth and can be helpful during a difficult time.

It's fairly common for young children to bump their heads, knees or elbows, but not to have an instant, emotional reaction. Instead, they look to their caregiver for cues. If it's a relatively minor bump, they'll probably follow their caregivers lead in either laughing or crying: 'Whoops, how clumsy, that was a bit silly' and a smile could trigger a laugh, whereas a howl of despair from the caregiver could trigger cries and tears from the child.

These patterns tend to build up and are reinforced through years of practice between parents and caregivers, and go on to shape the personality of people through to adulthood (Livesley, 2003; Magnavita & Anchin, 2014).

3. Parental behaviour (either neglectful or over-protective)

Neglectful parents can create a profound lack of confidence and ability to act independently. When they don't actively participate in children's emotional development, give limited social and emotional cues to children and do not help children learn to understand and develop their emotional range, this can be a risk factor in the development of personality disorders.

Over-involved and over-protective parents can also inhibit social and emotional development in children. Clearly it's a difficult line to balance for parents; as children grow and develop they look for more autonomy and independence, but are still fundamentally reliant on their parents or caregivers.

At the same time that children are learning about the development of social relationships, of sharing one's own emotions and picking up the emotional reactions of other people, children are also exploring their internal and external worlds and moving towards greater physical, emotional and psychological independence. It's a process that takes decades and never really finishes. But when a person gets to the point that they can function independently without harming themselves or others, they're psychologically healthy. How they get there is their business.

But when over-protective or over-involved parents obsess over their children, micromanage their lives and don't allow any self-direction or independent social development in their children, they can also be setting them up for a series of difficulties and putting them at greater risk of developing personality disorders.

Paranoid, over-protective parenting (Lukianoff & Haidt, 2018) risks setting up cognitive distortions in children in a few different ways. First, *discounting the positives* means parents and children can view unstructured or unsupervised time as too risky while playing down the potential benefits (excitement, learning problem-solving skills, resilience, independence). Second, *negative filtering* means everything is viewed according to risks, with safety and comfort as the only priority. Third *dichotomous thinking* means that anything that isn't 100 per cent safe is viewed as too big of a risk.

Then that risks the child developing similar paranoid beliefs (the world is an unsafe place, strangers are out to get me, other people, strange environments or new situations are not to be trusted) or dependent beliefs (I'm unable to take care of myself, independence is terrifying, I'm not able to deal with conflict, the consequences of failure are unthinkable).

And of course, parenting is not always consistent. Some caregivers can swing wildly or mildly between the two extremes, being extremely over-protective, and then, when seeing the developing dependence, swinging to the other extreme in order to encourage independence. These kind of inconsistencies can also lead to fascinatingly complex personality dysfunction in adolescents and adults.

4. *Emotional maltreatment or abuse*

People with personality disorders report higher levels of childhood abuse than those in the general population. It is important to say that the majority of people who experience abuse in childhood do not go on to develop personality disorders, but certainly are at greater risk of developing a personality disorder.

Abuse of any type (whether sexual, emotional, physical) can fundamentally distort someone's understanding of social relationships and disrupt the development of healthy, reciprocal and social relations. Children, too, have a tendency to think that their *parents are acting in their best interest* and that whatever bad things happen *tend to be their own fault* even when this is far from the truth. So that tension, traumatic memories and consequent negative feelings, emotions and memories can lead to people understanding and making sense of social relationships in distorted ways (as described in detail in Chapters 12–14).

5. Positive relationships: a protective factor
There are protective factors too, which can reduce or prevent the development of disordered or dysfunctional patterns of emotions and behaviour. Positive relationships with even one adult in childhood can be a protective factor. Just one strong and positive social relationship with a friend, teacher, family member or other close social relationship can act as a protective factor and mitigate some of the long-term effects of abuse or neglect in a family environment (Huff, 2004). In some cases it takes just one caring, kind and empathetic adult to model that behaviour and to show that other people can be kind, loving and treat others with respect. Some people never grow up to see or expect pro-social behaviour from adults in their close family circle or peer group. When children are isolated in an extremely dysfunctional or abusive environment, they may take on many of the characteristics that are shown and reinforced in the family environment. Whereas even one, strong positive role model and confidant may provide some context and understanding – the dysfunctional family environment is neither the fault nor the responsibility of the child – and learning to survive within the family environment is not the same as learning to survive and thrive outside of a dysfunctional family environment.

DIATHESIS-STRESS MODEL

Why do some people with large genetic risk factors for a disease or disorder never go on to develop symptoms, while others do? Why do some people who seem to grow up in the perfect environment still go on to experience mental health struggles or go on to develop personality disorders? Or why do two children brought up in the same environment turn out very differently?

There's a complex range of inputs that affect how people develop and that may impact personality dysfunction later in life. We talked about how there is a genetic component, but also some of the risk factors in the family and social environment, and the way all of these factors stack up can be very different for different people. Or, as was mentioned with positive social relationships acting as a protective factor, sometimes when people go through serious adversity or abuse early in life, one positive relationship can act as a lifeline.

The diathesis-stress model explains how genetic, environmental, family or social risk factors can interact with potential stressors in the environment.

Most people will have the experience of being 'at full capacity' in the load of stressors they can handle. They're just about managing in their relationships, their finances, their work or in their family life. They may even be thriving, managing everything fairly well and keeping on top of difficulties, while still enjoying the problems. Then, suddenly, crisis strikes. It pushes them over the top, everything that once seemed manageable or even enjoyable is too much. They are pushed over the edge and what used to be healthy coping strategies or outlook suddenly turns toxic.

Then everything that seemed to be in balance before starts to become unhinged. What was previously a healthy social life becomes a desperate and constant need for attention and validation. What used to be a moderate amount of drinking turns into heavy drinking. A healthy imagination turns into unrealistic and distracting flights of fancy. A healthy appetite for risk-taking turns into hedonistic or self-destructive impulsivity. Or enjoying a moderate amount of alone time escalates into shutting out friends and closing off social ties.

It's not just a flicking of a switch that causes a physical health condition, mental illness or moves personality from functional to dysfunctional.

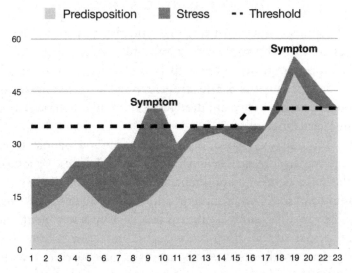

FIGURE 5.2 Diathesis-stress model

It's a cumulative effect of natural and genetic predispositions, risk factors and manageable levels of stress.

That does have two important implications:

1. In some cases, it is possible to prevent other people (or yourself) from going over that threshold, and keeping things at manageable and healthy levels.
2. It's harder to pull things back and put things back together after they've gone past that threshold and broken down, but it is completely possible. Better to act sooner rather than later.

This concept can be comparable with health conditions. Diabetes is a good comparison. Anyone can get diabetes, but some people are predisposed to develop diabetes. And if you put people in the right (or the wrong) environment or, situation, or expose them to certain risk factors, the combination means that they are far more likely to develop the disorder.

Case Study: Donald Trump (part 1)

A great deal has been written on US President Donald Trump, including 37 psychiatrists' and mental health experts' evaluations in a 2019 book put together by Yale University psychiatrist Bandy Lee. In 2020, Donald Trump's niece, psychiatrist Mary L. Trump, wrote a psychobiography and family history that is a fascinating exploration of the development of the personality disorder(s) of President Trump.

We will return to this case study in various places throughout the book because it's a relevant and interesting example that has been neatly tied into the early development of personality disorder by Mary Trump (2020). It's also useful and instructive because there is a substantial amount of publicly available behavioural data about Donald, including more than a decade of constant social media activity that provides a great deal of insight into his temperament and behaviour.

And interestingly, as Mary Trump (2020) explains, this case really demonstrates how later in life certain circumstances can further exacerbate personality dysfunction. For example, factors like those of the toxic triangle (see Chapter 21), when destructive leaders meet up with colluding followers, and a threatening environment can make personality and its dysfunction effects worse, and much more destructive.

This section explains the importance of early childhood experience in the development of personality disorders, and how we can see how patterns develop and crystallize very early, then tend to establish behavioural patterns that continue to be repeated and reinforced later in life.

Early childhood development

As a child, Donald was shaped by a domineering father (Fred Trump), who was almost certainly a sociopath (antisocial personality disorder), and a mother (Mary Trump), who neglected his development partly because of physical and psychological health problems, and partly because of a family that enforced gender norms that were strict and outdated even for the time (1940s and 1950s). This meant his mother was mostly absent, while his father's only concern was in raising his boys (he had no interest in the upbringing of the girls). He wanted a subservient castellan while he was alive who could turn into an acceptable heir to the family business after his death. He needed a 'killer' with no appetite for patricide and wanted a son to be raised in his image: an 'iron-fisted autocrat' at home and in his office (Trump, 2020, p. 34).

Unfortunately, although Fred Trump had high hopes for his sons, Fred had little interest in children. Mary Trump notes of Donald that 'neither of his parents interacted with him in a way that helped him make sense of his world' and that his father 'short-circuited Donald's ability to develop and experience the entire spectrum of human emotion' (p. 43). Fred Trump shut down any display of emotional needs in his sons, which he thought of as weakness, and any display of warmth, kindness or emotion was met with humiliation.

Children generally seek warmth, comfort and attachment from their parents, but Donald received no attention or warmth from his mother and the only attention he received or witnessed his father doling out was retribution in response to perceived weaknesses. Any sort of emotional needs were viewed as a sign of weakness and humiliation. Having a lack of emotional development in childhood meant Donald never really had the chance to develop a full range of emotional responses, and because there was little or no emotional interaction with his parents, no *mirroring*, he never developed empathy (Trump, 2020).

When we look at the risk factors for personality disorder, Donald's family environment was certainly dysfunctional and emotionally abusive (in terms of both neglect and frequent emotional abuse in the form of humiliation, hostility and the punishment of any affection). Fred Trump could never be described as 'protective', but certainly over-involved, taking interest in his children only as far as they could be useful in his business or to build up his company and legacy. Fred used and co-opted Donald's personality, because that's how sociopaths tend to operate – using people when they can to achieve their ends and discarding others who they don't perceive as useful. And like his father, Donald almost certainly meets all of the criteria for antisocial personality disorder (Trump, 2020; Dodes, 2019).

Mirroring is when one person unconsciously imitates the behaviour of another. It takes place in everyday interactions where people tend to automatically emulate the nonverbal cues of the person they are interacting with. Gestures, expressions, tone of voice are all mirrored to demonstrate empathy and connection with another person. This is part of the social learning theory that was described in Chapter 4.

Mirroring is especially important for the social development of children. It's how children learn to interact with people around them, and it helps to develop a sense of self. It also helps children learn which emotions and responses are expected in particular situations.

Why it's important: Mirroring helps children to develop empathy (Pfiefer, 2008; Trump, 2020). Replicating and reflecting back the emotions of others is part of an important neural mechanism in understanding the actions, intentions and emotions of others. Mirroring and the development of empathy is a critical task for people to be able to develop and maintain healthy social relationships throughout their lifespan.

In school

Donald had behavioural problems in school because the rules he learned for surviving in the family home were grossly out of step with the rules to thrive in the social environment at school. The fundamental lesson he learned about life from his father, Fred, was that there could only be one winner in any situation and everyone else was a loser. Behaviourally,

Donald learned that you had to project toughness at any cost, lying was acceptable and apologizing was an unforgiveable sign of weakness (Trump, 2020). The consequences of failing in any of these areas was met with hostility and harsh public humiliation.

That was a recipe for problems, because the essential requirements in school are that children know not to take other children's toys, they don't hit, insult or are mean to other children, and they are honest and apologize for bad behaviour. These deficits got Donald into trouble regularly, because insults, violence and lies were the social currency he picked up from his father. The lessons he learned at home were incompatible with what was required of a child in a school environment – which created more tension and resentment but did little to diminish the self-aggrandizement that masked a fundamental insecurity.

The bullying and aggressive behaviour went unchecked for Donald, and he did not face consequences for that at home, partially because neither of his parents took much responsibility for managing his behaviour and partially because Fred Trump liked and encouraged Donald's arrogance, aggression and disregard for other people's rules. It fit within Fred's worldview that only one person could be a winner, and everyone else was a loser. This helped to instil a belief in Donald that the rules didn't really apply to him, and although he was not yet being directly rewarded for his rigid and combative personality, there were no consequences for it either.

We'll return to this case study later to demonstrate how dark and dysfunctional personality traits can actually help people succeed in college or in business, with examples from Donald's later education and early career.

The Continuum of Personality and Optimality

6

The dark side of brightness

What is healthy functioning? What is a healthy level of a personality trait? The answer depends on whom you ask and in what context. In a work context, there tends to be optimal levels of different traits depending on the job and the situation. Being exceptionally perfectionistic can be useful for complex, detail-oriented tasks, but it can be a distraction when it leads people to focus on minutiae and forget about the bigger picture.

Self-esteem is another factor (which will be discussed in much more detail in Chapter 13), which tends to be helpful in modest doses. Inflated self-esteem is sometimes helpful in the short-term but can lead to problems in the longer term when confidence outpaces ability. Someone who is good at showing off their talents is more likely to get hired or promoted. But if their talents and abilities do not measure up to their boasts, then reality eventually catches up with them. We'll discuss this, in relation to the Peter principle, later in this chapter.

Section 1 prepared the ground with discussions of general psychological principles, especially in social psychology. We talked about the social and environmental factors that shape people, impact how they learn, change behaviours and potentially can even lead a person astray.

This section will focus more specifically on how people's personalities and attributes can interact with the environment to create success or failure, especially in the workplace.

THE OPTIMALITY MODEL

What are the best personality traits to have? What is the right level of a trait to have? Some people assume more is always better and treat a personality test like an aptitude test. However, having a higher score on a personality test does not necessarily mean that a person's traits are more adaptive.

Conscientiousness is a good example of this. People who are high in the conscientiousness trait tend to be more organized, better at setting goals, tend to be more intrinsically motivated and are more oriented towards long-term planning. Those are attributes that tend to be highly valued in many careers. However, there's two things to consider.

First, while high conscientiousness may be optimal in some situations, and this is especially true in some careers, the optimal zone varies. While a company that is selecting someone for a senior leadership position like a CEO may have an extremely specific optimal range, the same may not be true for other workplaces or other social situations.

Corporate boards may want a highly driven, well-organized person with a great eye for detail to run their company. But are those the same traits you look for when deciding who to spend time with at a social situation outside of work? Perhaps not. If we want to hire someone for a position that requires sustained high performance, we are likely to look for someone with a commensurate level of conscientiousness. But if you are looking for someone to spend a relaxing Sunday afternoon with, perhaps that is not the same person and those traits are less desirable in a different environment.

Second, more is not necessarily better. Optimal scores do not necessarily mean the highest scores. Conscientiousness is a prime example because excessive conscientiousness can be counter-productive. There's a level of organization and planning that is fairly helpful in day-to-day situations, and then there's a level of planning, spending so much time out of the day organizing, making lists and goal setting that nothing productive gets accomplished. When rigid perfectionism is taken to the extreme, a person can be so critical of their own work and other people that nothing is ever good *enough* so nothing ever gets done. When normal personality traits go to extreme levels, they can become pathological.

Optimal in the context of general wellbeing

Optimal functioning is also quite different depending on whom you ask. For a psychotherapist, most people would be in the 'normal' range. Anyone within the normal range has a general degree of independence and ability to sustain themselves, they are capable of setting goals in the short- and longer-term and they can maintain positive relationships with other people. That is not to say we expect anyone to be perfect. Everyone has days or weeks where they struggle to motivate themselves and most people wrestle with their long-term career and lifetime goals at some point. Similarly, everyone will have disagreements, arguments and differences of opinion with their friends, family and colleagues from time to time.

All of life's ups and downs are well within the range of psychologically 'normal' behaviour. The problem is when a person's life is characterized by ongoing and persistent problems with setting any sort of realistic goals, or when someone's relationships are chronically plagued with conflict throughout the course of their lifetime because they struggle to develop intimacy or empathy with other people. When these problems are persistent and widespread, then it may be a personality disorder. Sometimes people say 'everyone else is the problem', when the story of their life is that no one can be trusted; it's not necessarily everyone else's fault – sometimes the calls are coming from inside the house.

When we describe someone as healthy, or a psychiatrist might say 'functional', we tend to mean that they can live and adapt on their own, function in a social group and provide for their own basic needs. In this case, we are not concerned with what type of work they do, who is in their circle of friends, what goals they set for themselves, or what hobbies or careers they choose. Basically we're just interested in whether or not they have the capacity to manage themselves and their relationships with others and that they don't cause too much harm or distress to themselves or others. That's a fairly basic level of functioning for most people, but it's an everyday struggle for some.

Looking at these areas, we can evaluate people on four levels of functioning. The American Psychological Association (2013) lays out four core components that fit into two categories of personality functioning (or potential dysfunction).

A. Sense of self

1. Identity

The person is aware of themselves as separate from other people, they understand who they are outside of a relationship or group. They understand that their emotions are distinct from other people, and that their thoughts and emotions come from inside themselves, not from other people. They understand boundaries and can maintain appropriate boundaries depending on the role or situation they are in. They generally have an accurate understanding of their own capabilities and have a level of self-esteem commensurate with their abilities. They understand and can manage a range of emotions.

2. Self-direction

They have a realistic idea about their own capabilities and can set realistic goals. They understand the difference between their own thoughts and their own behaviour and don't blur the lines between what they imagine they could do and what they have actually done. They also understand the appropriate standards of behaviour in a particular environment (they don't expect constant praise for the most simple tasks, nor do they hold themselves to impossibly high standards).

B. Healthy relationships

3. Empathy

They need to be able to understand that other people have their own experiences and motivations that may be different from their own. Even if they disagree with others' perspectives, they can still understand and appreciate others' points of view. Most importantly, they understand the effects of their actions on other people and understand that not everyone will react the same way to their behaviour.

4. Intimacy

They can maintain mutually satisfactory relationships over long periods of time. They seek out and have interest in caring, close and reciprocal relationships. Importantly, they seek out activities and relationships that have mutual benefit, they understand that healthy relationships have elements of give and take, and they can be flexible in reacting to other people's ideas, emotions and behaviour.

These levels of functioning are important and will be revisited throughout later chapters. Continuing from the previous examples, we can see what happens when conscientiousness becomes so excessive it is obsessive-compulsive personality disorder. Those four levels of functioning (Identity, Self-direction, Empathy and Intimacy) become dysfunction for someone with obsessive-compulsive personality disorder (APA, 2013) or, as the normal range of obsessive-compulsive disorder will be referred to in this book, *perfectionistic style*.

How excessive conscientiousness becomes dysfunctional

Identity – The person's sense of self is tied completely to workplace success or productivity; the person doesn't know who they are or how to express themselves outside of their work.

Self-direction – Inflexible and unrealistic goals make success unachievable. Difficulty completing tasks because of unrealistic expectations.

Empathy – Difficulty understanding, appreciating or connecting with the feelings or behaviour of others. Has difficulty seeing value in other people's definitions of success, fulfilment or happiness outside of work or productivity.

Intimacy – Relationships subordinate to work and productivity; stubbornness and rigid thinking makes it difficult to connect with others.

When we dive in a bit deeper, we can look at these different types of functioning either *generally* or *specifically*. For example, when looking at healthy relationships, it is important that people can have positive, reciprocal relationships in one or more areas of their lives (general functioning). Whereas when we look at more specific domains, like the workplace, there may be interpersonal problems at work that are not present in other parts of the person's life. That's a crucial distinction, because if someone is *generally* able to form and maintain positive relationships but unable to do so in a *specific* setting, then it's important to look at the situational and environmental factors that could be at play.

When looking at personality disorder and dysfunction, generally these patterns would be persistent and pervasive in all relationships. People with narcissistic personality disorder (or *confident style*, see Chapter 13) have a limited capacity to recognize the feelings or needs of other people, except for the effect others can have on the person's own self-esteem or sense of self-importance. A personality disorder like obsessive-compulsive personality disorder or narcissistic personality disorder is not something that someone can 'turn off' at home or at work or in certain environments; it pervades all situations and all relationships.

It is also relevant when considering a person's health and psychological wellbeing in general compared with a specific job or role. Some people are perfectly capable of goal setting and maintaining empathetic and intimate relationships *in general* but find the demands of specific jobs are impossible. There's nothing wrong with steering clear of some occupations and favouring others, selecting particular roles based on one's own abilities and preferences. That tends to come with a healthy sense of self-awareness. Yet, often people get steered, goaded, flattered or persuaded into workplace roles and positions that they find are specifically dysfunctional, even though they are generally healthy and satisfied elsewhere.

Optimal in the context of workplace performance: the Peter principle
Most people get promoted to rise to their own level of incompetence. That's the core idea of the Peter principle (Peter & Hull, 1969; Robson, 2020). Laurence J. Peter was a Canadian schoolteacher who, in the 1940s, saw things going wrong all around him. Wherever he looked people were failing, derailing and messing things up. Journalists, politicians, civil servants and corporate professionals: incompetence seemed to be everywhere.

Peter wrote a bestseller in 1969 to explain the phenomenon. Generally, people are selected into roles that they are expected to perform well in. When the right characteristics are selected for (experience, ability, intelligence, personality traits) the right position, the person tends to perform well. This person is then successful in their role, and they learn how to perform even more effectively in that role.

When people are high performers in a particular role for long enough, then they are identified as high potential and selected for a promotion. Then that person might succeed in successive jobs and promotions, climbing the career ladder to positions that are more challenging, require greater levels of proficiency, have greater demands in terms of time, stress and complexity. Eventually people are promoted beyond their own capacity for success.

The work was originally intended as a satirical look at career progression within companies or organizations, however the insights remain relevant, and the psychological principles behind the idea are quite sound.

The Peter principle is a great explanation for the common problem in organizations of a high-performing specialist being promoted to a position of people management. For some reason, the assumption is made that expert technicians somehow will make great managers. Even though, in many professions, people work intensively to learn a specialized skill and spend years of time and energy mastering their profession. And promotions are sometimes seen more as an award for good work than an exercise in finding the person most likely to be effective in that role.

Experts, technicians and specialists are not always willing, able or capable of transferring their specialist skills to a very different type of work. The role of managing people is a very different type of work to technical or specialist occupations. People management career trajectories are fundamentally a different type of job than mastering a particular role (MacRae & Furnham, 2018). So it is often true that people get promoted into a role beyond their capabilities. This is why it's so important to identify potential success criteria, and optimal levels of individual skills, knowledge, intelligence and personality and other relevant factors.

CASE STUDY: DONALD TRUMP IN EARLY ADULTHOOD (PART 2)

This case study of Donald Trump, and his experience moving into early adulthood and relative independence, is an interesting one, because it is a perfect example of how a person's dysfunctional coping mechanisms and survival strategies that are developed in childhood can carry over into adulthood.

And it's particularly interesting because children tend to develop strategies for dealing with their environment that are adaptive in their home life, within their family bubble, and for getting by under whatever circumstances they live in. When these are healthy, happy and supportive home environments, children learn to expect the same from wider social environments and from the world as a whole. But when they learn that the world is a threatening place and their psychological or physical wellbeing is under constant threat, they adapt strategies to deal with that. And most (Livesley, 2003) develop healthy ways of adapting to the world even when faced with trauma and abuse at home. Most children learn how to adapt to the wider world, have positive social relationships with friends, teachers, colleagues and peers. A lot of children get caught at one point or another, lying, stealing, cheating or intimidating, and then have to face the consequences. They learn the important, early lesson that this kind of behaviour is not tolerated or rewarded. Some, however, do not. And this brings us back to the case of Donald Trump.

Donald Trump's early life had been shaped by a combination of rejection and neglect from his parents, combined with only the occasional reward or recognition for bluster or bravado. Donald's father was certainly a real estate tycoon and what is colloquially referred to as a 'killer'. Obsessed with building his business, maximizing profit, and using relationships with powerful and influential people to get ahead, he had little concern for the consequences to anyone else.

Yet, Donald's father Fred Trump was born in 1905 and shaped by the prevailing values and culture of the time. Although he possessed business acumen and a ruthless drive, he had little ability to be charming or charismatic. He used aggression and ruthlessness as a blunt instrument to act autocratically within his family and to get what he wanted and dominate others in his business.

Donald Trump never demonstrated exceptional aptitude for business (Trump, 2020), nor did he distinguish himself in school for any admirable reasons, but one of the traits that Donald developed and Fred encouraged was Donald's ability to talk, to charm and to aggressively promote himself. Recognizing this ability in Donald, as well as recognizing that Donald's need for approval and recognition made him malleable, Fred was happy to fund Donald's self-promotion. It was extraordinarily expensive, and Donald was unreliable and bad at managing money – but Fred was happy to run the business quietly while Donald attracted attention and promoted the Trump name and Trump business.

Donald's talent for self-promotion, constant marketing and an ability to play to a crowd and captivate the New York media was the perfect opportunity. Fred got a mascot in Donald, and Donald got to playact as a self-made entrepreneur (although his income was completely derived from his father's business). This is an interesting point in his adult development, because the lesson for Donald in his adult life became that shameless self-promotion gave him attention from both the press and his father. As long as Donald could get the Trump name in the headlines, his father was happy to bankroll Donald's exploits.

The problem, though, was that Donald also learned how to ingratiate himself with powerful people and make himself seem to be a keystone in the Trump empire. He would make promises, commit people to projects, inject himself into everything and get people into tight spaces for which failure would be costly and embarrassing to everyone involved. He would put his own, and other people's, reputations on the line, trapping people into positions where the costs of failure or quitting seemed to be more disastrous than the risks of following through with Donald's worst impulses and desires.

When the economy crashed in the 1980s, Donald was so embedded in the Trump businesses that there was no getting rid of him; Fred couldn't separate himself or distance himself from his son's incompetence. The consequences would be too severe and the repercussions would be too widespread, so the only thing to do was to keep Donald inside and do damage control (his creditors later had the same problem – they were in so deep and Donald was in so much debt that the consequences of Donald going bankrupt were too severe). There's a quote from American Industrialist Jean Paul Getty: 'If you owe the bank $100, that's your problem. If you owe the bank $100 million, that's the bank's problem.' Deutsche Bank loaned Donald over $2 billion (Enrich, 2019).

Donald never learned the lessons from his casinos about how to make the house win, but he seems to be extraordinarily adept at playing another gambler's fallacy: the sunken cost fallacy. The sunken cost fallacy is when people spend good money chasing bad money, or the idea that 'I've already put so much money into this, there's no point in walking away now'.

Many people who get caught up in Trump's orbit seem to be faced with a similar problem. Once you get too close to him, things become too big to fail. He ingratiates, manipulates or possibly even blackmails people into working relationships. But the consequences of falling out with Trump are made to seem worse than the consequences of giving him what he wants. When people are no longer useful to him, he loses interest. But when people slight him, he wants to dominate or destroy them.

In this way, for most of his life, Donald Trump managed to 'fail up' harder than most. The final part of this case study will be in Chapter 19.

7

The bright side of darkness

Personality exists on a continuum, but even along that continuum there are nuances. It's not simply that one side of the continuum is 'good' while the opposite side is 'bad'. Dysfunction in one area of a person's life may be incredibly adaptive in another area of their life. As we looked at in Chapter 5, the coping strategies and relationships people build with, for example, their parents may be extremely effective in their home environment, but completely inappropriate and dysfunctional in wider society. Behaviours that might be extremely successful with friends or romantic partners may not work well in the workplace.

Most people adapt their strategies and behaviours to some degree when in different environments or with different people; that's a healthy way of adapting to the demands of different environments. Whereas one of the defining characteristics of personality *disorder* is the rigid patterns of thinking and behaviour that the person cannot adapt to fit their circumstances.

In some personality disorders, this may create problems and conflict. When people have personality disorders that mean all of their social interactions are aggressive, confrontational and self-serving, they will have difficulty forming and maintaining close relationships.

However, there are many other personality patterns, some of which can be quite adaptive in work, in relationships and in friendships. What about people who just like to put their head down, get work done, but dislike the spotlight? Those can be invaluable employees in many roles. What about people who are extremely conflict averse? These people can be peacemakers and bridge builders. They may not be competitive or aggressive, but can play an important role in bringing people and groups together to work pro-socially. What about the people that just want to get their job done, but don't have much interest in their colleagues? They can be difficult to work with in some roles, but can work quite happily and effectively in roles that suit those preferences.

THE BRIGHT SIDE OF PERSONALITY STYLES

While personality disorders are characteristically maladaptive, personality styles exist somewhere in the middle. They can occur at different levels of intensity, but the discussion of whether or not they are adaptive depends highly on the environment. How people with different personality styles work, and their effectiveness, is nuanced and complex. While they may come with some challenges, there is always a bright side (Oldham & Morris, 1995). Just as anything of substance casts a shadow, every shadow betrays a source of light.

This chapter will review the different personality styles in more detail, and these styles will be discussed further in later chapters. For the purpose of the following sections, the positive elements will be emphasized to demonstrate when they may be optimal or at least functional (keep in mind, there is a dark side). In this chapter, we'll flip the perspective on personality disorders and look at when and how different styles can be useful.

CLUSTER A

Wary

Some people are constantly on alert for threats, they are hyper-aware of their surroundings and are continuously concerned about what is going on around them. They are particularly aware of how other people view them and they spend a lot of time thinking about their social interactions with others.

Since they are hyper-aware of the environment and people around them, they can be particularly good at picking up subtleties in conversation and nonverbal cues. They tend to be sensitive to criticism and worry about what other people might be thinking or saying about them. Anyone who has worked with a colleague who is always vigilant knows that their perceptiveness, care and good observation skills can be extraordinarily useful when they are channelled constructively. However, the quality of their work can be very dependent on the quality of their relationships. They struggle to work with people who they don't entirely trust.

Since they are so vigilant, they may also be keenly aware of any slights or criticism (real or imagined); they may spend a lot of time worrying about what others think of them, and protect their independence at the expense of developing close relationships with their colleagues at work.

Working with wary colleagues
Most people have some level of scepticism or at least curiosity about the motivations and intentions of other people. A natural hesitancy or caution with new people is entirely normal. Yet when someone is already highly cautious about other people, high levels of stress can easily tip them over into unreasonable states of paranoia.

Wary colleagues take a long time to trust people. They open up to others very slowly and are quick to withdraw if they see other people as a threat. It is more difficult to earn their trust and easier to lose it, so it's best not to push too hard and understand that they can develop positive relationships. Their defensiveness may be off-putting, but it's ultimately about worry and a desire for self-preservation. They worry that if they let other people in or if they give away too much about themselves it would be equivalent to losing control.

They can be extremely sensitive to power dynamics and really need to feel appreciated and respected to develop positive relationships with others. They may appear distant and cold, but there is a lot going on internally, which typically comes from a place of anxiety or fear.

However, when they are in a supportive environment, with trusted colleagues, their keen attention to detail, capacity to understand nuances and pick up social cues that others miss can be a huge asset.

Solitary
This style is an interesting contrast to many of the other types of personality in this chapter. While many are very outward focused, seeking to dominate, influence, charm or attach to other people, the solitary style is far more inward focused. They prefer their own pursuits and are highly focused on their own objectives – which tend to be objectives that they can complete on their own.

Unlike some other types (wary, sensitive, dependent) that tend to be anxious or ambivalent about their feelings towards other people, the solitary type has little interest in other people at all. They are comfortable on their own and are content with solitude. While some people would be anxious going out to a restaurant, going to the cinema or theatre on their own, someone with solitary style would be quite content with their own company.

They tend to be self-confident, but difficult to coach when they have their own way of doing things. They tend to take criticism or feedback easily from other people, but also may be less inclined to listen to it. Although they are not highly social, and probably prefer to get their work done on their own without distractions, this means they can be incredibly focused and dedicated workers who do not get distracted or demotivated easily. When they find an objective, they have a strong internal drive and focus, and therefore are hard to distract from that achieving their goal.

Their attributes can be effective when they are placed appropriately, but these tend to be solo pursuits and independent work. They are likely to struggle to connect with many other people in a job role that is incredibly social or involves influencing others, such as leadership. They are more likely to be direct and honest in providing and receiving feedback but may not always be tactful.

Working with solitary colleagues

Generally, most people will find solitary people easy to get along with but difficult to get to know. They are probably good colleagues who are focused on their work, try to complete things to a high standard and deliver what is expected of them. However, they probably avoid small talk, office gossip and politics at all costs. To develop a good relationship, it's important to understand that they need their space. Relationships may develop, but they are often not interested at developing relationships at the same speed, intensity or volume that others enjoy (especially their self-confident, dramatic and selfless colleagues).

These are people that tend not to make grand gestures, dramatic speeches or develop tempestuous relationships. Things progress a bit slower, and they show their caring and affection in smaller and more subtle ways – and sometimes a great deal of thought and care will go into those small but meaningful gestures.

In the workplace, logical appeals will be much more effective than emotional persuasion. They struggle to work with people they see as too clingy, mercurial or overly emotional. Developing a positive relationship with them probably involves a few shared interests combined with a healthy dose of independence. They enjoy and crave time on their own, so don't take their independence as a personal insult.

Unconventional

There are some people who just have their own unique approach to life. They don't seem to think quite the way everyone does, they probably stand out from the crowd and that's exactly the way they like it. Their approach and style can be eccentric, unconventional or even strange – but at their best people like this have a magnetic attraction. Their unique style and way of approaching things is interesting, different and fun to be around.

They draw on their own differences, their own understanding of the world and how it works. They probably have a rich, intense and sometimes exotic way of looking at things that other people might find mundane. They are unlikely to change or compromise their style for other people.

They can be abstract and creative thinkers and may be drawn more to artistic or creative types of work. This can be useful when they are good at working with others but can sometimes lead to distractions and diversions: they may have trouble staying focused or doing things in the same way as everyone else. They are likely to get bored or frustrated with tasks that don't fit within their worldview. They can be successful but will be most effective in an environment and workplace where people are accepting of their quirks and they, too, will have to make some effort to fit in and build relationships based on mutual respect.

Working with unconventional colleagues

The main thing to remember about people with this type of personality is that they are unique, they pride themselves on that and are unlikely to change. If they are challenged on their core beliefs, they are unlikely to change their mind or their approach. Instead, they will resist or disengage. But when they build strong relationships, they can be an incredibly effective part of a team when supported by others who are more practical and grounded.

They may have big ideas but forget about some of their more practical responsibilities, so they may need a bit of a nudge or some assistance dealing with administrative work or routine tasks. They've probably got a wide range of interests, so vive la différence, but don't expect to change them.

Cluster B

Aggressive
There are certain types of people who worry about very little, are fearless in the face of adversity, enjoy taking risks and like to live their life and manage their business on the edge. They are motivated by challenges and use excitement to propel their careers or their business forward. They can be innovative and resourceful, spurred to action by circumstances, and seem to perform better under pressure. While some people fret in a crisis, others are propelled into action, not just surviving but thriving in the face of adversity.

These types of personalities can be incredibly attractive in business, and their risk-taking and thrill-seeking encourages others to follow along in their adventure. When they share their success with others, they can win the loyalty and admiration of those around them. They are persuasive, good at influencing others and excellent at delegating.

When they can moderate their less savoury impulses and sublimate their drive towards the good of the team and the company, they can be effective leaders. However, their enthusiasm and bravado sometimes covers up the fact that their thrill-seeking is ultimately self-serving, and although their actions and charm may be inspiring, they are not quite as good at follow through: they need other people to be responsible for implementation, operations and finishing projects. Their approach may be effective when surrounded by a good team. But their instincts may sometimes be less constructive, and they can be mischief-makers and agitators. When they get bored they may be as likely to stir up trouble within their own team as to attack their competitors or disrupt the market. Their attitude of no guilt and no regrets has a bright as well as a potentially very dark side.

At the extreme ends, mischief can turn into criminality, bravado turns into bullying, and when they do not get what they want, they may be willing to break whatever rules get in their way. It's a broad spectrum from mischievousness to psychopathy – but either way people with these personalities are always ones to watch (and watch out for).

Working with aggressive colleagues
These types of personalities can be charming and exciting, but make sure to be self-aware, hold firm to your own values and ethics, and don't get taken for a ride. Listen to what they are saying, and make sure they are taking responsibility for their own decisions and actions. They may have great ideas and bold strategies, but pay attention to the details and make sure one or more people on the team are responsible for the finer points – they are probably thinking more about the grand strategy than any rules or regulations that might get in the way. Oversight is important and necessary.

Working with these types of personalities also requires a healthy amount of self-esteem and a sense of self. They are less sensitive to the needs of others, so when working with these people make sure you are looking out for your own wellbeing, work-life balance and your own ethics. The aggressive personalities probably push themselves hard, sometimes with little care about their own wellbeing as well as the wellbeing of others around them. Their grand ambitions tend to take precedence over the people responsible for implementing those visions. Stay grounded, be self-aware and do not expect to change them, and don't let them unduly influence you.

Impulsive
The intense passion and excitement of new friendships, new relationships and new ideas can be exhilarating and infectious. These types of personalities really experience the depths of the best and the worst, the highs are always higher, and the lows are lower, but impulsive people feel each extreme with intensity and passion.

They can be great connectors, networkers and motivators because they love to meet new people, spark new relationships and they tend to jump in headfirst. This means relationships can grow and intensify extraordinarily quickly when they meet other like-minded people. That energy can help to spark new ideas, develop new business and build teams. The impulsive people might develop close relationships in weeks or months when it would take other people years to develop that kind of connection.

They can be great salespeople, excellent for introducing and onboarding new employees, and bringing passion and excitement to their work. They tend to be emotionally uninhibited; they wear their heart on their sleeve and are quick to attach to new people. They can be spontaneous and fun-loving. They are open-minded, and like new people and new experiences.

The downside comes when they get too attached too quickly or build up relationships to feel more close or more intense than they really are. While they warm up to people extraordinarily quickly, the spark can burn out equally quickly, with passion turning to boiling rage or seething resentment. Since they never take relationships lightly, when friendships or relationships don't live up to their high expectations, the consequent conflict can be equally intense. They can't help themselves from getting caught up in office politics and drama, and sometimes they become more intensely involved with their colleagues than is appropriate.

Working with impulsive colleagues

It's important to remember that they tend to feel *every* emotion intensely, often more intensely than others. People who have solitary or avoidant personality tendencies probably find this level of emotional intensity terrifying, while others may find passion attractive or endearing. Just remember that impulsive personalities are quick to both heat up and cool off emotionally, and they can benefit from someone who reminds them to slow down and make sure they understand other people's points of view.

When you work closely with impulsive people, it's important to have regular discussions about the reasons for their actions and reactions. They can stew over conflict and amplify emotions relatively quickly – sometimes a minor disagreement can turn into a raging conflict when insignificant cues are taken as evidence to confirm their wildest suspicions. They are driven by instinct, so in stressful situations they should take some time to slow down and consider the middle ground. Most importantly, don't get caught up in their mood swings or shifting allegiances – that will only add fuel to the fire.

Dramatic

Dramatic personalities love to be the centre of attention. They are natural entertainers, are comfortable being in the spotlight and they can be very skilled at commanding attention. They seem to wear their emotions on their sleeve, talk openly about their professional and private lives and love to tell a good story. They may embellish details or add colour to an anecdote, but that's all done in the name of entertainment.

They probably have a vivid imagination and see most events in life as colourful and exciting, and they like to pass that on to other people. Sometimes when they get caught up in events; they may even be thinking more about how they will re-tell their story to others later, instead of worrying too much about what is going on around them at the moment.

They probably pay a lot of attention to their appearance, but that can take either dramatic or subtle forms. They may dress and act strikingly, or they may use more subtle and traditional cues with the intention of portraying a very specific and purposeful image (think: university colours or cufflinks, signet rings, family tartans or monogrammed apparel).

Their appearance, mannerisms and apparent openness means that they make striking introductions, get to know other people easily and develop relationships quickly. They express their emotions openly and directly, so other people find them easy to read and connect with. They also tend to be responsive to others' opinions, open to new ideas and can even be a bit suggestible – their emotions and behaviours are flexible and they will adapt to whatever gets them attention.

The downside is that, although they are natural performers and good communicators, their flamboyant style, apparent openness and attention-seeking behaviour may be a bit superficial – they have a tendency to be who they think other people want them to be instead of having an underlying set of guiding principles or core beliefs. They are people-pleasers, which can be an incredibly useful trait in some circumstances but can get them into a great deal of trouble in other situations.

Working with dramatic colleagues

They tend to be energetic and excitable, and like to take the lead. So if they are performing well, giving them recognition and the spotlight will encourage them to keep up the good work – but be wary of them taking all the credit. It may create conflict if they demand praise and attention at the expense of others – and they enjoy getting caught up in drama and office politics. If they are not getting recognition for positive contributions, they are likely to act out and attract attention for bad behaviour.

They enjoy spontaneity, excitement and they will probably try to charm those around them. They are great in positions that require good communicators, relationship building and motivating and inspiring others – but they sometimes have problems with impulse control and boundaries. Make sure they understand where they can use their discretion and what policies are red lines that must not be crossed. However, they tend not to hold grudges, so a stern reprimand may be necessary, as will be reminders and oversight.

Confident

High self-confidence can certainly appear to be a positive trait. People with these confident personality styles like attention and seek it out, so they find it easy to get recognition for their work and their achievements. They are natural (and sometimes shameless) self-promoters, so they fit right into environments and industries where getting noticed is an essential part of success.

They project a strong sense of self-assurance and use their confidence to stand out in crowded spaces. Their self-confidence is noticed by others, so they are more likely to make a good impression in an interview, and more likely to get singled out for a commendation or promotion.

They identify with people who have high rank, status, fame or respect. They believe that they deserve everything good that comes their way, and sometimes expect and demand even more. They do not hesitate to ask for recognition, call in favours and sometimes make demands of other people. This high self-regard can be extremely useful in the workplace when their self-esteem matches their capabilities, but there is a tendency to over-exaggerate their own achievements and take credit for any success, no matter how peripheral their role.

At moderate levels, they enjoy praise and recognition, but as this gets to be a more extreme personality trait, or when they are under high levels of stress, they need even more praise to bolster their ego. Often this self-confidence is a mask that hides insecurity, so without regular attention they may lash out at others and feel they are being treated unfairly.

Because they are highly ambitious, they try to develop an astute understanding of organizational politics and group dynamics and won't hesitate to play to win. They enjoy competition when they are winning, but tend to be sore losers.

Dealing with confident colleagues

People with this personality style can be relatively transparent; motivating and engaging them at work is easy for those who are prepared to play along. They love attention, praise and recognition and have a desire not just to be perceived as a good performer, but the *best* performer. They enjoy winning, but they may also enjoy seeing others lose. It is easy to get their attention (with praise and commendation) but hard to hold it, because they lose interest in people who are not helping to boost or bolster their self-esteem. They aren't great at reciprocal relationships, so don't expect praise and goodwill to be returned.

They are also relatively easy to offend. Remember that even though they appear extraordinarily confident, there's a soft core underneath and their tough exterior of confidence is actually fairly brittle and easy to shatter. That's why they spend so much time projecting strength: it masks a fear of failure, and an insecurity about relationships that are built on relatively shallow foundations. Difficult conversations and conflict therefore must be approached tactfully. If you want to resolve conflict and preserve the relationship, do not make personal attacks. Give them a clear path to a 'win', instead of direct criticism.

CLUSTER C

Sensitive

People with this sensitive personality style like comfort, familiarity and emotional security. They like to feel insulated and safe, preferring to work or socialize with the same, small social circle. They feel comfortable with people they know and trust, and they like to blend into the group: they dislike the spotlight and have no desire to be the centre of attention.

They care deeply about what other people think of them, and consequently they tend to be people pleasers who are very sensitive to criticism. They want to do the right thing, and they want to be liked by other people and are extremely careful to avoid offending or hurting others. Consequently, they are circumspect about what they say, and they tend to be polite and reserved in social situations and in the workplace.

They don't like surprises and being unprepared can be a source of anxiety. They like to have a script, understand the rules and know exactly what is expected of them. They are usually happy to do what is required of them, but just the thought of being in a situation where they don't know what they are expected to say or do can be a source of intense anxiety. They tend to question and doubt themselves, and because other people's opinion of them is so important, they worry about saying the wrong thing.

They tend to be private people; they are not quick or easy to disclose personal information except to very close friends or family members who they trust. Their social reserve typically comes from not wanting to burden or bother others with their personal problems.

Working with sensitive colleagues

Sensitive styles tend to work best when they stay within their comfort zone. While some others may function best when pushed outside of their comfort zone, sensitive people may find that counter-productive, and if pushed too hard outside of unfamiliar work, relationships and support networks, they may find their anxiety and insecurity to be overwhelming and detrimental. Structure, clarity and consistency is extremely important to them, and they do their best work in a small, close-knit team with high levels of trust and mutual respect.

They are great team players, because they dislike the spotlight, do not want a great deal of attention and get more pleasure from team success than individual achievement. Just because they don't like the spotlight doesn't mean they don't appreciate recognition. However, a quiet 'thank you' or a small token of appreciation will be much better received than a large, public display of recognition. They like to feel appreciated but don't like to be put on the spot.

Because they are not natural self-promoters, their achievements and contributions may go unnoticed. If they are looking for career advancement, promotion or want to take on extra responsibilities, they are unlikely to be assertive about pursuing those goals. These types of personalities need a bit of encouragement to open up, so during performance management discussions make sure to ask them about their goals and career objectives and give them opportunities to express these in a comfortable and private setting.

Selfless

People with the selfless personality style care deeply about others and tend to put the needs of others first. They want to see their team, their group or their organization do well, and they tend to care more about the needs of other people than their own. This means that while they can be dedicated friends, excellent employees and kind and generous colleagues, sometimes they neglect their own wellbeing. They care so deeply about other people that sometimes they may get caught up in the stress or anxiety of problems that aren't their own and find it difficult to disconnect from the emotional challenges of other peoples.

They like and need to be around others, and they love to be appreciated, needed and respected in a group. They much prefer to be followers than leaders, they are good at taking feedback, are receptive to criticism and always open to helping other people. They prefer to defer to others, take on the advice of experts and are hesitant to offer their own opinion (even when they have the experience and expertise to offer contributions). They are unlikely to offer their own opinion unless asked directly, so don't assume they will chime in to a discussion without prompting.

They find group conflict absolutely unbearable; they have a strong need to see harmony and cooperation in their own relationships as well as among those around them. They will even take on the burdens or responsibilities of others to keep the peace or promote group harmony, so it is important not to take advantage of their naturally generous and self-sacrificing approach to relationships.

Working with selfless colleagues
These are the peacemakers in an organization; they are warm, caring and expect the best from everybody and try their utmost to see things from their colleagues' points of view. They are diligent workers who don't crave a lot of praise or attention, especially when people are getting along in the team. They have a strong desire to be productive and make a meaningful contribution to the team. Explain to them how they can help, and how their contribution will be valuable, but try to avoid criticizing them personally, questioning their motives or using guilt.

It is also important to remember that because they tend to prioritize the needs of others, their own needs may go unmet. Particularly in times of stress they will sacrifice a lot to help others but taken to extremes this may lead to unhealthy and unproductive behaviour. Encourage them to take some time for themselves and remind them that rest and relaxation are good for them, as well as being good for their contribution to the team. Some of their insecurities may stem from the fact that they don't believe they deserve rest or relaxation, or that they feel guilt for taking caring of themselves. Ironically these types are the least narcissistic people, but they may worry that spending any time thinking of themselves will seem narcissistic.

Perfectionistic
The perfectionistic personality generally fits extraordinarily well with the requirements of most workplaces. They are achievement-oriented and obsessed with productivity. They have a strong work ethic, have a firm moral compass and like to see a job well done.

They see hard work and thrift as a virtue and like to see things done 'the right way'. This means that they tend to work hard, put in long hours and take on many and varied responsibilities. This can be a useful trait, but the drawback is that they tend to micromanage and have difficulty delegating work to other people. Loss of control of their work or the products of their work can be a source of anxiety.

They tend to be perfectionistic, which can be a great asset at times, particularly for work that is extremely detail-oriented or where errors can have serious consequences. However, in some areas of work this can create problems, because they have trouble letting things go until they are perfect: for them there is no such thing as 'good enough'. This can lead to problems when time sensitivity is more important than perfection – opportunities can be missed because of delays.

They also tend to be good long-term planners because they are preparers, accumulators and strategizers. They may hoard objects, documents or supplies that they think might be useful in the future. They tend to be financially cautious in their personal life and in business. They like to have contingency plans, rainy-day funds and backup plans, making them great at long-term goal-setting and strategy. The downside of this is that they may miss opportunities in their immediate environment or be unprepared for rapidly changing events: they are better at planning for the next five years than adapting to the next five days.

Working with perfectionistic colleagues
For perfectionistic people, their work and productivity is their focus, and of central importance in their life. They derive value from the work they do, and their self-esteem is tied to viewing themselves and being

viewed as competent, organized, determined and effective. To motivate them, it is far more meaningful to praise their work or their work ethic than personal compliments or flattery. Vague or generalized praise is probably less effective that specific recognition. For example, focus on a particular project they worked on, an endeavour they spent a lot of time completing, or the specific details of their work.

They probably work very independently, need little or no help setting goals and do not like to be micromanaged. When they see themselves as competent, telling them how to do their job may be perceived as an insult, so a hands-off management approach is generally more effective. They don't need someone looking over their shoulder to get their job done.

They may have a more limited emotional range than some of their colleagues – preferring to put their energy and focus into productivity instead of relationships. In the workplace they probably find it easier to connect with work-related discussions than wide-ranging topics about families and personal lives.

While they are thinking about long-term goals, they may find it difficult to be flexible or change course. They expect a certain level of stability and consistency in their work, so they are less likely to be agents of change and innovation in the workplace – but they tend to be consistent performers and reliable workers.

SELF-FULFILLING PROPHECIES

One of the interesting features of personality disorders is that they are enduring patterns of behaviour that tend to create self-fulfilling prophecies. People often act in ways that elicit exactly the behaviours they fear from others. People who are too demanding for the attention and affection of others can be so pushy that they push others away. People who are always suspicious of others, and alert for any criticisms or possible insults, will likely find what they are looking for. People who avoid social interaction and only seek solace in solitude will tend to find it.

There's no magic bullet or miracle treatment, although for people with personality disorders, Cognitive Behavioural Therapy can be effective at building more adaptive ways of thinking, feeling and behaving in the longer term (Beck et al., 2016).

8

Teams, personality clashes and conflict

Clashes and conflict at work often happen between people with very different personalities. Although there are many different reasons people get along (or don't get along) at work, personality is a powerful influence that shapes people's approach to work, and how they think, feel and behave in the workplace.

When people have fundamentally different or opposing personality traits they are more likely to come into conflict with people whose behaviour is rooted in a fundamentally different understanding of the meaning of people's behaviour and the correct way to behave at work and interact with others.

When we look at personality styles and the corresponding under- and over-developed strategies and behaviours, we can see how misunderstandings are likely to occur. For example, some people may have over-developed suspicion and vigilance, which they apply to everyone they meet, while others default to trust and openness. That is not something that is easy to overcome or change, but it can easily lead to misunderstanding.

Or, for some people who are highly conscientious, or even obsessive-compulsive (perfectionistic style), people assign value that is focused on productivity and work. For them, all of their behaviour, thoughts and emotions are caught up in that focus on productivity and achievement. Because they are always goal-directed and self-motivated, they may find it incredibly difficult to understand people who have opposing styles. People who are more casual and spontaneous, and put less value on productivity and work as a core component of self-worth, may seem radically alien. Both sets of people might just think, 'Why doesn't the other person just change?' Yet it's not that simple; personality traits are not preferences. They are systems for understanding and interpreting the world: it is far easier to understand that other people are fundamentally different, *and that's okay,* than it is to change someone else's personality.

GROUP DYNAMICS

Similar personality types may automatically understand each other more. Of course, understanding someone does not always align with liking them or working well with them. But under the right circumstances they may work well together.

That also means people with fundamentally contrasting traits, who have opposing over- and under-developed coping strategies, feel unconnected and may have trouble understanding each other. The divide may feel incredibly wide, their differences can feel like they are not just slight variances but major chasms where one struggles to comprehend how and why someone else would act in completely the opposite way to one that feels natural to them. They might think 'Don't they understand how people see them? Don't they understand the consequences of their behaviour? Why don't they simply do things differently?'

One of the most important parts of improving team dynamics is helping people to understand each other, especially in understanding those who they think are fundamentally different. This does not have to be a deep dive into someone's personal history and family life, not everyone needs or wants to dive in that deep in the workplace.

However, it can help to talk about the thoughts and emotions that underlie people's behaviours and the explanations and rationale people use. 'When I'm really stressed I need time alone; other people just add on pressure, especially when they think they are helping. Having to explain myself just makes me feel worse.' Or 'When I'm really stressed I need to have other people around. I like to be the centre of attention and entertaining other people distracts me from whatever else I'm worried about.'

Understanding these differences and accepting that there is no 'right' way to think, no perfect way of managing stress, can be helpful in reducing conflict within teams. Not everyone can or will become close friends in the workplace but understanding people who have their own ways of succeeding in their work and of controlling stress can build understanding and respect (Oldham & Morris, 1995).

This chapter will outline each of the personality styles, which ones tend to work most effectively together, and which are most likely to have conflicts and flashpoints.

PERSONALITY STYLES AND WORK RELATIONSHIPS

Wary

Wary people are highly aware of potential threats, challenges and risks, so tend to work well with those who they see as safe, secure and highly trustworthy. Sensitive and selfless people tend to be the most collaborative, trusting, and make more of an effort to reach out and build bridges. While wary people tend to be suspicious of some individuals when they trust people they use their attention and concern to look out for those they care about and work well with – which can be complementary because sometimes sensitive and selfless styles forget about looking out for themselves.

Perfectionistic and wary styles can work cooperatively when based on mutual respect and expertise. Both styles can have strong and uncompromising approaches, so they can work well together as long as they don't step on each other's toes too much. They can be a very effective team, but need to give each other space, respect and avoid trying to micromanage each other.

People with the wary personality style are more perceptive when it comes to assertiveness, inconsistences or unnecessary risk-taking. That means there can be conflict, particularly with aggressive and confident styles. The impulsive style also has significant potential to get into conflict with those who have a wary style: unpredictability and the highly emotional nature of impulsive styles can be seen as a threat by people with the wary style.

FIGURE 8.1   Partnerships and conflict for wary personality style

Solitary

Relationships tend to be more challenging for solitary styles than for most others. Their default mode and comfort zone is not in a social setting, so building and sustaining relationships takes more purposeful effort. They tend to develop fewer close relationships, and this may be especially true at work – but once they develop strong, positive relationships, they value them and hold on to them closely. This means they prefer to develop close, long-term relationships with people who they find consistent, trustworthy and reliable.

One of the best working relationships for people with solitary style will certainly be those with perfectionistic style. Both styles are more likely to be outcome-focused instead of relationship-driven in the workplace, so connecting over shared work objectives is likely to be a solid foundation for a positive relationship. These two styles may find it easier to develop mutual respect when working towards common goals and objectives. Both styles are perfectly happy to work towards shared goals individually, while both probably have limited tolerance for small talk, office gossip or distractions from the task or objective at hand. That means it is likely to be a positive working relationship where both are perfectly happy to give the other space – but it's important for both to remember to keep communication open.

The selfless style can be a good partnership with solitary style too. Someone with solitary style tends to prefer working with people who respect their need for personal space. Those with moderately confident style can be a good fit as well, when they have similar values and respect each other's approach. The confident style can be a great networker, communicator and relationship-builder but doesn't need too much attention from colleagues and can be an effective business partner. When the solitary worker prefers to perform in the background but avoid the spotlight, it can be useful to work with another who can focus on the social and public-facing parts of the job.

Any personality style that are more emotionally driven and more volatile will be the most difficult for solitary people to work with. They are less responsive to emotions, find emotional outbursts off-putting and probably do not give people with these styles as much attention as they would like. For the solitary person, interactions with those with dramatic, impulsive and aggressive styles will likely feel exhausting and invasive.

FIGURE 8.2 Partnerships and conflict for solitary personality style

Unconventional

People with the unconventional style have their own unique way of looking at the world, but can get along well with people who are more accommodating and understanding, like sensitive and selfless styles who can also bring a bit of practicality into the mix. They can also develop a mutual respect and healthy working relationship with people who have a dramatic style. Both might have their own unique flair, style or interests so can appreciate each other's strengths without stepping on each other's toes.

People with the unconventional style sometimes use their differences as a defence mechanism, staying apart from people they think are likely to reject them. They tend to be highly independent and can be inflexible when it comes to their own attitudes, beliefs and approaches to work, so this can create clashes with confident, wary or aggressive people who also have their own uncompromising approach. Confident and aggressive people may have an attention-seeking and assertive style that the unconventional person finds abrasive.

FIGURE 8.3 Partnerships and conflict for unconventional personality style

Aggressive
People with the aggressive personality style generally have the most challenges in maintaining healthy and productive relationships over longer periods of time. Since they tend to get bored easily, it takes more work on their part to make the effort to sustain long-term relationships. Any styles that seem too dependent or needy will create friction, which individuals with an aggressive style might find frustrating.

Those with the aggressive style will likely find their best potential collaborations are with people who have a clear and independent sense of themselves and who don't get too caught up in other people's risk-taking behaviours. Interpersonally, they will probably have the most affinity with dramatic styles that are lively, exciting and engaging, and like to act in the spur of the moment.

Partnerships or working relationships with perfectionistic styles can be extremely effective when both styles can complement each other's limitations. Someone with the perfectionistic style can be good for long-term planning, steadying the course and guiding risk-taking behaviour to be more sensible and outcome oriented. Having a diligent working partner to make sure the team stays within the rules and maintains focus can be extremely helpful. Short-term partnership or projects between aggressive and impulsive types can be intense, fast-moving and productive but also run the risk of meltdown. If disagreements happen, they have the potential to escalate quickly and can be extremely volatile if things go wrong.

There are more risks for aggressive types working with sensitive or selfless personality styles, because the aggressive person may have a tendency to take advantage of the other's good nature, eagerness to please and hesitation to stand up for their own interests. These working relationships all too often have the potential to be a toxic leader/ colluder/enabler type of relationship. People with the aggressive style may tend to bully people who they see as weak.

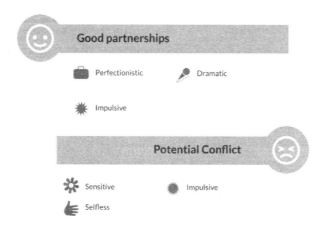

FIGURE 8.4 Partnerships and conflict for aggressive personality style

Dramatic
People with the dramatic styles tend to be outward looking and social, but also easily influenced, so they work best with people who can provide focus or individuals and groups that help to bolster the energy and excitement they can bring into their work.

They tend to work best with the perfectionistic style, which can be a good counterbalance between the head and the heart. This can be an effective working relationship where one brings logic and data while the other brings an emotional range and good ability to connect with other people. This frequently happens when you see a flamboyant and engaging entrepreneur who partners with a skilled and dedicated operations or finance manager. Selfless and sensitive styles can be good matches, with the dramatic person providing connection with people and members of their group, bringing strength and support to the team in the background.

They are mostly likely to come into conflict with other dramatic types. Both tend to compete for attention so they may see each other as natural rivals, and dramatic competitiveness can quickly spiral out of hand. The impulsive style is highly likely to clash with dramatic styles because neither hesitate to dive into confrontation, and sometimes people with dramatic styles enjoy the show. They would rather be the centre of attention for destructive behaviour than to fade into the background. Wary and dramatic people can come into conflict too: wary individuals are highly analytical, vigilant for signs of inconsistency. They can become particularly mistrustful of people who are unpredictable and overly dramatic.

FIGURE 8.5 Partnerships and conflict for dramatic personality style

Confident

People with the confident style tend to have a very clear idea of how they want to present themselves and they like the spotlight, so they work best with people who can accommodate this. They can work well with sensitive or selfless styles, if they are not looking for too much praise or recognition. When they can work together in a constructive and mutually beneficial relationship, the confident person can fill the strong, outward-looking and outgoing role alongside colleagues who prefer to work behind the scenes in supportive and collaborative roles. As long as credit is shared fairly, this dynamic can be effective.

People with the confident style may have conflict with those with aggressive styles, as the two tend to clash and get involved in power struggles. When both tend to be confrontational, direct competition between the two can become counter-productive. People with the wary style are likely to be suspicious of the motives and approach of people with the confident style and their tendency to exaggerate their achievements or contributions.

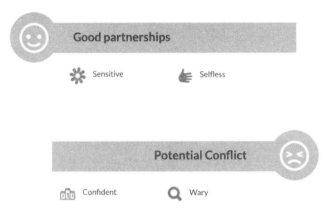

FIGURE 8.6 Partnerships and conflict for confident personality style

Impulsive

People with the impulsive style can be slightly unpredictable, so work most effectively when balanced out by those who bring a sense of calm, balance and purpose to a team. Individuals with the perfectionistic style may be good matches in long-term business or working relationships, but they might find each other's styles frustrating. This can be an effective business relationship but may not always be a close relationship where they always see eye to eye, so needs to be tempered with respect and competence on both sides.

Unconventional people may also work very well with impulsive people because they like and appreciate those who are a bit different, so may not mind a bit of volatility in a team. They also tend to be good at seeing the value of difference, so that can help to develop a mutually respectful and appreciative working relationship.

People with a wary style are naturally likely to come into conflict with those with the impulsive style. The natural suspicion of people with a wary style will pick up on the inconsistencies and rapid changes in mood and find those threatening, whereas the suspicion and social distance has the distinct potential to trigger negative emotional responses in the impulsive personality style. People with the dramatic and impulsive styles also like a lot of attention and tend to be spontaneous so they may either clash, or have a tendency to egg each other on and get each other into trouble when they work closely together without oversight.

FIGURE 8.7 Partnerships and conflict for impulsive personality style

Sensitive

People with the sensitive style don't like the spotlight but do like to contribute to a successful team. They worry a lot about their work and social relationships and can take criticism very personally, so they may struggle to work with those who are highly aggressive.

They work best with individuals who are more outgoing, socially confident and can communicate directly. People who are confident and dramatic can be valued and respected colleagues because their quite different strengths mean that they can take on separate roles in a team. People who are dramatic or confident may be a bit self-centred at times, so should remember to appreciate their sensitive colleagues in order to maintain an effective working relationship. Those with the perfectionistic style can also have very complementary relationships with sensitive people.

The greatest potential for conflict will be with those who have aggressive styles. Anyone who tends to be confrontational or assertive will be more difficult for people with the sensitive style to work with, and they may find aggressive styles stressful. Unconventional people, too, may trigger many of their anxieties as they prefer the workplace to be stable and predictable (which means the impulsive style can also cause conflict).

FIGURE 8.8 Partnerships and conflict for sensitive personality style

Selfless

Selfless people tend to be able to get along with other styles more easily than most. Co-workers tend to find them caring, warm and collaborative, and because they tend to minimize conflict and like to act as peacemakers, they are less likely to have conflict.

It is important for people with the selfless style to maintain awareness of their own career goals and maintain their own wellbeing. The most effective workplace relationships can be with perfectionistic or wary personalities. The combination of a perfectionistic long-term planner can help to make sure the group is pursuing meaningful, far-reaching goals. And work collaboration between people with wary and selfless styles can help to develop trust as both can temper the other's worst impulses (being too trusting v. too suspicious).

The challenge here can be working with confident or aggressive styles. Although individuals with confident and aggressive styles like people with selfless styles, the selfless person must be careful not to spend excessive amounts of time and energy when their work will not be acknowledged or appreciated. There are environments where the two *can* work effectively but the selfless personality should be very careful about making sure their own goals and career objectives are not set aside exclusively in service of others.

FIGURE 8.9 Partnerships and conflict for selfless personality style

Perfectionistic

People with perfectionistic styles tend to focus on work and productivity more than any other style, so in the workplace they will find it easy to develop effective relationships around shared work values and productivity – and will come into conflict with those who don't take their work seriously or whose behaviour at work negatively impacts the performance of others.

Perfectionistic styles may work very well with people who have a dramatic style because the combination of a showperson and someone who likes to work hard in the background can be a very effective relationship – especially in small teams and start-ups. The relationship combines being grounded and being flashy: if they both have respect for what the other does, it can be a remarkably effective and complementary combination. While the dramatic style is flexible and suggestible, they are happy to take guidance from the perfectionistic person. Moderately aggressive business partners can be a good and effective match too, as they can build on each other's strengths and decide on reasoned risk-taking that fits within a long-term plan.

People with the perfectionistic style tend to have conflict with confident or wary styles. When both sides always need to get their own way but approach their work from very different perspectives, it can be difficult to find middle ground. Wary, confident and perfectionistic styles all want to get things done their own way, like to be in control of situations and feel stressed when they don't feel they are, so there is a significant potential for clash between these styles.

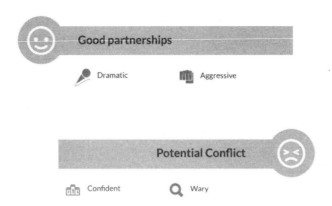

FIGURE 8.9 Partnerships and conflict for perfectionistic personality style

MANAGING CONFLICT

While we can talk about which personality styles tend to naturally find it easier to work together, and which styles are likely to be flashpoints for conflict, these should not be taken as strict rules. Just because people may be more likely to clash does not mean they are destined to do so. Most people will find ways to work with others irrespective of their various styles. Those who are self-aware can also overcome their initial reactions to other people's styles and see the value in others' contributions to a team or organization.

One of the best inoculations against conflict and misunderstanding is to understand other people and have a common language for discussing potential problems, reasons for conflicts and more effective ways of behaving to avoid conflict.

These personality styles are only part of the picture in the workplace too: if everything becomes about personalities, it is more likely to emphasize difference and lead to conflict. There are other reasons people go to work, and reasons people are effective or ineffective at work. Shared values and a constructive company culture can go a long way towards bridging divides. Effective managers and leaders who structure work around shared vision and objectives make it easier for people to overlook or overcome potential conflict.

Good selection, development and retention practices also go a long way. When the right people are selected and properly trained in their roles, the value of having individuals who are good at their jobs makes it far easier to accommodate and understand difference. Everyone has quirks and eccentricities and times in their life and career when they do not handle stress as well as they might like. It is far easier to put this aside when someone is competent, does their job well and doesn't detract from the performance of others.

When people are unsuitably selected for reasons of poor management processes, nepotism or incompetent leadership, personality clashes are far more likely to occur, to escalate, and even to characterize the workplace. Incompetent or corrupt managers may allow or even encourage infighting when conflict distracts from their own shortcomings (MacRae & Furnham, 2018).

9

The 'true self' online and offline

Do people act the same online and offline? It's a similar question to asking whether someone is the same person at work compared with at home. Or asking if someone is the same person with their romantic partner as with their family or friends.

The short answer is generally yes, most people act quite similarly online and offline. Most people's behaviour is generally consistent across different environments and social contexts. Of course, with human behaviour there are always exceptions and surprises. Most people behave in the same way most of the time in similar environments. Behaviour is also strongly influenced by stable, consistent and predicable factors like personality.

There are also clear factors and conditions where behaviour can change. Wearing a mask, hiding one's identity for example, has been studied extensively by psychologists for decades. We know that when people hide their face or hide their identity, they tend to be less inhibited: some of the social pressures and sense of personal responsibility is eased by anonymity. People are more likely to get caught up in group behaviour and feel less like an individual. They tend to feel less personal accountability for their own actions when wearing a mask or hiding their identity (Zimbardo, 1969; Mullen et al., 2003).

Research shows anonymity has the same effect on people's online behaviour (Huang & Li, 2016). When people are anonymous, they may be more likely to engage in negative, aggressive or destructive behaviours like trolling, provoking and bullying others (Connolly et al., 2016). However it is not always the case that anonymity online leads to bad behaviour: some people like to be anonymous to talk freely about their intense but harmless passions, such as knitting or flyfishing or video games or any other hobby. Others use anonymity to protect themselves; anonymous groups for survivors of abuse, violence and trauma can provide safety.

That leads to a second question: Which is really the person's true self? The image they put on display to other people, face to face, throughout the day? Or their actions when they hide their face or identity, let their guard down and allow personal accountability to fall away? That's what we will discuss in this chapter: the nature of identity, impression management and the sense of self while online and offline.

Understanding the three domains of the self

Who is the real you? What behaviours represent the 'real' person, and how is this different from the way a person acts when wearing a mask or in a different environment or social setting? It's a complex question. Philosophers would have their own answer, but we're not going to go there in this book. Those are interesting discussions to have, but a bit too lengthy to include in this chapter. Psychologists also debate the nature of the self, and have come up with some clearly structured frameworks. A good way of looking at, and examining, the self is from the brilliant humanist psychologist Carl Rogers. Rogers said we can look at the self as three different but interconnected domains.

Self-image is everything that we know and understand about ourselves, including physical features (like height, hair colour and eye colour), psychological features (like personality and intelligence) and our social relationships (partner, friend, employee, manager, doctor). This includes all the knowledge we have about ourselves and the mental systems we use to organize that information. For example, we might talk about something being very characteristic of ourselves, 'Oh that was so Karen.' Or uncharacteristic, 'I would never normally do something like that.'

Self-esteem is the value we place upon ourselves and our social roles and behaviour. This tends to involve social comparison, where value judgements are made in comparison to other people. Self-esteem can be based on highly subjective valuations of different attributes and factors, and they may or may not be objectively correct. Self-esteem can be high in one domain but low in another. For example, 'I am particularly good at my job,' but 'my colleagues don't like me very much.' Or these valuations can be interconnected in complex ways. 'I'm so good at my job other people don't like me because they are jealous.' 'I'm very productive at work, but do not have close relationships because I spend more time on getting more work done than getting to know people.'

Ideal self is the person that someone would like to be. It can include someone's dreams, ambitions, goals and ideals about how people should act and feel in general, or more specifically about how people in a certain country, region, group, class, family, friendship group or social structure should think and act. This can vary significantly based on timing as well: someone's ideal self for the current moment may be different from what they think is their ideal self in 10 or 20 years.

This can also impact self-esteem, depending on how people evaluate themselves. If they use social comparison, their self-esteem may be intricately linked to how they feel about themselves compared to the people around them. If they use self-comparison, their self-esteem may be more impacted by the perceived difference between their actual self (self-image) and their ideal self. Incongruity between the two helps to explain problems with self-esteem.

To understand why people tend to be very consistent (or not) between the online and offline world, we're going to use two examples to see why online behaviour might be highly variable in one person and extremely predictable in another.

THE SELF AND PERSONALITY DISORDERS – TWO EXAMPLES

Self in borderline PD (impulsive style)

People with borderline personality disorder tend to have their intense emotions driven by fear of vulnerability and the need to feel close connections with other people. Their core beliefs about themselves tend to revolve around them being broken, defective, vulnerable and needing protection from others. They generally see other people as warm and caring but have an intense fear of rejection, which is why they can be ambivalent in their relationships. They feel the need to identify with others, and they crave close relationships to have 'allies' and 'protectors', but then may feel inadequate in that role and act out recklessly, pushing others away or in order having explosive emotional outbursts because of the ambivalence and tension they feel towards people they become close to.

Because people with borderline personality disorder often define themselves so clearly in relation to those they intensely like and dislike, and because they have tempestuous relationships, they can bounce between different people and rapidly change their ideas about themselves. For example, they may form an intense and close relationship with one person, only to fall out with them later and then define themselves in opposition to that previous relationship. When in a close-knit social circle or a workplace, they may then form a close relationship and bond with someone who is also in conflict with the person they have just fallen out with. Because they tend to identify with the idea of 'the enemy of my enemy is my friend', they tend to get caught up in complex and shifting relationships that vacillate between extreme adoration followed by intense dislike, and then latch on to another who shares their current evaluations of those within that social group.

The same can happen online, and they may be extremely susceptible to fads, memes or intense political ideologies. They could dive deeply into an extreme ideology on one side of the political spectrum, getting absorbed in the concepts, rhetoric and the online communities that espouse that ideology. Then, when they get in too close or too deep, their fascination with that ideology turns to disgust, but instead of toning down their intensity, they are more likely to bounce across to an equally extreme and opposing ideology – not just moving away from their previous beliefs but directly and actively defining themselves in opposition.

Self in obsessive-compulsive PD (perfectionistic style)
People with obsessive-compulsive personality disorder tend to have core beliefs about themselves being accountable and fastidious (Beck, 2015) and see themselves as positive role models who are conscientious and responsible for themselves as well as others. They tend to be driven by

models of their ideal self, pulled along by so many things they 'should' do, things that they believe people, their work and society expects of them and that they demand of themselves. Complex systems, orderliness and an overemphasis on processes and control masks a concern that they may become overwhelmed, helpless or unable to function. Order, stability and contingency plans are all methods to counter a fear of failure and anxieties about not being useful to themselves or others.

They try to exert this control on themselves as well as others and have very specific and rigid definitions of the right thing to do, the right way to behave and the correct way to measure success and achievement. This is difficult to change, and this type of personality is probably remarkably consistent in different circumstances and social environments. They have the same focus, drive and need for rules at work as well as in their personal life. They have the same way of communicating in person and online, in a document and on a text message. They probably use full punctuation in instant messaging apps and always respond promptly, irrespective of the communication platform.

People with obsessive-compulsive PD also tend to have fixed, long-term goals, which makes their behaviour more predictable over long periods of time. Once you understand their motivation, it's easy to see how they pursue goals single-mindedly and are difficult to distract and may be insensitive to the physical or social dynamics around them.

IMPRESSION MANAGEMENT

Everyone manages the information, image and cues they present to other people to some degree. Different people may present an extremely diverse range of impressions, just as people value different types of imagery, communication style or desired outcomes in their life, their work or their relationships.

Impression management is a normal process people use to navigate social relationships and contexts.

> **Impression management** describes a conscious or unconscious process of selectively presenting an image or information about the self to show the most socially desirable dimensions of the self.

Personality disorders can be explained as under- or over-reliance on specific behavioural and coping strategies. That means people with different personality styles will use impression management in very different ways. For example, those with unconventional personality style under-rely on impression management. They tend to have little interest in the opinions of others and consequently might seem quite odd or eccentric. People with the confident style have over-developed impression management strategies and tend to focus excessively on their personal image and reputation, sometimes to the detriment of their workplace performance or inter-relationships.

Any social situation, or an environment where a person is being observed or monitored, elicits some level of impression management. And the type of observations makes a big difference. For example, when people are working from home and their work is monitored but their visual appearance is not monitored, they tend to modify their behaviour to match. When going into an office, people might spend more time on how they dress, wear their hair or how they visually present themselves. That is impression management. Whereas, if they are working from home and no one can see them, their impression management is likely to affect their written communication (e.g. emails, instant messages, written reports), while they may be less concerned about their visual appearance.

People can also be affected by impression management when they themselves are the observer. For example, even when working from home, some people like to get ready for a day's work the same way they would if they were working in an office. They may have a similar routine and even wear the same professional clothing that they would were to an office. That is because these routines, rituals and their own appearance impacts how they feel about themselves – impression management kicks in because they are keenly aware of their own self-image. Impression management will take different forms based on the technology that's used and the cues available. Whether it's text-based (email, instant messaging), audio-based (phone call, VoIP, voice messages) or visual (video calling). Each will elicit different forms of impression management.

SURVEILLANCE AND IMPRESSION MANAGEMENT

Impression management occurs when people are in a situation where they know they are being observed. Often this refers to social observation, where other people like colleagues are the observers. Surveillance can have similar effects on behaviour, and potentially on performance in the workplace, but rarely in a positive way.

People generally tend to be open to have their performance monitored when it's clearly linked to their job function, their responsibilities and objectives. Collecting data to measure performance is generally good practice, but constant and indiscriminate surveillance is quite different. Studies of workplace surveillance tend to find that surveillance reduces quite a few positive workplace outcomes, like causing increased tension between managers and employees (Oz et al., 1999) and leading to lower job satisfaction. Surveillance tends to be counter-productive, especially when it is non-specific, non-consensual and unnecessary (MacRae, 2018b).

There are companies that make decisions about job interview performance by conducting a computerized analysis of their facial expressions (Selinger & Hartzog, 2019), and with the rise of remote working, there are all sorts of indiscretions that can be accidently revealed over a videoconference.

If you have an electronic pass to enter various rooms and buildings, your employer can monitor your movements. It is possible for an employer to monitor everything you do on a company computer or mobile phone. The rise of remote working has made digital surveillance more appealing to some employers, and it is relatively easy to implement. While it may be unethical to install tracking and monitoring devices on employees' home computers, that has not stopped some companies from jumping at the opportunity.

While one of the largest experiments in remote working took place in 2020, many employers turned to surveillance software. Some surveillance software takes employee tracking to the extreme, by capturing screenshots of an employee's computer every few minutes, tapping into the GPS on an employee's phone to track their physical movements and even taking control of phone cameras and webcams to regularly take pictures of the employee, which are then automatically sent to the employer (Satariano, 2020).

The software includes a minute-by-minute breakdown of the employee's activities, from time spent on email, Slack and writing documents to time spent on social media platforms, food deliveries or whatever website the employee happens to browse during their waking hours. It's possible and relatively simple to implement from a software perspective. Yet from a privacy and employee wellbeing perspective, constant and intrusive surveillance is not conducive to developing trust and autonomy with employees.

There can be no doubt that surveillance is pervasive, and is somewhere between difficult and impossible to roll back, so the question must be raised: 'How far are we prepared to go?' To explore this, we will look at an extreme case study from Amazon surveillance tech, which is used to improve productivity and even to predict social workplace behaviours before they happen.

CASE STUDY: AN EXAMPLE OF EXTREME SURVEILLANCE

To look at an extreme case of employee surveillance, let's examine how tech behemoth Amazon tracks workers in their distribution centres. Amazon is often a pioneer of new technologies and has been at the forefront of tracking employee behaviour in an effort to measure productivity, output and any employee behavioural metrics that can be collected.

Amazon combines traditional surveillance technology like CCTV cameras with more advanced surveillance tools like thermal cameras combined with software to analyze people's movements and behaviour. In addition, they use wearable technology such as wristbands to track the hand movements of pickers in their warehouses.

A white paper from the Open Markets Institute (2020) describes how Amazon uses their complex surveillance technology to track more than just individual productivity, they also use surveillance data and socioeconomic metrics they collect about employees to predict potential behaviour and group activities. The research indicates that Amazon analyzes metrics like diversity statistics and employee satisfaction to predict which site locations and groups of employees are more likely to unionize. Then, they use that data to assign people to different roles or sites to reduce the likelihood of employees forming unions.

Amazon does not just use their surveillance footage to monitor employees, they also use footage as a tool to send messages to their employees. They use giant TV screens in their warehouses to display compilations from past security footage to show how surveillance has caught past employees stealing from the warehouses. The giant screens are a constant reminder to their employees that everyone is always being watched. It's a reminder that any bad behaviour will be not just disciplined, but also shown to others, to shame and humiliate the perpetrators. Although this may be effective as a behavioural change tool, it's difficult to argue that the psychological strain that emerges from that level of surveillance is justified.

To reduce human error, Amazon also use surveillance techno-logy to reduce individual autonomy. Wristbands on warehouse employees monitor how many products the employee picks per hour, sending them notifications when they are moving too slowly (a metric known as 'Task Time Off'). Delivery drivers are tracked and are required to stick to the route suggested by Amazon's GPS navigation, and they must deliver 99.9 per cent of packages on time or risk termination.

The concern is that people are being treated like automata, or robotic workers, where every action and movement is monitored and tweaked in the same way that an algorithm in a computer program might be modified. Using this type of mass surveillance combined with testing behavioural modification initiatives may improve a specific measure of productivity (for example, how many packages a person can ship per hour) but tends to be harmful to other aspects that are not being measured (for example, mental, physical and social health).

Excessive surveillance can create suspicion, stress and distrust between employers and employees. It also reduces individual employee autonomy, which is an important part of motivation and improving performance (MacRae & Furnham, 2017). If you take away workers' autonomy and flexibility, it dampens their motivation. Pervasive surveillance can send the message that the employer does not trust the employees' ability to do their job independently.

In the case of Amazon, workers report a feeling of constant, underlying stress or 'low-grade panic' (Open Markets Institute, 2020). And this doesn't just apply to their working life; because Amazon has used such intense and effective psychological techniques in an attempt to modify employee behaviour, employees report that intense stress spills over into their home lives, even making them unable to sleep because they are so strongly conditioned to react to the stimuli generated by their wristbands or other wearable tech. Reports also suggest physical injury rates in Amazon workshops are up to five times higher than in other logistics companies.

SURVEILLANCE, OVERSIGHT AND PERFORMANCE MANAGEMENT

As we are interested in behaviour and performance at work, it is important to clarify that not all data collection or monitoring is unethical, unwanted or counter-productive. Surveillance is an indiscriminate collection of data. Usually surveillance is intended to reduce negative behaviours like stealing, malingering or even misuse of time. Yet the evidence for surveillance improving performance is limited.

If you watch people closely enough, can you prevent them from stealing? Research from de Vries & Gelder (2015) indicated individual differences in personality were a far better predictor of misbehaviour in the workplace (explaining about 34 per cent) than a culture of surveillance (10 per cent). An ethical culture was also more effective at preventing bad behaviour (15 per cent) than surveillance. This suggests that surveillance *can* have an effect, but the benefits are relatively minor. The small benefits may not outweigh the consequences in costs to employees' physical and psychological health.

Oversight is a better way of reducing bad behaviour; generally most people behave quite well and when you give them more independence and flexibility along with the clarity of what they are expected to achieve, they tend to perform very well (MacRae & Furnham, 2017). Oversight tends to be more effective than surveillance. Oversight involves having structures and mechanisms to pick up on bad behaviour, without constant, invasive monitoring.

There are systems and processes that can be put in place to mitigate risks, prevent misbehaviour and even to promote and encourage positive behaviours that don't have the same negative consequences as a surveillance culture. The difference is between *surveillance*, which is blanket operation, and *oversight*, which is a more targeted and flexible structure for dealing with potential problems, along with *performance management*, which is when processes and data collection is focused on encouraging positive and desirable behaviours (see Table 9.1).

TABLE 9.1. Components of surveillance and oversight

	Oversight	Performance Management	Surveillance
Feature	Proactive	Proactive	Reactive
Purpose	To provide a flexible structure that can adapt to different problems if they arise, identify root causes and prevent them when possible.	To monitor specific measures of good performance and desirable workplace behaviours with the intention of achieving and reinforcing it.	To identify, record and observe all behaviour (good or bad) displayed by the employee.
Structure	Reporting structures, accountabilities and levels of management are in place to identify potential and current problems, and address them from personal and situational perspectives.	Key behaviours, output, results or deliverables are identified, pre-defined and measured and monitored to track their performance and meet targets.	Monitoring systems record and store all available data on employee behaviour to react to events and data.
Responsibilities	Different individuals and groups are accountable for the functioning of the system.	The employer is responsible for defining success criteria; employers and employees come up with a plan to meet those success criteria.	Technicians and technology are responsible for monitoring and recording data about all individuals or select groups.
Culture	All individuals are responsible actors within the system, with clearly defined roles and accountabilities.	All individuals are responsible actors within the system, with clearly defined roles and accountabilities.	Employees are conditioned to be aware of 'good' behaviours that will be rewarded and 'bad' behaviours that will be punished.
Framework	Flexible structure that is adaptable to change.	Clearly defined structure, targets and goals that are adaptive based on employee and employer's focus.	Rigid structure with proscribed and prescribed behaviours.

Examples

1. **Oversight.** The role of oversight in a company is more like watchful, considerate and knowledgeable observation. It may involve being alert to potential warning signs for damage or derailment. It also stipulates that specific individuals should be responsible for acting on and resolving any potential problems before they become too difficult or too problematic. For example, a board of a large company should ensure the senior leadership is taking appropriate, but not excessive risks and has the right strategic objectives. Yet they are not directly involved in the day-to-day operations nor do they issues diktats – they observe and guide instead of surveil and control.

2. **Performance management.** When it is done effectively, performance management is a continuous progress of setting individual and team goals (Armstrong, 2017). It involves continually reviewing and assessing people's performance using specific measures with the intention of improving skills and abilities.

3. **Surveillance.** An example of a surveillance system is when a company collects and stores copies of all employee emails. This may not have any stated purpose, other than monitoring, collecting and storing all employee communication. It may or may not be used, read or analyzed by others within the organization.

AN EXTENSION OF THE PHYSICAL WORLD

As the virtual world becomes more integrated with the physical world, it becomes more difficult to separate the two, or distinguish between the effects of one on the other. Virtual social environments are not separate from in-person social environments, and the methods to monitor or control people in one area do not limit the effects in others. When people are monitored, micromanaged and treated poorly in their work, even if it is using 'virtual' tech, the physical, social and psychological effects carry over into other areas of life, including at home, family life and social relationships.

Most people don't use cyberspace to have a different life, or to live a separate or imaginary life (although some do). The social relationships and connections people have tend to encompass both in-person and the virtual spaces. People do not have different personalities or different senses of self online or offline. They use both spaces, and bring their background and personality to fit into the spaces that are available.

How leaders succeed

There is no one single metric that predicts or measures success. Success or achievements are relative and reflect values, vary depending on specific outcomes and environments and have a range of different contributing factors.

Yet, when looking at success and achievement in work, there are a few common factors that generally predict workplace performance. Personality is one component, and there are other core psychological traits that can be used to assess potential performance, and understand who is likely to perform well, and why.

When determining the factors that contribute to success, it is necessary to clearly define success. Labelling a person or a team successful or 'high potential' is meaningless without a qualifier. The important question is really: Potential to do what? It's necessary to define either what the person wants to accomplish, or what they need to achieve in a particular role. To define this, use indicators such as:

- What type of performance is desirable.
- Current examples of high performance.
- The *process* used by high performers to get results.
- Why certain types of performance are more or less important depending on the context.

Defining success requires defining the position and the success criteria. Instead of a vague suggestion of performance, there should be a clearly articulated pathway, where the stepping stones and the end goal are obvious. Then, after defining what the position is and what success looks like, we can examine what predicts success in that domain. For a senior, strategic leadership position with a history of achievements, learning from failure, the capacity to develop mutually beneficial relationships over a long period of time, to set goals, meet targets and set a strategy that is beneficial for the employees and stakeholders, there are a few common attributes that consistently predict success.

INTELLIGENCE

Intelligence is one of the longest-researched, most thoroughly validated and best predictors of workplace outcomes. It is also a basic attribute linked to survival. The capacity to perceive patterns, understand circumstances and adapt behaviour to survive and thrive is not even limited to humans. We can even assess levels of intelligence in different animals by observing their capacity to solve 'problems' of varying levels of complexity by taking in information and making decisions or judgements based on that information.

Some people are just naturally quicker, sharper and more insightful than others. Some people are better at solving 'problems', whether those problems are fixing an engine, writing computer code, making business decisions, resolving interpersonal conflict or designing scientific experiments.

In general, people with higher levels of intelligence tend to learn faster, process and make use of information more quickly. There is even a neurological component: for those with higher intelligence, the signals in their brain actually transmit information more quickly and use the brain's resources more efficiently (Deary et al., 2010). Intelligence is intimately associated with reasoning, problem solving, adaptation and learning; all the characteristics that are necessary to perform well at work.

There's a ceiling effect, though; more intelligence doesn't necessarily make someone more competent. Like most traits, there is usually a sweet spot or a 'good enough' level of intelligence. Simple tasks do not require as high levels of intelligence to perform well, and the more complex the task, the more intelligence predicts success in that area. There are also situations where intelligence is counter-productive, especially when smart people over-estimate their own abilities. For a thorough and thoroughly good read on this topic, see David Robson's *The Intelligence Trap: Why people do stupid things and how to make wiser decisions* (2019).

Smart people tend to learn more quickly from experience, perform better in training and on average have higher levels of work performance. The more complex or cognitively challenging the job is, the better intelligence predicts performance (Bertua et al., 2011). Intelligence is, quite simply, one of the best predictors of workplace success. It's not a guarantee of success by any means, nor is it the only indicator, but it's a good one.

There is also the question of motivation and potential personality disorders. Psychological traits always interact with other factors, they don't exist independently. A highly intelligent psychopath could be a good performer but they also have a huge potential to be extraordinarily *counter*-productive or even destructive. Remember: there's an American saying that stupid psychopaths get arrested, smart psychopaths get into Congress.

Personality traits

Given how much this book has discussed the effect personality *dys*function can have at work, it should be clear that personality traits within the normal range have profound effects on the way people work too. Just as some personality disorders actually fit fairly well within certain roles or types of work, normal personality traits can also match well with certain types of work.

Next to intelligence, personality traits are the next best stable predictor of performance in the workplace, and an excellent predictor of leadership potential (MacRae & Furnham, 2018). Not all personality tests are created equal, though. Personality tests like the Myers-Briggs Type Indicator or Insights have little predictive validity (meaning they don't predict workplace performance). Whereas the most effective and most predictive measures of personality are generally accepted to use the Big Five model of personality.

The Big Five
The Big Five model of personality has emerged as one of the most commonly used measures of personality in psychological research. Its

development and research started in the 1980s and it has emerged as a valid model of five major personality traits, each of which has a number of facets that make up the major trait. The facets are smaller, inter-related components that make up each trait. The factors and facets of the Big Five personality traits are shown below in Figure 10.1.

The High Potential Traits Indicator (HPTI)

Other personality measures have adapted the Big Five model and theory to different applications, such as the HPTI, which measures personality as six traits in a workplace context. This removes some of the facets or factors that are not directly related to workplace performance. For example, extraversion is an interesting personality trait in relation to interpersonal behaviour, but it is not a predictor of workplace performance (Barrick et al., 2001). HPTI also omits some facets like fantasy and aesthetics and focuses on measuring openness in relation to new ideas, approaches, people and methods in the workplace.

Personality traits, especially in the context of the workplace and behaviour, are only briefly mentioned here because they will be discussed in more detail in Chapters 15 and 19.

EXPERIENCE

While there are stable psychological attributes that change little over time, like intelligence and personality, these traits are obviously insufficient to fully understand a person's success or potential to succeed. You

FIGURE 10.1 Factors and facets of the Big Five personality model

Trait (Factors)	Facets
Conscientiousness	Competence, Order, Dutifulness, Achievement, Striving, Self-discipline, Deliberation
Neuroticism	Anxiety, Hostility, Depression, Self-consciousness, Impulsiveness, Vulnerability
Openness to experience	Fantasy, Aesthetics, Feelings, Actions, Ideas, Values
Extraversion	Warmth, Gregariousness, Assertiveness, Activity, Excitement-seeking, Positive emotions
Agreeableness	Trust, Straightforwardness, Altruism, Compliance, Modesty, Tender-mindedness

could identify and select someone with optimal intelligence, optimal personality traits and absolutely no specialist knowledge or experience and make them CEO of a multinational company. The results would not be pretty.

Experience is an essential component of success that no one is born with: it has to be learned, trained, practised and developed over time. Some people are more naturally predisposed to certain talents or abilities, but without practice latent talent will never be realized or developed to its full potential. Even from the earliest age (Subotnik, Olszewski-Kubilius & Worrell, 2011), providing opportunities for those at all levels of performance to further hone and develop their skills improves performance, and increases confidence and motivation.

Gaining experience affects someone's overall performance and potential over time in a cumulative way. While factors like intelligence may be unlikely to change over the course of someone's life, experience can build on the advantages of higher intelligence, or even compensate when people are a bit slower to learn from experience or pick up new skills.

The benefits of experience also tend to compound over time. Those with more social, career or educational experience early in their life often have more opportunities and advantages to use that later, often giving them an edge over their peers. Expertise compounds the opportunities and the benefits of gaining more experience over time. And second, lack of experience can also have compound effects over time: those without many opportunities early on may struggle to gain the necessary experience later in life. This can create two different effects:

A *virtuous cycle* is a process where a few successful results or a few good opportunities lead to many more. Gaining new insight, knowledge or skills can open many doors, and those who demonstrate talent early on tend to be given more opportunities to demonstrate their abilities again and again. This often leads to improved competence and confidence, praise and, consequently, more opportunities to continue on the upward cycle: 'For everyone who has, more shall be given.'

The opposite is a *vicious cycle* where little experience or poor experiences lead to fewer offers to gain experience and hence a serious lack of growth. Early setbacks tend to compound, and it becomes harder and harder to catch up. Sometimes early blows to confidence or competence have very long-lasting effects. This can start early, and it's one of the reasons that improving opportunities at early ages are so critical. Lack of opportunity and falling behind early on has a compounding effect. Poor schools, lack of educational opportunities, limited access to social programmes, after-school clubs and work experience can all compound into a vicious cycle.

Of course, life is rarely a straight line or a continuous cycle. Everyone throughout their life and career will experience major setbacks and lucky breaks. Experience can provide a guide on how to navigate these and work to minimize the negative consequences of setbacks and take advantage of opportunities.

Ten thousand hours?

Experience is important, but the value of experience depends on a lot of other factors. There's a simplified explanation of experience and expertise popularized by Malcolm Gladwell in *Outliers* (2009), which suggests the main factor in becoming an expert or mastering a skill is practice. Apparently 10,000 hours is the magic number: 10,000 hours of deliberate, coached and structured practice. That's about 20 hours a week over a period of 10 years.

The idea is that anyone who has mastered anything from a musical instrument, a sport or becoming a chess grandmaster has one commonality: 10,000 hours of deliberate practice. Gladwell tends to stress the importance of practice over natural talents. It very much fits in with a certain American idea that anyone can do anything, they just need the grit and determination and to spend the time building their talents. And anyone who hasn't mastered their skill of choice just has not practised enough, or has not practised in the right way.

Practice is important, but hardly sufficient. A good coach, hard work and a good practice schedule can all improve someone's success, but without the natural talents, abilities or capabilities, practice alone is not enough. Practice in most areas has limitations that cannot be overcome by anyone and everyone. Athletic ability is a good example to use: basketball players, long-jumpers, sprinters and swimmers all have natural physiological differences that give them substantial advantages. Someone who is less than five feet tall can certainly become a good basketball player, practice can improve their skills, but no amount of practice will give them the height needed to become the very best of the best.

The hours spent in practice cannot explain the very real and manifestly apparent differences between elite or expert performers. Take 10 random people, put them through the same well-designed but gruelling 10,000-hour training programme and one is a star, another barely manages to finish. The same limitations are true of factors like intelligence. Someone with relatively low intelligence can certainly improve their performance with determination, practice and hard work, but they still would not be the most desirable candidate to run a large company if they struggle to learn from their environment and adapt to change.

Furthermore, recent research shows that practice doesn't necessarily make perfect, that spending more hours practising does not necessarily get one closer to mastery and that natural ability may actually be more important. Researchers Macnamara & Maitra (2019) replicated the 1993 study with violinists that Gladwell (2009) cited as key research supporting his 10,000-hours hypothesis. This more recent research did not support Gladwell's idea about the very best being set apart by the amount of deliberate practice.

The research by Macnamara & Maitra (2019) shows that volume of practice doesn't actually separate the good from the best, and that the good and the great generally practised about the same amount of time. So in this case, practice was obviously necessary to achieve a good level of skill but it didn't account for the highest expertise or the very top talent. The authors go on to say that the factors that influence top performance are far more domain specific than just practice. For example, intelligence and working memory would be essential in chess, whereas a person's physiology would be essential in sports.

Of course, the authors don't diminish the role of deliberate practice in improving performance. Experience is certainly an important part of any individual's development. People can improve their own performance, beat their own personal bests or improve their skills

(Sample, 2019). It's just not necessarily a route to elite performance, or becoming more skilled than peers or competitors. Some people undeniably have natural advantages.

MOTIVATION

Motivation operates differently than traits that are stable and change little across a person's life or career span. Motivation can change from day to day, month to month or year to year. It is far more affected by a person's circumstance: it's an 'energizing force that induces action' (Parks-Leduc & Guay, 2009). Whereas intelligence and personality explain *how* people are likely to react, motivation explains *why* people are likely to behave in certain ways. Motivation also helps to explain why people with very different personalities and levels of intelligence can act very differently. Take two highly intelligent and conscientious young people. If one has always been wealthy and has never been motivated to earn a living or work and another has had a strong motivation to earn money and be self-sufficient, these two people are likely to approach their early career and work experience very differently. They're both smart and have the capability to be top performers, but without the motivation, success is less likely.

Motivation has been studied for more than half a century, and the study of motivation has been dominated by one theory that is still one of the most researched, cited and applied theories of motivation today. It's an effective and parsimonious theory suggesting that motivators essentially fall into two categories: intrinsic or extrinsic. Boosting internal motivators boosts job satisfaction whereas lack of extrinsic motivators is the main cause of dissatisfaction.

Jobs provide different things, from achievement, independence, power and influence to pay, perks, security and comfort. When people receive intrinsic benefits like independence or contribution to a team, job satisfaction and engagement tends to increase. Whereas when people receive low pay, poor job security or insufficient perks, dissatisfaction tends to result.

It is also possible for people to be both satisfied, because of the intrinsic motivators, and dissatisfied with the extrinsic motivators at their work: the two are not mutually exclusive. There are plenty of jobs where people love the satisfaction they get from their work while also being unhappy with the pay. The reverse is also possible: someone can find the extrinsic rewards extremely amenable, but still feel unfulfilled by a lack of extrinsic motivation.

Motivation can be categorized according to two major factors, then split into facets of motivation or even individual motivators.

Intrinsic factors are internal drivers where people value the enjoyment or satisfaction they get from a task or a job. That could be challenging work that brings a sense of pride, satisfaction from contributing to part of a team, work that allows one to be autonomous or independent, or even having power or influence. These boost positive work factors like job satisfaction and drive work engagement, which are connected with a host of other positive workplace outcomes.

Extrinsic factors are external inputs that drive a person's performance. They are a core component of any job, and can create intense dissatisfaction when removed. These factors include motivators like job security, working conditions, pay or benefits. There tend to be base levels that need to be met to avoid dissatisfaction, but no amount of extrinsic factors can compensate for the lack of extrinsic motivators.

These factors have been further developed. MacRae & Furnham (2017) explain the facets within the factors of intrinsic and extrinsic motivation in the workplace.

Intrinsic factors

Autonomy revolves around personal development and growth at work, which involves core factors like work engagement, active participation and stimulation. Those who are motivated by autonomy want a job that is consistent with their own development or self-expression.

Accomplishment means being motivated by achievement, advancement and visible success. It's often related to a desire for promotion, power, status and recognition. People who highly value this want to be known either publicly, within the company or within their team for their accomplishments at work.

Affiliation. Social responsibility, passing on knowledge, teaching and instruction and working with others. Those who value affiliation prefer to work with others, like to pass on their knowledge and experience, and value the social aspects of work.

Extrinsic factors

Security involves job security and personal safety as well as consistency and regularity. This could mean a job in a company or profession with a long-established history, consistent reputation or clear organizational culture. Valuing security is a focus on stability, consistency and reliability.

Compensation includes material rewards, such as pay, insurance, bonuses and job perks that are easily measurable, counted and defined. It may also include other perks or advantages that make work life a bit easier: a convenient location, a nicer office or a more desirable working schedule.

Conditions include elements of safety and security and personal convenience. Conditions require that a job fits within the person's lifestyle and provides an environment conducive to their needs and comfort.

Each of these factors help to explain what motivates people, and what they are working towards in their jobs and careers. As a general rule, the intrinsic factors drive positive work-related factors like work engagement and fulfilment, whereas a lack of sufficient extrinsic motivators are a driver of work dissatisfaction. Remember, some careers can be incredibly fulfilling while at the same time the work can be underpaid, insecure and poorly equipped.

Go further: Want to test out your own motivation and see how it compares? Go to highpotentialpsych.co.uk and take the test for free.

Case Study: The new manager

How much does each of these criteria matter? Can someone who doesn't have an optimal psychometric profile still be a good leader? I was recently asked this by a young, high-performing employee at a tech company in continental Europe. This was a new start-up, an extraordinarily successful company, growing fast, with a small but expanding team, very profitable and in a niche industry. This guy was in a technical position, with a tech background and was being offered a leadership position and was strongly considering accepting.

He had enough self-awareness to know that this was a fundamentally different job; his experience was in the technical side of the business, and he was in his mid-20s and had limited experience managing other people or groups. He had taken a few different psychometric tests and had done a substantial amount of reading and development work on people management styles and skills. He thought, from his experience, he would have a more technocratic management style (he was in both a company and a country where this approach is well respected).

Generally his psychometric profiles showed he had high potential. Highly intelligent, conscientious, he wanted to develop his emotional intelligence and people skills further. His approach suggested he wanted the position but was cautious. He knew it would be a challenge and he wanted to learn a lot more to be effective in the new role. He was keenly aware of some of the limitations both in his experience and the challenges he would have in becoming a people manager.

His main question was whether someone who was not a 'perfect' fit for a role, but a fairly good fit, could succeed. The answer of course, is that the missing link is the question of motivation. Do you want to do it? And why?

If you know the challenges in a role, you understand what is going to be difficult and you still want to do it, then success is absolutely a possibility. If someone is motivated to learn from experience and develop skills they know they have not yet mastered, that's a key ingredient in development and growth. Go in knowing that it's going to be challenging, stressful and difficult at times, but if you are confident in knowing what you want to do, and crucially *why* you are doing it, then that's an important ingredient.

Conversely, there is absolutely nothing wrong with *not* wanting the job. Sometimes people are pushed into jobs they do not like, aren't good at or simply have no interest in because they feel like it's something they *should* do.

In this case, he really did want to do the job, and did take it on. His reluctance stemmed more from insecurity about his own experience: but a bit of nervousness can be extraordinarily adaptive when it is channelled into personal or career development.

11

How leaders fail

In any employee selection process there tends to be a list of desirable criteria. Typically these are picked as a combination of traits, attributes, skills and knowledge – all of which would fit in the previous chapter. A healthy combination of intelligence, conscientiousness and experience in the right field are a list of desirable traits. But often, this focus is solely on positive traits, selecting for attributes that are desirable. That is a great start but it is also important to look at factors to *select out*. It's rare to pick up on information that you're not looking for. If someone is bright, conscientious and hardworking, they may be a great employee. But what if they have a history of bullying others? What about if they have a long history of causing chaos in all their previous jobs? That is something to look for and select out for.

Then, it's also important to identify the factors that can derail someone. Generally workplace development looks to create, improve and enhance positive qualities. Development is about building on skills, cultivating values, expanding expertise and improving proficiency. That is all useful and desirable, but development should also consider how to avoid creating bad habits and encouraging counter-productive or destructive behaviours.

There are a few common paths to leadership failure or derailment. And as we've discussed previously, sometimes people get promoted beyond their level of competence (The Peter principle, Chapter 6). Sometimes a person's personality is well suited to the environment, but when faced with extreme stress or difficulty, their optimal traits have a dark side.

Later in this chapter, the case of former chairman and CEO of Nissan, Carlos Ghosn (now an international fugitive), will be explored as a recent example of how an extraordinarily successful leader can derail, and how the traits that initially help people get ahead can go off the rails.

THE HUBRIS SYNDROME

Lord David Owen, former British Foreign Secretary, has written extensively about the factors that may cause leaders to go astray and derail: ultimately, many leaders find the traits that bring them to power ultimately lead to their downfall. This is what Owen (2008) refers to as the 'hubris syndrome'.

Owen talks about how power, combined with the right conditions that often encircle people of significant influence or power can create a toxic, insular environment that creates conditions which lead to poor decision-making and ineffective leadership.

Owen also explains how the key qualities that make leaders successful also have a dark side. The traits of charm, charisma, the capacity to inspire others around them, willingness to take risks and grandiose aspirations alongside very high self-confidence are all extremely attractive qualities. They are also qualities that, in excess, can be characteristic of dramatic or confident personality styles.

In Owen's view, the dark side of these attributes are a refusal to listen to others' advice (excessive self-confidence), impulsivity (excessive risk-taking) and inattention to detail (big-picture thinkers). These attributes can contribute to a unique type of incompetence when enabled by colluding followers. The people around the leader, or people looking in from the outside, may think that, as the leader's successes start to decline or reverse, the leader has lost it. For someone on the outside looking in, the events leading up to derailment may seem obvious. Yet for the leader who is suffering from hubris, they may not see when they have gone down a dangerous path. For them, they have always been on the same path and their decisions have emerged from a logical and continuous process. Their stubbornness, focus and single-mindedness in pursuing their goal is what got them to the top position – why stop there!

The more successes they have had, the longer it takes the facade to crumble too, and the longer it takes for loyal followers and enablers to question the behaviour, resign or even confront someone who is taking actions that are ineffective or even destructive.

The development of hubris is not the same as a personality disorder. Personality disorders are pervasive patterns that endure throughout someone's life and the patterns generally start in early adulthood. Owen's description of hubris is unique and within a specific context. It's a development over time within a context of significant power over multiple years and has the following features:

1. Sees the world as a place for self-glorification through the use of power.
2. Tendency to take action primarily to enhance personal image.
3. Shows disproportionate concern for image and presentation.
4. Exhibits messianic zeal and exaltation in speech.
5. Conflates self with nation or organization.
6. Uses the royal 'we' in conversation.
7. Shows excessive self-confidence.
8. Manifestly has contempt for others.
9. Shows accountability only to a higher court (history or God).
10. Displays unshakeable belief that they will be vindicated in that court.
11. Loses contact with reality.
12. Resorts to restlessness, recklessness, impulsive actions.
13. Allows moral rectitude to obviate consideration of practicality, cost or outcome.
14. Displays incompetence with disregard for nuts and bolts of policy-making.

David Owen describes how power, combined with the right conditions, can create a 'bad barrel'. In his early exploration of hubris, Owen talked about the examples of George W. Bush and Tony Blair's handling of international relations following the September 11, 2001 attacks on the US, and lead up to the Iraq War (Owen, 2012). In later writing Owen explores Donald Trump in relation to his definition of hubris syndrome. However, given the behavioural data about Donald Trump from a lifetime in the public eye and media, it is unlikely the characteristics of hubris syndrome in Trump are a recent development – but are much better explained by personality disorders and behavioural patterns that have been present over a lifetime. In the case of Donald Trump's leadership, it is unlikely the role has changed his behaviour, although the stress and demands may have exacerbated it.

Better examples of the hubris syndrome are demonstrated in both Tony Blair and George W. Bush. Both were described as charismatic and energetic figures by their supporters. They connected with people, were likeable and seemed energetic and warm. Although their styles differed substantially, they reflected the national and regional cultures they emerged from. While George Bush had an easy-going and personable style, he relied heavily on the advice of people around him and didn't worry too much about details. In the aftermath of the September 11 attacks, Tony Blair saw an opportunity to use his charm and charisma, and his vision of Britain as an international leader, to launch himself on to the world stage in a show of solidarity with his close American ally and defender of the free world.

However, a big dream and massive ambitions combined with poor planning and a limited grasp of nuances and details can lead to substantial mistakes. A series of blunders, misrepresented intelligence combined with a bungled approach to UN Resolutions, forever destroyed Tony Blair's reputation and left the rest of his premiership fighting to preserve and revive public respect for his leadership. Hubris took a far more public and absurd form when George Bush decided to proclaim success in Iraq. Bush stood under a huge banner on an aircraft carrier off the coast of California reading 'MISSION ACCOMPLISHED'. It would be another eight years before the last American troops left Iraq in December 2011, only for the US to return in December 2014.

The key point here is that leadership environments, especially those that are accompanied by exceptional power, come with a host of potential problems. Generally democratic and corporate governance structures are designed to act as a check on the excesses and pitfalls of power and the powerful. However, the most appealing leaders are often those who appear able to 'get things done' irrespective of rules and norms (as the next example in this chapter lays out). And generally, people tend to be quite forgiving of rule-breaking when it appears to be benevolent, but over time it tends to become self-serving and self-preserving.

There's an irony that many people who follow, support and prop up toxic leaders rarely appreciate in their own time: 'I knew this leader was chosen to throw other people under the bus, but I never thought he would throw *me* under the bus!'

CASE STUDY: THE RISE AND FALL OF CARLOS GHOSN

At the time of writing, ex-Nissan Motor Company boss Carlos Ghosn (to pronounce his name, Ghosn rhymes with scone) maintains that he did nothing wrong, that the Japanese justice system was rigged and would never give him a fair hearing (Dooley, 2020).

However, when you have to flee house arrest, when you're smuggled out of a country in a wheeled box by ex-special forces mercenaries (Raymond & Shepardson, 2020), something has almost certainly gone wrong in your career.

Like many who have a spectacular fall, Ghosn's rise was equally spectacular. He worked his way to the top of the car industry, becoming 'one of the most powerful, colourful and charismatic figures in the global car industry' (*Autocar*, 2020).

Ghosn was born in Brazil, raised in Lebanon, then at 17 moved to Paris, France, for university. At 24 he started his career at the Michelin tyre company, quickly being promoted to plant manager, then to Head of Research and Development. At 30 he returned to his birth country of Brazil to become Chief Operating Officer at the struggling country office of Michelin Brazil.

Ghosn continued his rapid rise. In 1989, Michelin acquired tyre manufacturer Uniroyal-Goodrich to create the world's largest tyre company (Hicks, 1989) and Ghosn was appointed to President and Chief Operating Officer of Michelin North America. The company struggled in subsequent years, with major corporate restructuring and layoffs. After managing the merger and restructuring, Ghosn rose to CEO of Michelin North America.

In 1996, Carlos Ghosn caught the attention of newly privatized French car manufacturer Renault. He moved from tyres to cars, joining Renault as executive Vice President and head of Renault's South American division (they were moving manufacturing to Brazil). As Renault had been struggling with profitability, and privatization did not solve their problems, Ghosn, who had a reputation for cutting costs and returning struggling operations to profitability, was made CEO of Renault.

His approach didn't change, and he earned the nickname at Renault 'Le Cost Killer' (Andrews, 1999). Under his leadership, Ghosn moved Renault from a company 'plagued by losses and inefficiencies'

(Andrews, 1999) into profit by the late 1990s. Ghosn can't be credited entirely with the decisions though; the French government still had a 44 per cent stake in Renault and decided that most of the factory layoffs should be in Belgian factories, to minimize job losses in French factories.

The 1990s was an era of massive mergers between global players, particularly in the auto industry. For some, bigger was better, but this was not true in every case, as Mercedes and Chrysler found out. However, under Ghosn's leadership, Renault invested USD$5 billion in ailing Japanese automaker Nissan.

In 1999, Ghosn took the same approach with Nissan Japan, promising that he, along with the entire executive committee, would resign if the company did not return to profit by 2001. He planned to close four plants in Japan and eliminate thousands of jobs at Nissan in his plan to return to profitability (Bloomberg, 1999). At the time there seemed to be plenty of opportunities for Nissan to return to profitability on paper, but as was reported at the time 'in practice, no one knows whether it would work' (Andrews, 1999).

But Nissan did return to profitability under Ghosn in the 2000s, and even surpassed Honda to become Japan's second-largest car manufacturer. Ghosn became a celebrity in Japan, but treated with equal measures of suspicion around his approach to business, and his showy and autocratic style. Many complained that his splashy style and extravagant demonstrations of personal wealth were at odds with Japanese culture and values (Chozick & Rich, 2018).

As his success grew, so did his lavish spending and approach, which seemed at odds with the early reputation he had cultivated as 'Le Cost Killer'. During the 2000s, his colleagues at Nissan said he was impermeable to criticism, had a sky-high opinion of himself and would not listen to the opinions of others around him. His personal spending (which mixed with company spending) accelerated. He paid a friend and artist from Lebanon USD $888,000 for a statue to place at the entrance of Nissan's Yokohama HQ. In 2017, he hosted a lavish second wedding reception at the Palace of Versailles. (For anyone taking notes: holding a Marie Antoinette-themed party at the Palace of Versailles may be the sign of growing hubris, or at least a lack of self-awareness on the part of 'Le Cost Killer').

Ghosn's compensation was also an issue in Japan, a country where a sense of pride in the company and the work itself is as important as the salary, and where even top bosses tend to take more modest salaries than their international competitors. In 2019, Carlos Ghosn made USD $16.9 million in salary, which was lower than the nearly USD $22 million paid to General Motors CEO, Mary Barra, but 11 times more than the salary paid to Takeshi Uchiyamada, the chairman of Toyota, the world's largest carmaker.

While he was at Nissan, Ghosn fought against Japanese regulations for executive compensation, complaining that he was underpaid in comparison to other global car manufacturers. And in the autumn of 2019, a whistleblower at Nissan reported that Ghosn was effectively creating two separate compensation pots for himself: an 'official' compensation package to be reported in the company's official filings, along with a second compensation package to be paid out after Ghosn left Nissan. The US Securities and Exchange Commission settled civil charges with Ghosn for 'false financial disclosures by the company that omitted more than USD $140 million to be paid to Ghosn in retirement'. Japanese prosecutors are currently pursuing Ghosn for four charges, relating to mismanagement of company money, offloading his private debts on to the company accounts and hiding compensation packages.

The leadership context
A bit of lavish spending was not Ghosn's only problem at Nissan though; his meteoric rise and fantastically successful early years at Nissan seem to have laid the path for his eventual downfall. Like many of these cases, leadership failures are often rooted in hubris that eventually leads to nemesis.

In the early 2000s, praise was heaped on his successes and his leadership style. A case study in 2005 by Millikin & Fu (2005) suggests that Ghosn knew there would be a cultural clash and a difference in values, but that could be used effectively to bring about positive change. The approach was that a bit of constructive conflict and cultural difference, if channelled and paced appropriately, could bring about the necessary change. This, combined with the three fundamental principles Ghosn brought with him for the business, are credited for Nissan's turnaround:

1. Transparency – an organization can only be effective if followers believe that what the leaders think, say and do are all the same thing.
2. Execution is 95 per cent of the job. Strategy is only 5 per cent – organizational prosperity is tied directly to measurably improving quality, costs and customer satisfaction.
3. Communication of company direction and priorities – this is the only way to get truly unified effort and buy-in. It works even when the company is facing layoffs.

(Millikin & Fu, 2005, p. 128).

His success may have come from breaking the rules of the company culture and national culture in Japan, but his downfall also came from pushing the wrong buttons and then breaking the wrong rules. From around 2005, he continued to strengthen his connections with the senior management team, but became more disconnected from the rest of the company as communication became less effective with the wider company (Ikegami & Maznevski, 2020), although he had built up trust and networks early on in his leadership, which he continued to benefit from for many years.

From the early 2010s, trust of Ghosn began to deteriorate even though the company performed well – suggesting that people's growing discomfort with Ghosn was not a result of company performance. There were a few growing problems with Ghosn's evolving leadership style. His past success and impressive achievements at Nissan meant he was growing increasingly inaccessible, refusing to tolerate criticism or dissent. Ghosn's relationship with shop-floor employees and front-line leaders deteriorated significantly over time. Ghosn, who was described as open and humble early on in his role at Nissan, was becoming the opposite: haughty and close-minded, insulated by his senior leadership team and own sense of grandeur.

Through the 2010s, as members of his leadership team stepped down, he struggled to replace them with trusted colleagues and so his circle at the top slowly narrowed. The leadership became more disconnected from the company, and Ghosn would not tolerate dissent. At Nissan, the parable of the 'Emperor's New Clothes' was often raised as a descriptor of Ghosn's leadership style. Because he relied so much on a few key relationships that he built up early on at Nissan, and failed to cultivate new relationships, he may not have realized how disconnected he seemed from the perspective of most within the company (Ikegami & Maznevski, 2020). A series of business miscalculations and deteriorating relationships between various levels of employees, management and leadership eventually built up and Ghosn seemed to be less aware or involved in solving the growing problems.

As is common with powerful people who isolate themselves in an ever-shrinking circle of close colleagues and confidants, blunders then tend to get blamed on people outside the leader's circle. Hubris and arrogance can lead to problems being blamed on other people and, as the leader further isolates his or herself, they get more indignant about their orders not being followed by other levels of management. Scapegoats get singled out, people get blamed, the trusted leadership circle continues to shrink, and even that inner circle starts to have serious doubts about the leader's continued capability to lead. But, when the leader becomes (or has always been) autocratic in style, everyone already knows that criticism of dear leader is out of the question.

Ghosn became disconnected from the Nissan senior executives and employees, who eventually blew the whistle on his allegedly fraudulent behaviours. Ironically, it seems that many of the factors that led to Ghosn's success at Nissan turned into factors that led to his downfall. He was willing to challenge cultural norms and chart his own path for the company. He listened to people and made use of that knowledge and information to make effective business decisions. Yet after making a series of good decisions, he started to explain *his* decisions as the main factor in the company's success: he appears to have forgotten that it was the culture of openness, innovation and listening that was also a main reason for adaptation and innovation. His initial successes and those of Nissan made him listen less to the people around him, and an initial push towards a culture of transparency turned opaque as Ghosn felt more entitled and determined to take what he thought he was owed from the company.

While it is possible to ride a virtuous cycle upwards for a long time, it is not a guarantee of indefinite success. Once that virtuous spiral is taken for granted, it can start to unravel. The tolerance of Ghosn's unconventional style (for Japan) and the culture clash was tolerable as long as he was making the company successful, but the fortunes of Nissan started to wane in the late 2010s. And once all of that rule-breaking, friction and team deterioration no longer appeared to be effective, people were much less willing to tolerate it.

Ghosn maintains that he did nothing wrong, and that he was the victim of a witch-hunt, although he did settle his case with the US Securities and Exchange Commission and agreed not to run any publicly traded companies for a decade. Nissan is trying to recoup USD $90 million in damages (Tsang, 2020) and the Japanese prosecutor's case is ongoing. Ghosn claims that people within Nissan colluded with the Japanese prosecutor to get him arrested (which is an interesting way to describe whistleblowers). However, that is likely to have limited effect on Ghosn while he remains a fugitive in Lebanon.

Ghosn has started up a programme to coach business leaders and to encourage tech start-up jobs with the Université Saint-Esprit de Kaslik (Gilchrist, 2020). He and his wife have also agreed to be the subject of a documentary miniseries (Amro, 2020).

Preventing derailment

Each case is different, people derail for different reasons and in different situations. However, the general structures that enable toxic leaders tend to follow similar templates (more on this in Chapter 21). Similarly, there are some general rules and principles that can help to prevent destructive people from captivating groups and organizations, can spot signs of derailment before they becomes too destructive, or can even remove toxic leaders who do manage to gain power.

There are four important components to prevent derailment.

1. Proper oversight

Good governance is essential in preventing derailment and leadership failure. In government this is often overlapping systems of checks and balances, oversight and accountability. Leaders have independent bodies and structures which ensure leaders are abiding by the rules, and there are consequences for breaking rules. The same should be true for corporate boards: the board should be a strong and active oversight body, not a rubber stamp to automatically endorse all of the CEO's ideas. A board should be perceptive and have a reasonable level of involvement and authority to step in, if and when things go wrong.

2. Sophisticated selection

Selection processes should use criteria that are meant to select for people with desirable traits (especially those laid out in the previous chapter), but also to select people out who have a history of destructive behaviours. Those involved in selection should have a good understanding of different selection processes, especially for senior positions. In senior leadership positions, extensive reference and background checks and vetting is strongly advised. It's always surprising how many people in senior leadership positions have histories of exaggerating their successes, making up qualifications or have consistent patterns of derailing behaviour that is never picked up until after the person has caused havoc in a company.

3. Personal support

Social networks, trusted connections and constructive relationships with personal support from other people can intervene to stop or mitigate derailment. One of the common problems that comes from the hubris syndrome is that when leaders become more powerful they tend to become more isolated. Fewer people understand their position or the demands, and the leader may push people away to avoid disagreements or dissent. However, that dissent from a trusted friend, colleague or partner can be essential in helping people to avoid potentially destructive behaviours or derailment.

The other problem is that sometimes when people know, or have an inkling, that they are doing something wrong, they are less likely to confide in others. That's why, when going into demanding, stressful and powerful positions, leaders like to have strong connections, trusted confidants or personal support. It is much more difficult to develop relationships that have strong foundations independent of the position of power or authority.

4. Self-awareness

Not all derailment is inevitable or a result of personal traits. People are shaped by their experience; personality patterns are consistent and stable but they are not destiny. The environment has an impact, and the most stressful and challenging environments can have even more profound impacts.

Self-awareness is an important buffer in derailment prevention. It takes a substantial amount of self-confidence, understanding and humility to notice signs of derailment in oneself. It could be behaviours that only come out under extreme stress (normally personality traits take a dysfunctional turn). It could be when healthy coping mechanisms (e.g. exercise, humour, social supports) are replaced with unhealthy coping mechanisms (e.g. substance abuse, over- or under-eating, avoidance). There may be all sorts of signals, but they show up differently for different people. Some people might start avoiding their normal, enjoyable social contact. Other people might have disrupted sleep or eating habits. Signs of problems often show up physically, so self-awareness and being aware of the physical and psychological warning signs can be extraordinarily helpful in identifying potential problems before they snowball.

Personality Styles and Work

12

Cluster A – The eccentric personality styles

The group of personality styles where people tend to be a bit eccentric, different and set themselves apart from other people is generally grouped into 'Cluster A' (APA, 2013). The best way to describe this cluster of personality disorders is *eccentric*. Generally people within this group of personality disorders see themselves as loners or outsiders. The way they think is different, and they have little interest in seeing the world in exactly the same way as everyone else. They typically don't see themselves as normal.

They're not like everyone else and they are quite happy with that fact. They use various strategies to keep some emotional and social distance between themselves and other people in order to avoid becoming vulnerable to conventional social pressures. When under stress they see other people as generally hostile, so use a variety of different techniques to keep themselves away from other people – or to keep other people away from them. Their over-developed survival strategies tend to involve keeping other people at a distance and developing ways of soothing themselves physically, psychologically or spiritually. Their social strategies may be undeveloped, so they have trouble opening up and connecting with other people. They are more likely to escape into their own world or imagination, and less likely to look to others for help and support.

At work, they tend to fit better in individual roles where they are judged by their own criteria. They might be brilliant technicians or tacticians but find working closely with a team more challenging. While they may be creative, independent or vigilant, they also need to be integrated into the communication structures of a team – left alone and out of the loop, they could quickly spin off into their own world, becoming more and more disconnected. For people in this category, it's important to balance the need for communication and connection with a team, alongside giving them enough space and time on their own.

The three personality styles in Cluster A are wary, solitary and unconventional.

WARY PERSONALITY

People with the wary personality style have a general distrust or scepticism about other people's motives. For them, trust always has to be earned; it is not something to be given freely. Their general approach to the world centres around beliefs that other people are only out for themselves, and they have to protect themselves from the malign intentions of others.

At work they have more difficulty than most getting to know people and developing relationships, and struggle to get to know those outside the group of people they are familiar with. They tend to be cautious about sharing any information, especially personal information. As direct reports they tend to be defensive, and as managers they are likely to become over-involved and are very keen on employee surveillance of all types.

People with this personality style can be great in analytical roles and in work where they need to be vigilant to potential risks. Their suspicions mean that they are often good at anticipating potential obstacles or challenges in a project, and may see potential risks that their optimistic colleagues do not even consider. When they build trusting relationships, they can be very good at taking negative feedback, learning from mistakes and applying those lessons to future projects.

Not all careers benefit from having a fully open and trusting approach to other people. A bit of worry and worst-case scenario planning is important for roles such as safety auditors, risk management, security and any role where people have to operate under the assumption that human, mechanical or digital systems could potentially fail, and the failures need to be anticipated and prevented ahead of time.

It's also necessary to differentiate between irrational paranoia and completely rational suspicion and caution. In many organizations, there are some people with ill intent, both inside and outside the organization. Banks do get robbed, networks get compromised, employees steal or commit fraud, equipment malfunctions, people get injured – there are all sorts of risks of varying degrees of severity in every organization. For those whose job it is to manage those risks, being wary and on alert is an asset not a hindrance. The problems occur when people over-apply that strategy and start to become paranoid about things, events and people that are not a threat.

FIGURE 12.1 Optimal and excessive characteristics of wary personality style

How it looks online

The most obvious place for people with a wary personality style to gravitate towards is conspiracy theories and the social networks that create and promote them. (The case study later in this chapter talks about InfoWars). People with wary personality style tend to see themselves both as smarter, more perceptive and more righteous than other people while worry that most or all other people are malicious. Everything bad that happens appears to be naturally connected, and people with this personality style feel that they naturally pick up connections: seeing patterns even where none exist gives a feeling of comfort and security. Even if the world is scary and dangerous, they think they see it for what it really is and that brings a sense of relief.

Online this will certainly create a desire to seek out new information, to find new sources of information that seem different or niche and appear to actively fight against whatever is normal or mainstream. (It also creates a vulnerability, a blind spot for people who automatically assume the worst and feel like people are out to get them).

Solitary personality

People with a solitary personality style prefer to be on their own and like to have a lot of personal space in the workplace. For people with this personality style, working remotely in their own space is likely to be the strongly preferred option. They find social interactions tiring, any potential interpersonal conflict extremely difficult and they need a lot of alone time to recharge. They also tend not to be very emotionally expressive. In the workplace this can make them seem to be detached and unlikely to develop a culture of passion for the work or develop strong emotional connections.

They tend to stay as far as possible away from interpersonal conflict or organizational conflict. This means any conflict they are involved in is more likely to be triggered by their emotional distance or seemingly disconnected approach to other people on the team. But they are the last people who will ever try to stir up trouble or cause conflict. They will withdraw instead of engage in conflict, but this can create problems when differences of opinion or resentments go unresolved.

Leaders with this style tend to retreat from problems. Their retreat is likely to be social and emotional as well as physical: closing the office door, going away on business trips, calling in sick or whatever they can do to isolate themselves from other people and the problems. For this reason, people with a solitary personality style may find people management roles quite challenging.

People with a solitary personality tend to work effectively in positions where they can work independently, where the role is very analytical, requires objective decision-making and minimal politicking. When they can manage their relationships effectively (possibly in a small, trusting team), they can be very useful in a crisis: they tend to take a solution-oriented approach to problems, maintain an outward reserve and sense of calm that can be reassuring to others in the team.

FIGURE 12.2 Optimal and excessive characteristics of solitary personality style

How it looks online

These are the people who are most likely to opt out of the most popular social media websites, and who use private or niche online networks. They are more likely to take up individual pursuits and centre any social activities around objects instead of people. Online they tend to be the most concerned about companies using, collecting or stealing their personal data. Instead of adopting eccentric behaviour online, they are the most likely to just turn it off, disconnect and shut down their social profiles. Although some research suggests solitary individuals communicate less with others on social media, they actually tend to write more on their profiles (Martin et al., 2015).

Their online activity is more likely to be individual: if playing video games online, it's far more likely to be expansive but individual pursuits where they can get lost in their own imagination, their own ideas and create their own worlds, without the risk of anyone else coming in to mess it up. Whatever strategies they can use to detach from social contact and attachment are likely to be preferred. Anonymity online is likely to be incredibly valued: they would rather be anonymous and disconnected.

If they do have social media profiles, they are probably much less emotive and more fact-based when sharing or publishing content. They tend to be much less forthcoming about their emotions and thoughts than other people. They tend to have fewer connections and initiate social contact less often. They are also more likely to use direct and private messaging as opposed to posting publicly in large groups. Generally, they are private, guarded and inward looking.

Unconventional personality

People with an unconventional personality style like to be seen, be different and show that they are unique. This can help them to stand out from the crowd, but that may or may not be for positive reasons. When they cannot channel their energy effectively, they have difficulty prioritizing tasks. They may come up with many different (and potentially good) ideas, but struggle to implement them.

They tend to be individualistic, irrespective of what anyone else thinks. At their best, this means they can tenaciously pursue ideas and projects with little support or encouragement from others – but this means they also have a tendency to get distracted, go off on tangents and may spend a great deal of time on ideas or projects that are not useful to their team or the organization.

They can be stubborn, have difficulty compromising and be averse to meeting others even halfway. This can make them challenging to work with, especially when their ideas are fundamentally different from those around them or their objectives don't align with the team. Their eccentricity may be a bit off-putting, and although they expect people to appreciate how they are different, they may be surprisingly intolerant of difference in others.

One of the challenges in the workplace is that people may not take them seriously. They may delight in odd behaviour, relishing the opportunity to stand out and make others uncomfortable. Generally this is a coping mechanism that has the dual effect of standing out in a crowd, but keeping others at an emotional distance to protect their own feelings of self and identity.

On the other hand, when they are willing to make an effort to meet others halfway and can find a confluence of their unique talents and the team's priorities, they can be fun, vibrant, productive and innovative colleagues.

FIGURE 12.3 Optimal and excessive characteristics of unconventional personality style

How it looks online

Crystals, tarot cards, numerology or unique spiritual or religious ideas tend to be attractive online to those with unconventional personality styles. There certainly is a substantial amount of odd and eccentric content online, and they are more likely than others to search it out, explore different ideas and get caught up in unconventional groups, ideologies and messages.

They also tend to be very resistant to social pressure, so once they latch on to an idea, whether it's a self-development programme, spiritual pursuit, religion, cult or ideology, it's difficult to change their mind. Resistance from other people tends to only strengthen their attachment to whatever idea or group they've come to identify with: one of the reasons they latch on to unconventional ideas and groups is to emotionally distance or insulate themselves from others.

THE SOCIAL MEDIA CONTEXT

4chan

While the largest and slickest social media companies like Facebook, Instagram, Twitter and LinkedIn now dominate the Internet and capture the most eyes, attention and time, there are other more chaotic, less polished and less moderated communities all over the Internet.

4chan is a fringe site that has far fewer users than most popular social media sites but tends to influence the overall web landscape. 4chan is an imageboard website where one user posts an image and discussion topic and then subsequent users can respond with images and text. Users are anonymous and posts are sorted only by time and date so the content can appear chaotic, disorganized and confusing compared to mainstream social media platforms.

4chan boards are sorted into seven different categories (such as Japanese Culture, Video Games, Adult, Creative and Interests) and dozens of sub-categories ranging from things like Anime and Manga, to Technology, Music, Weapons, Business & Finance, LGBT, Science & Maths, etc. It also includes some quite niche categories. The topics range widely, but the 'Politically Incorrect' imageboard tends to get the most attention because the combination of (almost) unmoderated content, user anonymity and ephemerality of posts is a haven for extremists, trolls and troublemakers and the memes that go alongside them. For those who are drawn to conspiracy theories, paranoia, suspicion, odd or eccentric content and the environment that surrounds it, this imageboard draws them in. It also serves as an incubator and platform for all sorts of hacktivists (like Anonymous) and extremists (like the alt-right).

Zannettou and colleagues (2018) found that while the source of 28 per cent of memes could not be determined, the most common identifiable sources for meme generation were YouTube (21 per cent) and 4chan (12 per cent). They also found that while the memes tended to be generated on 4chan, they then tended to filter down to Reddit, which amplified their reach.

Over many years, 4chan's Politically Incorrect board has been a significant generator of Internet slang, culture, memes and content. In recent years, it has received attention for generating and transforming a huge volume of right-wing content like the 'God Emperor Trump' meme and a host of other content related to far-right and authoritarian ideologies. Papasavva and colleagues (2020) conducted a study of over 134.5 million posts on 4chan from a period of 3.5 years, which form the start of interesting research because: 'A non-negligible portion of these nefarious activities often originate from these "fringe" platforms.'

Much of the content eventually filters down through and across different platforms (Zannettou et al., 2017). Twitter tends to be the earliest and most influential source in popularizing mainstream news articles (e.g. BBC News, *The Guardian*, CNN, *New York Times*), whereas 4chan and Reddit tend to be the most influential sources for popularizing fringe, conspiracy theory or alternative news articles (such as Breitbart, RT, Sputnik).

CASE STUDY: INFOWARS — HOW DO SOCIAL MEDIA COMPANIES DEAL WITH MISINFORMATION?

InfoWars is an interesting case study, partly because the rise of InfoWars and Alex Jones tracks the apparent rise of conspiracy theories and their spread on social media, and partly because of the reaction by social media companies to remove this content in 2018.

InfoWars started in 1999 (Bloomberg, n.d.), and is presented in the format of a news programme, emulating the style and content of many American far-right news media. The site trades in conspiracy theories and manufactured news, but its revenue is primarily derived from products marketed as nutritional supplements, such as 'Brain Force Plus' and 'Super Male Vitality', which purport to improve brain function and male reproductive processes respectively. Other products like 'Alpha Power' and 'Survival Shield' iodine drops are clearly targeted at the discerning yet impotent far-right man who lives in fear of an impending apocalypse and subsequent mental and physical performance problems. Much of the air time focuses on selling these supplements and survivalist products.

It certainly caters to (or perhaps even exploits) people with paranoid and schizotypal personalities. The content then uses a panoply of garden-variety conspiracy theories: plenty of Illuminati and secretive New World Order organizations controlling the world, airplanes being used to spray mind-controlling chemicals into the atmosphere. All completely untrue, and in various cases retracted, such as when it accused a yogurt manufacturer of deliberately hiring sex offenders from overseas (Montero, 2017).

InfoWars fits into this chapter because it's a combination of conspiracy theories, intensely aggressive presentation and the odd fusion of both fake news and entertainment: if it wasn't taken so seriously, InfoWars could almost be seen as satire. However, it is clearly designed for people who gravitate towards odd or eccentric beliefs and conspiracy theories of a right-wing flavour. And one of the reasons it spreads so well on social media is that both the style and content seem so ridiculous that many find it amusing. There are a host of memes, videos and stylized content with millions of views online turning Alex Jones' more infamous rants into music videos. At the time of writing 'Alex Jones rants as an Indie folk song' had 6.4 million views, whereas 'Gay Frogs (Alex Jones Remix)' had 14 million. Former design ethicist at Google and co-founder of The Center for Humane Technology, Tristan Harris, said that Facebook's algorithm recommended Alex Jones to Facebook users over 15 billion times (Patricof et al., 2019).

Now, the memes and fairly benign videos of Alex Jones that circulate mask a far darker depth of conspiracy theories, hate speech and troubling content. It's just the tip of the iceberg into an online sales and advertising platform that promulgates conspiracy theories. It creates a serious problem for social media companies because they publish and promote some or all of the content to an international audience.

In 2018, YouTube, Facebook and Apple banned Alex Jones and InfoWars content from their platforms (although much is still available in various forms). Their rationale for the ban was not the conspiracy theories but because, as Spotify said, it 'expressly and principally promotes, advocates or incites hatred or violence against a group or individual based on characteristics' (Coaston, 2018).

It marks an interesting development, because it shows that social media companies are taking more steps towards moderating or removing content from high-profile cases of people violating their terms of service. It also shows how social media companies have moved from being (at least ostensibly) smaller personal networks to now more closely resemble mass media and advertising platforms. The most popular, and often controversial, content is prioritized instead of focusing on content within local social networks. But as social media platforms have become a popular news source, now almost one in five people use social media as their primary source of news (Mitchell et al., 2020).

It shows that although most of the platforms have been loath to remove any content for most of their history, some are starting to take a more active role in moderating content or removing users. In the past few years, and especially leading up the 2020 US election, they have been removing more spam, bot and troll accounts (BBC, 2018) and removing hate speech (Wagner, 2019). Twitter first highlighted one of Donald Trump's more than 17,000 Tweets as inaccurate before the 2020 election, and then banned him from the platform after he lost the election.

ECCENTRIC BELIEFS ONLINE

The Internet has certainly made access to information easier for anyone with a connection. However, one of the challenges is that the main content providers online are the social media companies, which do little to curate information based on veracity or responsibility. In fact, social media companies tend to promote content that triggers an emotional reaction (which will be discussed in much more detail in Chapter 22). Widely distributed content tends to be that which delivers the most intense emotional responses: fear, lust, anger, righteous indignation or derision.

For people with eccentric beliefs, or who find conspiracy theories and paranoia a natural response, for those who believe other people are a threat to their own psychological or physical safety or for the people who want to find ways to really distinguish themselves as fundamentally different from what they see as the average person, they will find everything they are looking for online. It will be easy to find information or misinformation to confirm their worst fears. Seek and ye shall find: especially if you look online.

13

Cluster B – The assertive personality styles

The group of styles where people tend to be more assertive, outward looking and show a desire to influence other people are generally grouped into 'Cluster B' (APA, 2013). When most people think of personality disorders, Cluster B personality disorders tend to be the most well known. Narcissism and sociopathy are the two personality disorders that have come to be most commonly known outside of psychological circles.

At the adaptive ends, people in this cluster (Cluster B) tend to be outward looking, gregarious, charming and adaptive in social situations. They can be charmers, performers, negotiators and charismatic leaders. When they have a moral compass, they can use their talents for constructive endeavours.

However, at the more dysfunctional ends of the spectrum they have a diminished moral compass, or in some cases there is none at all. At the more extreme cases then, they tend to be egocentric, self-serving and arrogant, good with relationships but only to the extent that relationships give them what they want. These are the people who are good at getting into power through any means necessary: lying, manipulating, exaggerating, breaking promises and taking advantage of others. This tends to lead to consequences, where meteoric rises can lead to spectacular falls. The problem with using dishonest methods is the short-term benefits almost always lead to long-term consequences. It's only possible to cover up a trail of destruction for so long.

The four personality styles in Cluster B are aggressive, dramatic, confident and impulsive.

Aggressive

People with an aggressive personality style have a sense of adventure, get excited about opportunities and jumping to new things. They can be argumentative, challenging and find conflict to be energizing and even exciting. They tend to see all risks as opportunities and seem happy to engage in any conflict whether it's large or small. They may have trouble prioritizing between calculated risks with reasonable returns and thrill-seeking but ultimately counter-productive behaviours.

They tend to like to show off their risk-taking behaviours too, wanting to make big displays of their physical courage, bold decisions and apparent lack of concern for the risks. They tend to enjoy pushing other people to take risks as well and will push as hard as they can to test the boundaries of others.

They get easily bored, so although they like starting projects, they are quick to jump to the newest and most exciting thing, forgetting about previous projects and preferring other people to be responsible for implementation. They like to jump in, stir the pot and feel like they are in the hot seat, but will jump out just as quickly when they get bored or are out of their depth.

They also tend to be quite skilled at hiding or covering up their mistakes or shifting blame, which it tends to be their go-to defence when they get into trouble. They will make use of ambiguity, and they have no compunctions about making other people or the entire team look bad to shift responsibility away from themselves. They tend to be good talkers, without a great deal of attachment to the truth, so deflection and smooth talking is a common technique they use to get themselves out of the trouble that they very likely got themselves into.

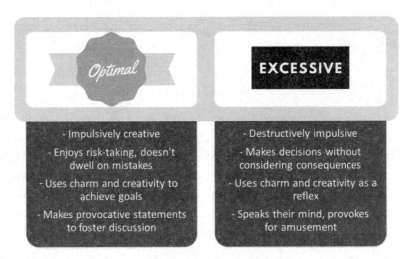

FIGURE 13.1 Optimal and excessive characteristics of aggressive personality style

How it looks online

This profile is your classic online troll. Add anonymity (or perhaps not) and this is the type of personality style that delights in causing mischief, stirring up trouble and provoking negative emotional reactions in other people. There are so many places online where people already have strong emotional reactions and controversial opinions are easily triggered. These places are easy targets for causing trouble, so tend to draw people in who find that to be an amusing pastime.

However, there are different levels of nuance; it is not all posting aggressive, violent or threatening messages from an anonymous account. In the workplace, and on workplace social media platforms, the aggression may not always be obvious or blatant. Some people are very good at stirring up conflict without looking like the aggressor. They may be adept at drawing colleagues with opposing views into arguments online with a few subtle mentions and tagging antagonists. They might operate behind the scenes, messaging people individually to encourage them to create conflict within the group. Sometimes they operate happily behind the scenes, acting as a confidant but advising courses of action that are bound to be destructive.

Depending on the behaviour, this may be easier to spot when it's an obvious attempt to stir up trouble. But it's not always easy to spot, and the motivations behind someone's behaviour are not always easy to discern. There certainly is valid discussion and debate: the question to ask is whether there is a purpose or a constructive objective behind a brash exterior, or is the person starting fires just because they enjoy watching things burn?

DRAMATIC

One of the hallmarks of the dramatic personality style is a colourful, bold and showy presentation style. They like to be the centre of attention, to be noticed and flattered. At their best they can be charming, interesting and exciting. They tend to exaggerate and hype things up, so they are good at getting people excited and building up expectations, but they sometimes have trouble living up to the fantastic image they project.

When surrounded by and bolstered by a good team, they may be effective in motivational speeches, selling products or attracting investment in their company. They make big promises, charm the people around them and are particularly good at using techniques to quickly build rapport and trust. When they can temper their colourful presentation with a healthy dose of reality, they can be exceptionally effective. However, when they are less disciplined or less scrupulous, they don't let reality get in the way of a good show.

They like to take centre stage whenever possible, so their showboating can make it hard for other people to contribute to the team when they are around, and they may fail to spot good ideas when they try to dominate the attention of a group. When someone with the dramatic personality style is in a leadership role, their direct reports quickly learn that there is no reward for speaking up, and anyone who steals the spotlight might be looked upon as a threat.

They may have trouble keeping focus and following through. They make grand pronouncements and big promises. Although they may not be deliberately trying to deceive, they can quickly forget about the promises they have made so easily when they wanted to be viewed favourably. They are also very easily influenced by others: they have an intense need to be liked, so they have a unique ability to pick up on what other people are looking for and play that character. It makes them a social chameleon, adapting quickly and easily to their group environment.

Their style makes sustained and constructive social connections difficult though. While they usually make a great first impression, other people notice that they change when around different people or in different environments. The ease at which they put on different masks or act to please other people in different ways over time means the people who have known them for long periods of time see that the charm and flash is superficial, but getting to know the 'real them' surprisingly hard, and they may seem to be hollow, unable to find any firm beliefs, convictions or ideas that they can sustain interest in.

Although the more functional end of the spectrum often involves positive emotions and more constructive behaviour, people with a dramatic style may be just as likely to use negative emotions and destructive behaviour to garner attention. If they feel powerless and ignored, they may be inclined to play the victim and make huge displays of negative emotions. While the confident and aggressive style hate admitting they were wrong, the dramatic style may relish the opportunity to make grand gestures of apologizing and anguished handwringing to achieve their goals. Any emotional display is just part of their repertoire and getting to use their whole range is part of the fun.

FIGURE 13.2 Optimal and excessive characteristics of dramatic personality style

How it looks online

Social media is the perfect platform for someone with the dramatic personality style. It affords the opportunity to put every experience, every emotion, on grand display for the world to see. It can be perfectly curated, crafted and developed to create the right responses in others.

These are people that present every feeling as bigger, bolder and more intense than anyone else. However, most of it is superficial and manufactured (unlike the impulsive personality style, which really does have intense swings that are difficult to control). Every picture and post is likely part of a grand narrative, their social media history is an epic journey of highs and lows, available for the world to see forever (unlike the impulsive personality style, who tends to genuinely regret past behaviour and is likely to delete previous posts).

CONFIDENT

Confidence certainly can seem to be an attractive trait, and there is no shortage of self-help books telling people that all they need to do is believe in themselves, trust their gut and never give up on their dreams. But somewhere between the *Power of Positive Thinking* and *The Secret*, talent meets reality. It's certainly true that many people would benefit from healthier feelings of self-worth and feeling a bit more self-assured. Overconfidence, however, can be a significant problem, and when chronic overconfidence and belief in one's own superiority and personal narrative at the expense of everything and everyone else, including facts, serious problems can emerge.

People who are exceptionally self-confident and project an aura of superiority and conviction often inspire others. People believe that if someone projects confidence, there must be a reason behind that confidence. Sometimes there is, but sometimes there is not.

People who have the confident (and potentially overconfident) personality style have such a confidence in themselves that they often have a diminished capacity to learn from experience or other people around them; they reinterpret information around them to fit in with their own worldview. This prevents them from learning, but also discourages other people around them from sharing information or having discussions. This can lead to the classic autocratic problem when a leader is supremely confident and impervious to outside information: the people around the autocrat know their contribution is only welcome when it will confirm the leader's worldview or need for reassurance.

In excess, the person with the confident personality style tends to internalize when things go well and externalize when things go badly. Every success comes directly from their own brilliance, ability and force of will. Everything that goes wrong is someone else's fault, or the result of some outside event beyond anyone's control. They tend to find scapegoats and can turn on people they were once close to when necessary to deflect from their own failure. This approach is as much about preserving their own fragile ego as protecting their image: they desperately need to see *themselves* as capable, intelligent and better than others. Deflection, blame and scapegoating is automatic because they struggle to integrate any negative information into their self-image. Every argument and every mistake is treated as an existential threat and a battle for self-preservation. An apology would be seen as a weakness, so they would rather ruin a relationship than ruin their image (as they see themselves).

The problem often emerges after some initial success(es). They tend to be stuck in a formula that gave them early success and achievement, and seek to dominate events, people and their work to fit those early models of success. This makes them resistant to change and they find different patterns of relationship or authority unacceptably threatening. Because they do not have the ability to recognize their own limitations, when their formula does not work in new environments, they blame the people or circumstances around them.

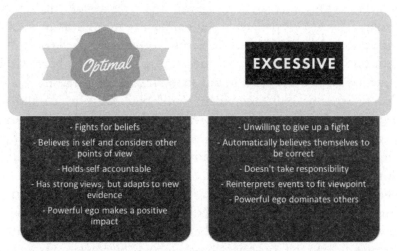

FIGURE 13.3 Optimal and excessive characteristics of confident personality style

How it looks online

The online environment absolutely abounds with opportunities for people with more confidence than talent. When it strays into the realm of a clinical personality disorder, excessive confidence is called narcissism.

Narcissism tends to be one of the easier personality disorders to spot based on online behaviour. A meta analysis of 62 studies (McCain & Campbell, 2018) found that this was related to:

- More time spend on social media.
- Increased frequency of status updates/Tweets posted to social media.
- Higher number of friends/followers/connections on social media.
- Frequency of posting pictures of self on social media.

One of the problems identified by Hawk and colleagues (2019) with the social media behaviour of those who are overconfident (or narcissistic) is that their aggressive or over-the-top attention-seeking behaviour online can lead to social rejection on social platforms.

This is the irony inherent in the behaviour of many different personality disorders: people tend to elicit the opposite behaviour in others to what they intend. Yet they tend not to see it as a failure of their behavioural strategies (e.g. aggressively showing off, displays of bravado and self-aggrandizement often pushes people away instead of drawing them in closer). Instead of trying different strategies, they see it as a failure of their effort – so their attempts at using the same strategy intensify, even when their behaviour continues to produce an undesirable result.

It is also important to say that there is no evidence that social media *causes* people to become narcissistic. It certainly may encourage the behaviour, especially if someone is in a peer group where that is normalized behaviour. However, social media activity is not a cause of personality disorder: people with certain personality disorders are drawn to specific tools that enable their preferred behaviours. Social media is certainly an ideal tool for people seeking self-aggrandizement, praise and attention.

IMPULSIVE

One of the main features of the impulsive personality style is that their behaviour and mood tends to be unstable, unpredictable and intense. People with this personality style feel passionately about events and about people and react accordingly. They tend not to be neutral or non-committal and are less likely to see grey areas. Life is black and white, good and bad, and everyone needs to pick a side.

Although they become intensely attached to ideas, plans and people, their allegiances and emotions can suddenly change. Their commitments also tend to depend on their relationship with the people involved. They may be intensely committed on one course of action, and highly involved with a person or a group who champions that cause. They maintain a firm and unshakeable belief that this is the right course of action – until they have a major disagreement with one of the key people involved. The emotions are so intense and tempers flare so high that instead of waiting for cooler heads to prevail, the person with impulsive style reverses course and suddenly and vehemently opposes the course of action (and the people involved) that they once ardently supported.

In extreme cases, the person with the impulsive style, in their outright rejection of a previous person, group or idea, may find joining an opposing camp to be quite appealing. Their antipathy and emotionality makes the opposing (and previously unthinkable) idea, ideology or strategy to be suddenly very attractive. Like-minded people, who may have been previous opponents, suddenly seem to have the right values and the right approach. The person can then find a new unity in opposition.

This pattern can continue over long periods of time, but the core component is an instability of emotions and relationships. The style can make it difficult to manage or work with someone because their emotions and their performance is highly dependent on the success of their relationships. When a manager or leader has the impulsive style, people around them probably spend most of their time 'managing up', and their focus is on reading the moods of their manager and navigating around these, instead of getting on with the job at hand.

This style can create significant bottlenecks in the workplace because people avoid delivering bad news, they avoid certain topics and they probably have to be careful about mentioning certain people or groups. It can be hard to predict who is in or out of favour week by week. People get emotionally distant, which can negatively affect relationships with colleagues because everyone is always walking on eggshells and trying to avoid information that would trigger negative moods in the person with the impulsive style.

This personality style is quite different from the previous styles in this chapter, in that the person's emotions really are not under control. People with dramatic and confident styles often use intense emotional responses in a deliberate, calculated and often superficial way. People with dramatic and confident styles can plan, predict and curate their responses to get the desired result. However, those with the impulsive style really don't feel in control of their own mood changes and have difficulty predicting their own behavioural changes. They may very sincerely believe a close confidant is their favourite person in the whole world and always will be, only to discover something new about them and suddenly feel intensely repulsed by that person at a later date.

There's a paradoxical effect in their behaviour: those with the impulsive style feel intensely and uncontrollably interested in, or attracted to, people in a very short period of time. They idealize and idolize others, which can spark intense relationships. Yet their intense and fiery approach can drive other people away.

FIGURE 13.4 Optimal and excessive characteristics of perfectionistic personality style

How it looks online

Instability will be characteristic in their online behaviour, just like in their in-person behaviour, although this is probably moderated by the severity. For people who can effectively manage this personality style, their intensity can be channelled into productive ideas and endeavours. They get excited about new projects, can maintain focus and are careful not to let their anger or frustrations take over. If they have developed effective coping skills, they will be reasonably self-aware and have a capacity to pause and think before they post intense emotions online for everyone to see.

However, when they are not very self-aware and have not developed effective coping strategies they will probably share a great deal of their personal views and private desires online. They may write very long posts, describing in detail what (or whom) they love and hate.

They also probably feel extreme regret about past actions, and may have difficulty understanding how they ever felt that way. They are likely to go through phases of making, then deleting, social media accounts or posts. They tend to be quick to reach out and share their thoughts but then are also very sensitive to criticism, meaning that having long, fiery engagements with acquaintances or strangers online has the potential to exacerbate their problems with emotional regulation.

Their tempestuousness, intensity and mood swings mean that the combination of alcohol (or other substances) and social media activity is an extremely risky proposition.

CASE STUDY: THE SOCIAL MEDIA
OBSESSED NETWORKER

Social media has created an interesting challenge for narcissists. It offers fantastic opportunities for networking, self-promotion, curation of one's own image and constant access to other people.

This case study is the perfect example of how someone's dark-side tendencies can be both a blessing and a curse at the same time, with both being perfectly apparent to anyone who is paying attention.

This colleague was a fantastic networker with an impressive CV. She had risen quickly in the non-profit sector, with an impressive list of achievements for someone of her age. She was good at moving both laterally and vertically – into different positions, on to different committees – and was great at picking up responsibilities related to judging, selecting, adjudicating – positions of influence and 'soft power'.

Being very attractive and charming certainly helped. She also used social media to maximum advantage. Generally, she would use social media in a way that was mutually beneficial for her and whatever organization she was working with. She made the organization look good, and she was always able to make herself front and centre. Even when she was only marginally involved in a project, she would manage to take an outsized amount of credit. On the surface, that was typically a welcome relationship. Some of her colleagues would put in the work and she could do the schmoozing of sponsors, networking with relevant organizations and using her connections.

Many people don't enjoy that kind of public-facing networking, schmoozing and subtly persuading people as a course of their work, so it's useful for an organization to find people to fill that necessary role. In this case, our charming networker seemed exceptional on one hand because she was 'always on', great at making connections and was convincing in person. The problem was, she posted *everything* on social media. She connected with *everyone* she possibly could on social media. She posted continuously and always publicly.

Even when she would call in sick (typically with an elaborate and compelling backstory, not just the flu), she would then post her daily activities on social media. Off to the gym at 10:30am. Champagne brunch with a large group of friends in the afternoon, long rambling post about the value of family, caring and trust later in the afternoon, then off to a cocktail party in the evening. All of her colleagues could see these posts and would know that it was likely she would be calling in 'sick' the following day as well.

As she progressed in her career, the pattern persisted (in different ways), but generally proceeded in the direction of collecting positions of influence, soft power, and wielding it skilfully. Yet the prevarication continued, the constant sharing on social media never ceased, and so most people around her knew that she was not very trustworthy, tended to shirk real work, but also tended to be quite effective in some roles and was willing to use her influence and connections for people she liked.

Now, some of the interesting questions in this case study are: Why don't people confront her? Why do people keep giving her positions of power and influence? There are five reasons for this:

- **The tendency to make a great first impression**. In many of these cases the charm comes on strongest at first; the person is most careful about impression management when it counts.
- **The opportunity for making connections.** Most people know the value of making connections in the workplace, but not

everyone is good at it. The help and favour of someone who is well connected and influential can be very attractive.

- **The risk of falling out of favour.** People who are willing to unscrupulously use their influence are *willing to unscrupulously use their influence*. So many people fall into the trap of thinking 'well I've seen them mistreat others, but they would never do that to me.' Often people who are manipulative attract people with the promise of great things, then trap them under the promise of terrible things happening to anyone who steps out of line.

- **The tendency to value the relationship.** It is not only for Machiavellian reasons that people maintain toxic relationships. It is often hard to lose sight of the person you thought someone was, or the relationship you thought you had, even after the situation has changed and there is much evidence to the contrary.

- **The desire for security and stability.** This is related to some of the previous points. No one's life only has 'one' problem at any given time. Often it *seems* easier not to rock the boat. It's not a 'good time' for the company/team/person. It seems better to wait it out or wait for the right opportunity to present itself.

In this case, like most cases, people around the destructive person or leader eventually find out about the dark side of the behaviour. Often the deception is done out in the open, or as in this case all posted publicly on social media. The clues are usually there: they may not be easy to miss, but they are very easy to misinterpret.

Case Study: The manipulative bully in Fintech

I spoke with a Director of Talent at an extremely profitable and rapidly growing financial technology company in North America. Her Chief Operations Officer/Chief Reputation Officer was 'charming, engaging, supportive in the beginning'. He always made a good first impression with people. However, that charm was short-lived for most employees.

The COO had zero tolerance for disagreement and no time for anyone who challenged his opinions. He had two different ways of managing disagreement on the team. In some cases, he would immediately fire someone who disagreed with him (or get his Director of Talent to fire them). His second approach was to slowly discredit and undermine people who challenged his authority.

She made the same mistake many people do in this situation: 'My biggest mistake was thinking I could influence or change the way he worked.' It's not unreasonable to think that people can be influenced or change their behaviour at work or as a result of the expert advice of their colleagues. However, it is difficult or impossible to change people with personality disorders, because their rigid patterns are inflexible. Also, if they have achieved positions of power, status and authority and have used their destructive behaviour to achieve success, then they are even less likely to change.

It's worth restating one of the messages from the case study in Chapter 23, about the leader in the oil industry: 'People change when the consequences of *not changing their behaviour* outweigh the demands of changing.'

Like many bullies and effective manipulators, the COO was exceptionally good at 'managing up', and working very differently with people who are more senior v. less senior. The COO deliberately isolated the CEO, so he was the only one with regular direct contact to the CEO. This is a common tactic in which bullies get away with treating their direct reports and employees badly while being effective at ingratiating themselves with people who are more powerful or influential. They can operate under the guise of the helpful deputy, 'taking on' many different tasks and responsibilities with the intention of fragmenting teams and departments and managing information to fit their agenda or narrative.

The COO's expectations of staff were unreasonably demanding and controlling, both in major and minor/unnecessary areas. He would expect employees to be on call at all hours of the day and night, and would regularly send angry emails at unpredictable times, which one employee called 'snot-a-grams'. But he would also demand staff carry out tasks to exert control over them: he would expect his staff to get him lunches or meals whenever he asked, and for the company to pay for it. Yet he ignored employees' break times and expected other people to do whatever he asked at whatever time.

People around him saw most of the aggressive and domineering behaviour as planned, not impulsive. It usually seemed calculated, and surprise firings or undermining of his employees generally served a purpose and was part of the culture he was creating intentionally.

He certainly hired some people in his own image and developed small cliques of favourites. He liked 'brilliant jerks', who were exceptionally skilled but also treated people badly. He liked and encouraged people to be aggressive as a rule but hated when people challenged him. While he expected others to cater to his whims, he would be deliberately unavailable and wouldn't let anyone else set an agenda: he refused to use Slack or email, but when he wanted something, he would barge in and out of meetings, shout people down, shout at people for not speaking up and dominate the conversations or hijack the meeting completely.

Part of his strategy was to keep people under constant pressure, instil fear of retribution and he 'created drama' as a method of 'controlling people'. There's a paradox in this, as when a company is growing exceptionally quickly, it can act as an incubator for a toxic leader and subsequently develop a toxic culture. Many problems can be shrugged off when business is booming, and rapidly expanding tech companies have a reputation for fostering destructive environments and ignoring bad behaviour as long as the company is growing. Sometimes the risks or the costs of destructive behaviour are ignored or accepted as the price of doing business. This company went through eight directors in a 12-month period (seven were fired; one resigned); they had four separate complaints of racism in the company (the COO fought against doing any diversity and inclusion work because he said he didn't see the value in it); and a half dozen complaints were brought against one of the COO's favourite employees (bullying, sexual harassment).

The Director of Talent at the company had been getting more distressed and frustrated with everything that was going on and had actively been looking for alternative work on what transpired to be her last day in the company. The COO informed her and another colleague in the morning that they would have to terminate six employees in a different department, and it had to be done by 10am. After they were finished, they were also both terminated at 10am. It had all been planned out well in advance, since a replacement Director of Talent was lined up the next day.

Conclusion

The damage done in this situation is difficult to tally up. Working for someone like this, and in a work environment like this, can be incredibly damaging to the employees who suffer under these bad bosses. The negative impact on people is profound, but some might argue that kind of environment can be overlooked if it's good for business. However, it's not good for business. The cost of high employee turnover alone is estimated to be around 30 per cent of an average employee's annual salary (Cappelli, 2019), and the cost of replacing senior executives could be over 200 per cent of their annual salary (MacLean, 2013). For a Fintech company that employs highly skilled, well-paid employees, the cost is substantial. It's the lost time, wasted hours, energy and effort that employees spend catering to a capricious boss that drain productivity. And the loss of progress and focus slows growth. Then there's the potential legal and reputational costs that can destroy an emerging business. That type of environment is never justified, and the negative impacts on both people and profits cannot be dismissed or excused.

14

Cluster C – The anxious personality styles

Cluster C personality styles tend to be dominated by feelings of anxiety and worry about themselves and other people. In terms of normal personality, these could be described as the anxious personality styles where people are generally more susceptible to stress. They are more likely to worry about what other people think of them, or be concerned about their own behaviour and performance. Two of the types – sensitive and selfless – tend to worry about their interpersonal relationships. Whereas the perfectionistic (commonly referred to as obsessive-compulsive personality disorder) tends to have a sense of self and their potential anxiety is tied up in work and productivity.

While people in the previous chapter (Cluster B) tend to have less concern with morality and may struggle with empathy, people with anxious personality styles (Cluster C) sometimes go too far in the other direction. They worry about doing the right thing, about being moral and empathetic and helping others. This certainly can be pro-social when the impulses and anxieties are channelled effectively and managed appropriately. But, as we know with personality disorders, sometimes too much of a good thing can be destructive (sometimes destructive to others, sometimes self-destructive). People in this group are more likely to fall into the self-destructive category; their obsession with doing the right thing can have unintended and undesirable consequences.

How can someone be too moral? Too conscientious? Too dedicated to helping others? In the case of helping others, that certainly is an admirable trait, but one which can be taken too far. It's usually a good thing to help others when they ask for it, less desirable to barge in and try to help people who have no desire for external intervention. Or, people who are incredibly selfless may run into problems when they are too trusting, or too focused on helping others at the expense of themselves. When people put other people's needs over their own financial, physical or psychological wellbeing, it can create its own problems. Or, sometimes the most diligent people are so convinced they know what is right and moral for them, that they believe it should be applied universally to everyone else. They can become so obsessed with their own rigid standards of behaviour that they berate, shame and denigrate the people around them: they may believe they are doing good when really they are causing harm to their relationships and others, and potentially even their own productivity.

The three personality styles in Cluster C are sensitive, selfless and perfectionistic.

Sensitive

People with a sensitive personality style tend to like familiarity (of places and of people), habit and routine. They like to feel comfortable and secure in their home, work and relationships and don't enjoy taking risks. They care profoundly about what other people think of them, so they want to do right by their friends, family and colleagues and worry about doing or saying the wrong thing.

At work they function best when they are around familiar people and know exactly what their roles and responsibilities are. The idea of improvising or being unprepared probably terrifies them and they get overwhelmed under pressure. While some people work well outside of their comfort zone, people with this personality style get too overwhelmed to be able to function effectively. They tend to be better in small groups with warm and trusting relationships and they struggle to cope with conflict. They are probably quick to apologize, and in an argument they tend to assume they are in the wrong or at fault (even when they are not).

They are good with collaboration, since they don't like too much attention and don't seek the spotlight. They would much rather contribute to the success of a group than be the team leader or publicly take credit, and they would never steal credit for someone else's work.

Although people with sensitive personality styles may not typically be identified and promoted into leadership positions as often, they can be successful managing smaller, closely-knit teams. They are probably very perceptive of what is going on in their team. They are far more likely to take the approach of leading from behind, encouraging their team members and sharing credit for success generally: this approach can contribute strongly to team cohesion, trust and loyalty.

They can also be effective in positions that require a keen perception of what could go wrong and perceptiveness to risks or conflict. They may have more trouble making decisions quickly and swiftly, but are good in roles that require more discussion, deliberation and fact-finding. Conversely, this can lead to delays, excessive caution and a focus on avoiding the worst-case scenario instead of searching for the best outcome.

Their worry, combined with constant consultation and over-planning, can create the impression of being 'busy' without actually being effective. Their constant movement sometimes creates the image that things are happening, but it's really churn and froth instead of real movement or progress.

Generally people with the sensitive personality style struggle to get started and to complete projects, so it's important that they focus on setting goals and objectives by importance and urgency. The temptation for them will often be to follow the path of least resistance or avoid doing things for fear of failure. Excessive risk-taking tends to lead to paralysis, so it is better to take reasoned and carefully planned risks instead of going too far and using failure at an impossible task as a reason to avoid other tasks.

FIGURE 14.1 Optimal and excessive characteristics of wary personality style

How it looks online

People with the sensitive personality style tend to prefer smaller, closer-knit communities. They are worriers who like to feel comfortable and secure, either on their own or in groups, so they are more likely to avoid platforms that tend to be fractious, controversial or aggressive.

However, they probably get drawn into things because they worry about leaving groups, muting, blocking or deleting people or standing up for themselves. Even if someone is posting content they find extremely offensive or disagreeable, they may still worry that the *other* person might be offended if they hide the content. Some social media sites, like Facebook, encourage people to have extremely wide circles of connections from family and friends to work and social clubs, to old school friends from years or decades ago. People with the sensitive style may feel like they need to accept every connection, even from a distant acquaintance with whom they would rather not be privy to their innermost thoughts, musings and political views. Yet they are torn by the fear of missing out, fear of rejection and worry about offending or appearing to reject someone else. They may become passive but continual observers in content that makes them worried or anxious, but they are equally concerned about the consequences of disengaging. They worry about what they are engaging in, but also worry about what could go wrong if they disconnect: consequently, they tend to anxiously hover somewhere in the middle.

People with this style would be advised not to participate in everything online but choose one or a small number of social networks and/or online groups that really share their approach and fulfil their needs. They should be mindful of how some groups or platforms make them feel and realize it's okay to stop participating in something that makes them very anxious or unhappy online.

Selfless

The selfless personality style shares some similarities with the sensitive personality style because both have a tendency to worry about other people. They both tend to be more passive and submissive compared to other personality styles and have under-developed social risk-taking behaviours. The difference is that people with the sensitive style tend to generally see others as potentially threatening or critical: everyone is a potential critic, and worry is an over-developed strategy to try and protect oneself. For the selfless personality style, all (or nearly all) other people are seen in an idealized way: they are warm, nurturing and supremely capable. Someone with the selfless style sees other people as impressive and capable. They have an over-developed need to be close to others, to rely on others combined with an under-developed sense of self-esteem and self-reliance.

This means that someone with the selfless style tends to be a bit over-dependent on other people. They can often be a bit too trusting of others; they rely so strongly on the approval, support and opinions of other people that sometimes they struggle to make decisions for themselves. They are great followers, loyal companions, extraordinarily caring friends, they feel profound empathy and find it easy to lose themselves in someone else or within a group. That can be a great, pro-social attribute when they are in healthy, constructive and mutually respectful relationships. But it also means they can struggle to distinguish between their admiration for someone and for the actions of someone they admire. When they like someone they have trouble separating the relationship and the behaviour. In other words, once they like someone, they see an idealized version of that person, and they will readily excuse any of that person's behaviour to preserve the relationship.

Conversely, they have a heightened fear of being alone and worry that they could not be self-sufficient. They generally tend to be amazed at other people's independence, resilience and capabilities but struggle to see that in themselves. They may very well have all of those capabilities (and struggle to realize how often other people feel insecurities or stress), but they don't see that in themselves unless it's reflected back off someone else. Even when they do act independently, capably or resiliently, they think to themselves: 'Oh well, I could only do that because of so-and-so's support.' Giving credit where credit is due is always great, but people with the selfless personality style have a tendency not to give themselves as much credit as they deserve.

In the workplace, people with the selfless style are the peace-makers, consensus-finders and compassionate colleagues. They value harmony within a team, sometimes to the exclusion of everything else. They avoid conflict, so consequently are more likely to carry something out unhappily, but without complaint, than to make a fuss. When they are effective, they believe that happy workers are productive workers (generally a correct assumption), but this means sometimes they tend to shy away from disputes that really need to be resolved.

They are great to have on a team when they support an effective leader, promote team cohesion, support their colleagues and are always willing to help others. However, they also make easy targets for bullies and can become colluding followers and enablers of bad behaviour. It's really important for people with a selfless style to have a pre-defined set of values and goals going into an organization and be willing to fight for principles that are worth defending.

FIGURE 14.2 Optimal and excessive characteristics of solitary personality style

How it looks online

Generally, people with the selfless style who have found effective coping strategies tend to have become part of a smaller, well-connected and supporting team, group or community. They feel a strong need to be close to people and are likely to use any communication medium available to meet those needs. They desire more constant support and a need to feel close to others, so are likely to post, message and share more frequently.

When they feel their needs aren't being met, they may increase their attention- and support-seeking activities. For some people, their constant need for comfort, affection and support (sometimes even from strangers) may seem off-putting. It can have the paradoxical effect whereby increasing the frequency and intensity of demands for affection or support actually diminishes the quality of relationships. While they are generally warm, friendly and cooperative (Sachse & Kramer, 2018), in some cases, this can lead to relationship asymmetry, where one person is demanding all of the emotional resources of another, which is rarely a sustainable foundation for a relationship (Overholser, 1996).

The problem people with selfless personality style often encounter is that they worry so much about being able to form, develop and maintain relationships with other people that they over-compensate in ways that others can find overwhelming or smothering.

PERFECTIONISTIC

The perfectionistic personality style tends to be associated with more positive outcomes in the workplace. When someone has the perfectionistic style and can effectively manage their stress, has healthy coping mechanisms and can effectively prioritize tasks, this can be an exceptionally productive style. Being driven, self-motivated and detail-oriented are some of the most sought-after characteristics in most workplaces.

Of course, everything has a dark side, and like with any of the personality styles there is much less productive behaviour that can emerge under stress. Being detail-oriented can go too far when people become obsessed with control and micromanaging, placing extreme limits on the autonomy and productivity of themselves and others. Being perfectionistic can lead people to focusing on minor details and appearance over the substance of the work. It can cause people to dither and delay, when 'good enough' is never enough. One of the features of the perfectionistic style when it becomes dysfunctional is an inability to deal with ambiguity (Wheaton & Ward, 2020). So often things become either black or white, perfect or unacceptable, right or wrong. They can struggle to see grey areas.

Of course, there are jobs where being perfectionistic is essential. Maintenance of aircraft engines, health-and-safety officers in mills or manufacturers, biosecurity lab technicians and nuclear power technicians have jobs that leave little room for error. In some types of work just 'good enough' can be lethal. However, most types of work leave more room for going through rough drafts, developing plans on the fly. Different job roles have to make different trade-offs between constraints on time, budgets and the need for perfection. People with the perfectionistic style tend to be more effective in roles that are detail-focused and may struggle in environments where quality has to be sacrificed for punctuality.

Another challenge for some people with this personality style is that they may focus on processes more than people. In a position of leadership they may thoroughly develop processes that would be extremely efficient if they could fill all of the roles. However, sometimes they find it difficult to understand other people who are not like them, and may have difficulty accounting for the broad range of different personalities, approaches and behaviours within a workplace.

They may struggle to understand and connect with people who place less value on work and productivity than they do. This means that they may have trouble forming positive relationships with people who they see as taking a more casual or laid-back approach to work, and sometimes they struggle to see the value in being spontaneous, agile or having a more easy-going attitude.

They can also be more prone to burnout when they struggle to disconnect from work; they internalize work problems and are more likely to bring them home. For some people with the perfectionistic style they may have trouble finding value in activities outside of the work and can have difficulty connecting with people who don't share their priorities. This often translates into their personal relationships, so they may have difficulty prioritizing their time for personal relationships or time with family.

Getting a healthy balance is challenging for everyone, and while a focus on work and productivity can certainly help with career advancement and feelings of satisfaction and achievement when their careers go well, it means they can also take career setbacks and failures even harder than most people. Because their sense of self and personal value is so tied up in professional achievements, failures at work can become overwhelming.

FIGURE 14.3 Optimal and excessive characteristics of unconventional personality style

How it looks online

In its darker side, the perfectionistic style can appear in the form of those obsessed with rules and regulations, and constantly preoccupied with the enforcement of those rules and regulations. Neighbourhood watch groups online sometimes have people like this: obsessively monitoring others for minor infractions or transgressions.

There's also some interesting research that would suggest people with obsessive-compulsive personality disorder (perfectionistic style) may be more vulnerable to cults and fringe groups (Rahmani et al., 2019). Many cults and extremist religious groups use an excessive attention to detail, strict rules and repetitive behaviours that can align with the perfectionistic style. Furthermore, many have specifically prescribed behaviours as a means of combatting obsessive thoughts or compulsions (e.g. what to do if you have 'impure' thoughts). While cults and conspiracy theories may seem to align with the general worldview of the Cluster A disorders, the rigid rules, structures and prescribed behaviours of cults may also appeal to people with the perfectionistic style.

Instead of being attracted to the unconventional thinking or counter-cultural elements of conspiracy theories and cults online, people with the perfectionistic style may find the strict rules and Byzantine structures of cults appealing, or in the case of conspiracy theories may find the attention to detail in building a conspiracy theory to be engrossing.

15

Personality styles and dysfunction at work

Personality traits can be measured and understood on a spectrum. The extreme ends of the spectrum tend to be dominated by rigid and inflexible ways of looking at and interacting with the world, alongside over- or under-developed coping strategies. At the generally healthy and adaptive ends of the spectrum, we have personality styles, whereas the extreme and dysfunctional ends of the spectrum are personality disorders.

So how does personality disorder and dysfunction relate to 'normal' personality traits? Chapter 10 briefly mentioned how personality traits are one of the strong predictors of success in the workplace and in leadership. This chapter will explain that in more detail and discuss how specific personality traits contribute to success and different behaviours.

The important components of functioning (or dysfunction) will be discussed later in this chapter, by specifically looking at:

1. Identity – The person generally has self-awareness about who they are and their impact on other people and can manage a full range of emotions.
2. Self-direction – The person has reasonable and achievable goals and is able to motivate and manage themselves to work towards those goals.
3. Empathy – The person is capable of understanding and interpreting the emotions and motivations of other people and can understand the perspectives of other people even when disagreeing.

4. Intimacy – The person is capable of managing and maintaining continuous and caring close personal relationships.

If someone can 'do' those four things fairly effectively, most of the time, then they can probably function reasonably well in day-to-day life. Of course, 'reasonably well' doesn't mean a person won't have arguments, disagreements, emotional outbursts or bad days from time to time. That happens to everyone, and is well within the range of normal behaviour; it's when there are sustained problems in some or all of those four areas that we look for personality disorder.

For example, if someone has a solitary style, they tend to keep to themselves, to seem emotionally unavailable to most people and to only have a few close relationships, all of which is not necessarily indicative of a personality disorder. If they prefer to just have a few close relationships, are able to manage their own personal life and career, work towards their personal and professional goals on their own terms and can fairly effectively navigate the relationships they do choose to have, that's not particularly concerning. It might not be the lifestyle *everyone* would choose, but that doesn't mean it's unhealthy.

The same is true of someone who has, say, a dramatic style. They may be a continuous entertainer, like to steal the spotlight and be the centre of attention, feel they need to 'perform' in social situations and want to be around other people as much as possible. Having some superficial relationships or many acquaintances isn't a problem if the person is also able to develop and maintain close, reciprocal and empathetic relationships with at least a few people. If their social activities don't get in the way of their personal or career goals (or if they can use this style to further their personal or career objectives), then that's perfectly fine.

Normal personality at work

Normal personality traits in the workplace can be measured using the High Potential Traits Indicator (HPTI), which is a workplace adaptation of the Big Five model of personality (MacRae & Furnham, 2018). By measuring personality in the workplace we can map out people's potential in different domains, understand optimal functioning and find ways to help people work together and understand each other better.

Each of the six traits can be mapped on to the personality *styles*.

- *Conscientiousness.* Those who rate themselves as being highly conscientious tend to be focused on goals and how to reach them. They will usually be self-motivated. Those who score lower on this trait tend to be more easy-going, spontaneous and open to new insight.
- *Adjustment.* High adjustment scores suggest calmness under pressure and fewer feelings of stress. Those who report lower adjustment tend to experience more stress and worry.
- *Curiosity.* Those with high curiosity scores often like novelty, learning and variety. By contrast, lower curiosity suggests a liking for tried-and-tested methods and consistency.
- *Risk Approach.* Those who score high on risk approach tend to bring a reasoned and rational approach to difficult situations and conversations. A lower risk approach characteristically indicates more instinctive or emotional decisions.
- *Ambiguity Acceptance.* Those with high ambiguity acceptance usually thrive on uncertainty and complexity. Those who find it more difficult to cope with ambiguity may like situations where there are clear-cut answers and solutions.
- *Competitiveness.* High competitiveness scores are typical of people who enjoy positions of power, influence and recognition. Less competitive people prefer cooperation and collaboration; they may dislike the spotlight.

Figure 15.1 shows how personality styles can be mapped on to traits, and when combined with levels of functioning, we can examine how those attributes could fit in with different roles and types of work. For example, your solitary style worker with low risk approach and adjustment may be effective in a safety manager role, or someone managing cybersecurity risk for industrial control systems. In that job, you probably want someone who has a low tolerance for risk and worries about what could go wrong. Whereas it is clear that the aggressive, confident and dramatic styles tend to have high risk approach and high adjustment, which may fit better in high-pressure, public-facing roles.

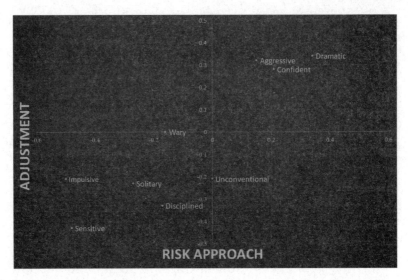

FIGURE 15.1 HPTI risk approach and adjustment, mapped on to personality styles

TABLE 15.1 Notable personality traits associated with styles

Disordered Personality Style	High	Low
Wary		Ambiguity acceptance
Solitary		Risk approach
Unconventional	Curiosity	
Aggressive	Competitiveness	
Dramatic	Risk approach (Interpersonal)	
Confident	Risk approach, Competitiveness	
Impulsive		Adjustment
Sensitive		Adjustment Risk approach
Selfless		Competitiveness
Perfectionistic	Conscientiousness	

Adapted from MacRae, 2015.

PERSONALITY TRAITS AND DISORDERS

There has been considerable effort by psychologists and psychiatrists over the last decades to unify models of normal personality and disordered personality, and while great progress has been made in recent years, there is still work to be done on bringing everything together into one clear model.

In the 1980s and early 1990s the first steps were made in mapping personality disorders on to the models of normal personality traits (Wiggins & Pincus, 1989; Costa & McCrae, 1990). This developed as the research on personality traits flourished. There has been continuous effort over subsequent decades to see convergence between models used for diagnostic and treatment purposes in clinical practice and personality models like the Big Five, and the progress has been successful in finding significant confluence (Morey et al., 2000). The latest version of the American Psychological Association's *Diagnostic and Statistical Manual of Mental Disorders* (APA, 2013) now incorporates a trait-based model of personality disorder (Watson et al., 2013).

We see some common trends here in the clusters of personality disorders, especially with Cluster B disorders having clear connections to higher scores on most of the HPTI personality traits.

Cluster A
These traits, which tend to be characterized by eccentricities and slightly odd thinking, have some similarities – the wary and solitary styles tending to have lower adjustment and being more sensitive to stress. However, their relationship with normal personality traits varies substantially within each style. The solitary style tends to be lower in nearly all HPTI traits, indicating someone who is generally more withdrawn from all aspects of the workplace. In terms of HPTI traits, we could describe these as lower in risk approach, competitiveness and ambiguity acceptance. Whereas the unconventional style has no relationship with sensitivity to stress (adjustment) but tends to have a higher preference for ambiguity acceptance, risk approach and competitiveness.

Cluster B

It's interesting to compare normal personality traits, because, in general, when we measure people with higher levels of subclinical personality disorders in the context of positive, *desirable* traits, people in this cluster tend to exhibit traits that are highly desirable in the workplace and especially in leadership positions (with the exception of impulsive style). Aggressive, dramatic and confident styles, however, all report high adjustment, which indicates a low sensitivity to stress along with more appetite for risk and ambiguity as well as high competitiveness.

Cluster C

Within this cluster, sensitive and selfless personality styles have a similar pattern compared with normal personality traits. They tend to be a bit more susceptible to stress (substantially more susceptible to stress in the case of sensitive), being more avoidant of risk and ambiguity, and being a bit less conscientious. Generally these would not be seen as an optimal leadership profile but more likely to be people who wish to contribute to the team without wanting to steal the spotlight.

The perfectionistic personality style, unsurprisingly, is related to higher conscientiousness, but is also characterized by a very low level of ambiguity acceptance. This would be someone who is both achievement-oriented and detail-oriented.

LEVELS OF FUNCTIONING

Other than personality styles, we can look to function v. dysfunction to see whether people's styles are adaptive or destructive. This could be particularly important in job selection because it offers us another lens to look at issues of 'selecting in' v. 'selecting out'. Employers should select in for positive traits like intelligence, knowledge, charm, interpersonal skills, work ethic and past performance. But they should also look to select out for undesirable traits such as a history of bullying, misusing company resources, difficulty with collaboration or cooperation and inability to work independently.

We can look at levels of functioning to address this. For example, if someone had a dramatic style, they could appear charming, engaging, quick, easy to talk to and clear about their career goals and their personal strengths. That may be true, irrespective of their

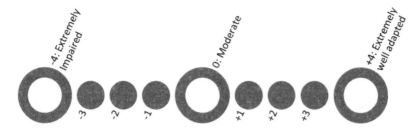

FIGURE 15.2 Levels of impaired and adaptive functioning

weaknesses, but what about those select-out factors? Should you hire someone with all of those traits, if they can't get along with others? Or if their promises, objectives and career goals change with the weather and depending on the person they are trying to impress at the moment? Perhaps not.

Psychiatrists use four levels of *dys*function (APA, 2013) to diagnose personality disorder (the areas of function and dysfunction were initially discussed in Chapter 6), but if we are looking at the full range of a person's potential, particularly in the context of work and success (instead of just focusing on the dysfunctional ends), and we are looking to select for good behaviour as well as selecting out bad behaviour, we can extend the matrix to look at variations in *high* functioning as well. For example, the range shown in Figure 15.2.

Then we can contrast personality dysfunction with what highly effective would look like on this spectrum.

Identity (high self-awareness)
Has an excellent understanding of self, with consistent, accurate and generally positive sense of self and self-worth. This means they have a good sense of their own strengths and how best to use them, their sense of self-worth is tied realistically to their strengths, and they work to make best use of their own strengths. They also understand their limitations and can accept that as part of themselves.

They understand a full range of emotions and can recognize those emotions in themselves and know how to effectively cope with them. This is true for positive emotions: excitement, happiness, feelings of energy and vigour can be channelled appropriately into healthy and adaptive behaviours. And negative emotions are experienced and understood and the person has healthy coping mechanisms to deal with those emotions. They can accept both positive and negative emotions as part of their overall experience.

Self-direction

They set and aspire to reasonable goals. It's important to note here that 'reasonable goals' are entirely contextual for that person.

The person can attain meaningful levels of fulfilment in different domains. That means the person can balance their time commitments and relationships not just in one area (work, family, romantic relationships) but strike a balance across the different domains that are important within reasonable limits. For example, someone who prioritizes work to the point that their goals in personal, family and romantic life are unachievable or unavailable is having difficulty functioning. Or someone who sets unreasonably high standards in all domains and consequently has difficulty living up to those standards in all domains is having difficulty functioning.

Empathy

They understand how other people feel, and even when they disagree with someone, they can respect the other person's perspective. They may show curiosity about the reason for others' thoughts, actions or beliefs when they don't understand: they make an effort to understand differences and are able to set their own prejudices or biases aside.

They also have a fairly good capacity to figure out how other people might react to different situations and can understand the emotional responses of others.

They use that knowledge and ability to understand people constructively and compassionately (those who have an excellent ability to read other people, but who use that callously or maliciously would be dysfunctional).

Intimacy

People who are well-adapted in this area are able to form positive and reciprocal relationships that can be sustained over time. That doesn't necessarily mean they will get along with *everyone* they work with or maintain *every* relationship they initiate. It means that they can adapt to social environments and have a capability and autonomy about who they do choose to form close and long-lasting relationships with.

LEVELS OF FUNCTIONING ONLINE

It's not a stretch to extend all of these areas of functioning into the online space. Having self-awareness, self-direction, empathy and developing intimacy are just as relevant when looking at online behaviour and whether it is healthy or potentially toxic.

Identity

Does the person have a clear and unified sense of self that is stable and consistent in the online and offline world? As has been discussed in Chapter 9, people emphasize and de-emphasize certain parts of themselves in different settings. People even engage in fantasy worlds in gaming, or with their friends, but still have the capacity to integrate and understand how that fits together with other parts of their life.

Self-direction

There are two components involved in self-direction.

First, is their behaviour self-directed online? Is the person choosing who to communicate with, what platforms to use, what behaviour to engage in and how they want to approach the online environment? Or is their online behaviour directed and dictated by someone else? If work emails, Slack groups and other platforms completely dominate the person's life to the point where they feel they have no control, or no ability to function and pursue their goals in other areas of life, this is clearly becoming dysfunctional. Or is their behaviour being dominated by some toxic organization or cult-like entity online (e.g. QAnon, see Chapter 21)?

Second, do people have a reason and a purpose to go online, and is their activity online goal-directed? These could simply be goals like talking to friends, catching up with family or communicating with family. It could be recreational: reading, gaming, watching movies or learning new things. It could be educational. Or is it compulsive behaviour that is purposeless and impossible to achieve fulfilment from (e.g. constantly refreshing pages, compulsively checking news, social media feeds etc.)? It should meet some needs while not compromising needs or goals in other areas.

Empathy

Trolling is a good example of dysfunctional behaviour because it indicates a lack of empathy. Going out to deliberately annoy, frustrate or elicit negative emotions in other people demonstrates either an impairment in understanding one's own effects on others or a callous disregard for one's effect on others.

This, of course, should be taken as highly context-dependent, especially in the online world of gaming: playing games like wargames, where the purpose of the game is to defeat an opponent, playing within the rules and the context of the game are entirely pro-social. Although there has been various hysterical reactions to violence in video games (there is no evidence to suggest violent video games cause violence, just like there is no evidence to suggest that people who read the Bible go out and crucify their neighbours), violent video games are not a concern. What may be a concern is when someone deliberately breaks the rules or cheats in a video game or online community in order to deliberately annoy, harass or humiliate other people. Playing within the rules is pro-social (whatever those rules may be); whereas violating the rules and norms is not.

Intimacy

Is the person able to maintain satisfying and reciprocal relationships online? This may mean being able to strike an appropriate balance between how much of the relationship takes place online v. offline, and how much certain relationships affect their whole social matrix. For example, it's not a problem to have relationships that are primarily or exclusively online – but when those relationships detract from someone's ability to interact with people in person, or all of the person's other relationships suffer as a result of online activity, then it is dysfunction.

Two examples

Let's look at examples for each area of functioning in describing personality styles. These are expanded versions of the optimal v. excessive comparison for the styles in Chapters 12–14.

Solitary – High v. Low Functioning

	Low Functioning	High Functioning
Identity	Don't feel like they have much purpose or meaning, feels lost in social settings.	May seem a bit odd or unique to other people, but has a clear idea of who they are and what is important to them.

	Low Functioning	High Functioning
Self-direction	Has difficulty setting goals or prioritizing, or identifying what is important to them.	Likes to be alone or in small groups and can focus intensely on goals and activities for long periods of time.
Empathy	Feels that other people are different. Shuts others out as a means of perceived self-preservation.	Takes longer to understand other people, but makes an effort with close connections, important relationships.
Intimacy	Has little to no interest in social relationships and gets no pleasure from social interaction.	Has close-knit social circle, needs personal space but has positive, reciprocal relationships with a few people.

Aggressive – High v. Low Functioning

	Low Functioning	High Functioning
Identity	Sense of self is impervious to the reactions and feedback from others; automatically defines self as opposed to perceived threats.	Can channel their behaviour into appropriate and legal forms of thrill-seeking and adventure.
Self-direction	Impulsive and thrill-seeking, gets bored easily and may have trouble controlling impulses.	Understands the potential consequences of actions, and works towards positive outcomes.
Empathy	Understands other people's emotions and reactions but uses this to hurt or manipulate others.	Can focus on positive outcomes and values in interactions with other people.
Intimacy	Outgoing and gregarious, but gets bored of people quickly and can't sustain long-term collaborative relationships.	Outgoing and gregarious, meets many different people and can connect with and maintain collaborative relationships with some.

Go further: Go online to highpotentialpsych.co.uk, take the test and see where you score on the dark-side personality styles, and how your results compare to other people.

16

Identifying personality disorders at work

Understanding, measuring and assessing personality, and some of the dysfunctional elements of personality, are essential for managing and improving behaviours. There has been an abundance of research in the past two decades (Fournier, 2015), but there are still ongoing debates about the best ways to understand and measure personality and how to describe personality disorders in particular. This continuing debate and development is excellent for the field because it has significantly advanced our understanding of personality and its dark side as we continue to learn more. This means it's also worth remembering that the science in this field is nowhere near 'settled'.

Personality disorders can be understood as either traits or types (see Table 16.1). This chapter focuses on different types of measurement in psychology, with tips and techniques for assessment in the workplace. Keep in mind that the development of psychological assessments is not something to be carried out without significant training and expertise.

TRAIT V. TYPE

In *type* models of personality, each person has a 'type' that corresponds with a category, and that type comes with a set of attributes. *Trait* theories describe people based on measured quantities. Instead of someone being of a single type, they exhibit a certain *level* of the trait.

TABLE 16.1. The differences between traits and types

Trait theory	Type theory
Concerned with universals possessed in different amounts	Concerned with preferences which are perhaps inborn or learnt
Involves measuring	Involves sorting
Extreme scores are important for discrimination	Midpoint is crucial for discrimination
Normally distributed	Skewed distribution
Scores mean amount of trait possessed	Scores indicate confidence that sorting is correct
Often used in 'normal' populations for comparisons between individuals	Often used in clinical populations for diagnostic criteria

So if someone has a trait they can be 'a little', 'a lot', 'extremely' or other quantities of that trait. Types describes people as either/or; traits describe *how much*.

Throughout this book we've tended to focus on different styles of personality disorder which are *type* models of potential dysfunction. Whereas models of normal personality like the Big Five or HPTI are *trait* models. The styles align particularly well with how personality disorders tend to be understood in clinical practice, and in the long-standing tradition of the DSM (APA, 2013) categories of personality disorder.

Personality types can be mapped on to traits (see Chapter 15), and there are clear relationships between the measures of 'normal' personality functioning and personality disorder.

ASSESSING PEOPLE AT WORK

There are four key methods that can be used to collect data about people. Each of the methods has different purposes, applications and practicality. They provide different information for different purposes. Assessment can be as much of an art as a science, that is based on practice, training and experience. Combining the right set of tools to develop a profile of an individual or group depends very much on the context and the intended outcome.

1. Personal history/biography

A biography is the history of a person's life. In a biography you can look for narrative examples of their personality traits, their intelligence, along with details about their education and work experience, as well as more nuance and context about experiences that are unique to them. In a biography, all of these different attributes and experiences tend to be presented on an equal footing: each contributing to the development of that person. In this way, biographies are an excellent way of trying to understand all of the different factors that help to understand a person and the way they act.

Biographies are a great way of zooming in on a particular person and a particular context. They are helpful in understanding how different psychological principles play out in specific cases. They are less useful at making generalizations that apply to everyone.

The case studies in this book are a good example of brief snapshots of people within certain environments, but they don't provide a detailed history or biography of the person – just a snapshot of their behaviour from one perspective. The extended case studies of Donald Trump throughout this book (Chapters 5, 6, 19) include far more biographical details, connecting early childhood development through to adolescence, middle and late adulthood alongside career development. This is a more thorough profile that helps to provide more insight: when you can observe patterns of behaviour over years and decades, it makes it easier to understand current and future patterns of behaviour. The more behavioural (and observational) data you can put together on someone, the more comprehensive and accurate the picture can be.

Personal history, though, is not scientific data, and not necessarily generalizable to any other person. It is most useful for understanding a person and their particular decisions, behaviours and actions throughout their life. At times, the lessons may be instructive or interesting to other people, but general rules and principles can never be reliably derived from the experiences of one person.

Business and leadership biographies are a good example of this. Often, leadership case studies and biographies like to list a few 'key elements of success' or 'things you need to know to succeed'. At times these are interesting and useful, and sometimes they even align with the more general principles. But what helped one person be successful may not be applicable to another person. Biographies are useful because they are instructive in a very unique context and set of irreplaceable environmental factors. The 'right' set of characteristics, the optimal levels of personality traits, vary depending on the environment. There are characteristics and traits that almost universally contribute to achievement (e.g. intelligence, conscientiousness), but many others that are that are best suited to specific social or physical settings.

It is impossible to recreate another person's life history, or to translate one successful person's achievement story on to a completely different person, so it is unwise to try. We can learn from the mistakes of others, and certainly gain insight from a person's biography and speculate whether or not we would like to work with them. But it is far more useful to take general, evidence-based principles and adapt them to personal or workplace contexts, than to try to recreate someone else's irreplicable experience.

2. Test performance

Test performance is very different from personal history, and it gives very different information into a person's capabilities. While personal history is subjective and qualitative, test performance is an objective and quantitative measure.

Test performance refers to how well people do on tests that measure some underlying characteristic or ability. Intelligence tests, for example, tap into a general capacity for information processing, retrieval and storage. Tests of ability or knowledge can be used to measure or demonstrate competence in specific skills. In the context of dark-side personality traits, one interesting use of test performance data could be assessing someone's insight or honesty. If someone says they are the most intelligent person, that they have exceptionally high intelligence, that is relatively quick and easy to test objectively.

In fact, psychologists have conducted this experiment. First, they ask people to estimate their own intelligence: are they above or below average intelligence? And by how much? This research into *self-estimated intelligence* and actual cognitive ability, as measured by tests of vocabulary, spatial reasoning, working vocabulary and similar measures, shows some interesting results (Gabriel et al., 1994; Furnham, 2005; de Ribera et al., 2019):

- Narcissists tend to over-estimate their own intelligence.
- Sociopaths tend to have slightly lower intelligence scores, particularly in sociopaths that engage in criminal behaviour.
- Personality is a good predictor of self-rated intelligence, but not a good predictor of actual intelligence.
- There are significant gender differences in men and women's estimates of their own intelligence. Men tend to *over-estimate* their own intelligence and women tend to *under-estimate* their own intelligence.

By testing intelligence, abilities and knowledge it is possible to reduce some of the problems in self-report and self-reported biography (such as a CV) and disentangle someone's self-confidence from their competence. It also has some capability to weed out some of the people who exaggerate their own abilities. It's easy to catch out exaggerators by making them prove their own claims and demonstrate their real abilities in an objective test.

Beyond detecting some of the more extreme dark-side attributes, measuring objective test performance also has the potential to reduce biases like gender bias: we know that in comparison to their own self-evaluations women tend to over-perform and men tend to under-perform. So testing can provide valuable insight into people's own self-awareness and the realistic estimation of their abilities.

3. Observation data

Observation data is second-hand data about another person. It can be structured to assess the same content as other types of data. For example, external observers, friends, colleagues could be asked to assess someone's personality, behaviour or performance at work as they have seen it. The purpose of observation data is intended to get a different perspective on that person's behaviour. No one can be truly impartial, but developing a composite profile based on external observers can create a more complete picture than a single observer alone, or a self-report.

Observation data can also be used very effectively to provide more comprehensive assessments of people as part of employee selection and development activities. The 360-degree ratings (multi-source feedback) use observations about an individual from others who are familiar with that person's behaviour. When done well, they should gather data from observers who have different relationships with the target of the

360-degree ratings: peers, director reports and managers all provide different perspectives on the person's behaviour. It can be interesting to detect similarities and differences. Does the person present themselves very differently to people who are more senior than them compared with less senior? Are they belligerent to some people while meek with others? Does their self-image match up with the perception of other people? Figure 16.1 shows how multi-source feedback can start to answer these questions.

There are three main limitations to multi-source feedback. As with any source of data, there are advantages and limitations. Being aware of the limitations can help to use the data most effectively.

1. **How well do the observers know the person they are rating?** The more closely people work together, the better they get to know each other. The longer they have worked together, the better the understanding of the person's behaviour in different contexts. A line manager only sees a certain set of behaviours, whereas a close colleague may have a more nuanced view of their colleague's behaviour. All ratings are coloured by the work environment, the relationship and the context.

FIGURE 16.1 Multi-source feedback model

2. **Are people willing to tell the truth about the person they are rating?** The rater's familiarity with the candidate affects the observer's objectivity: based on their experience with the person, are they motivated to be more or less honest about that person?

3. **Who is selecting the referees?** Who selects the rater and how they are selected can have a significant impact. Is the candidate selecting their raters? And are they selecting people who they think will make them look good, or people who will give them honest feedback? Perhaps the two will align for some people, but certainly not for everyone.

The 360-degree data can be especially useful in detecting the behaviour associated with low self-awareness, or the rigid and inflexible thought and behavioural patterns that come with personality disorders.

4. Self-report

Self-report methods are extraordinarily common, especially in testing and psychometrics. Self-report methods are what people say about themselves. They can either be very open-ended questions: 'Tell me about your responsibilities at your last job,' 'How would you describe your work ethic?' The person is asked a question and draws on their own experience and understanding of how to respond to the question. Or, as in most psychometric tests, there are closed-ended questions: 'Rate your agreement with the following statements.' Closed-ended questions have a limited number of possible responses, so tend not to be used when there are opportunities for conversation, more open social interaction or opportunities to prove the nuances of the responses.

Self-report methods tend to be favoured in employee interview and selection processes because they are familiar and cost effective. Most candidates are familiar with the format and requirements of writing a CV, and most employers think they know how to evaluate a CV. Interviews are equally familiar, and most hiring managers feel confident that interviews are an effective method and are useful for judging personal characteristics. Yet interviews and CVs are some of the least valid or reliable predictors of an employee's potential.

Another familiar self-report questionnaire is the closed-ended, quantitative method for collecting data, such as in personality tests.

In these tests, the participant is asked to respond to a pre-defined number of statements. Each of their responses is mapped on to a clearly defined structure of different traits (or factors) that can be measured and explained quantitatively with objective comparisons between different people.

There are three limitations to self-report methods:

A. **Self-insight.** Most people have reasonably good insight into themselves and why they think and act the way they do. The vast majority of people have an idea of who they are, who they want to be, and the actions that help or hinder that. However, not everyone has that insight. Those who don't have insight into their own behaviour or the reasons they act the way they do are not able to provide an accurate description to other people, because that insight is not available to them.

B. **Social desirability.** Even when people are self-aware, have a clear self-image and understand their own behaviour, they may not want to disclose that information to other people. Most people have a tendency to act the way they think they *should* act based on cues from the physical and social environment.

C. **Lying.** The majority of people will tell the truth, or the truth as they understand it, when asked. However, a small number of people will set out to deliberately lie, or try to fool psychometric tests. There are various measures that can detect this, like measures of social desirability and response bias, and there are even good tools that can be used to detect when people lie or exaggerate (Paulhus, 2012).

People tell untruths for different reasons and in different ways. Although the idea that there are certain tips or tricks in detecting deception is popular, there is no universal way to tell if someone is lying. Some people play with their hair or look to the side, but others don't. Some start to breathe more rapidly or cover their mouth or look ashamed. But others will open their body language, intensify their stare and remain still. It's not possible to accurately detect lies based on someone's body language unless you are familiar with their behaviour. Body language can signal discomfort or distress for many different reasons, not just deception (Navarro, 2018).

It's not easy to detect deception in strangers. However, it is much easier to detect deception when you are familiar with someone's behaviour and potential motivation. What can be helpful in understanding how and why people lie is greater knowledge of the different ways that people can tell untruths.

Max Eggert (2013), an expert on employee selection, explains the different types of lies and deception people use.

- **Errors of commission or fact.** Errors of commission involve adding some information that doesn't really belong. These are the types of lies most people immediately recognize as a lie. It often means deliberately manufacturing a story that has no basis in fact; there is no truth in it and if found out there is no explanation other than it is a lie. These are explicit, verifiably, false claims.
- **White lies.** Minor mistruths are not necessarily malicious, but might be stretching the truth. Someone might start an interview with: 'This office is very nicely decorated,' 'Oh, look at that photo, what beautiful children you have,' 'I also like that sports team you are so proudly displaying your affiliation with.' They are not lies about substantial issues, but often related more to social desirability and impression management.
- **Altruistic lies.** Lies that are told 'for the greater good' or ostensibly for someone else's benefit. These might be covering for a friend or a colleague who made a mistake and would face serious consequences, 'I have no idea what happened' or even providing an alibi, 'They were with me at the time, it couldn't have been their fault.' The content of the deception matters here: For whose benefit is the lie really told? And what are the consequences of deception?
- **Lies of omission.** Is missing out a few dates or details really a lie? It might be convenient to gloss over a few years of employment on a CV, or omit certain details that do not cast a positive glow. Sometimes the details are important, and sometimes they are not. 'My colleague punched me' may be a serious accusation, especially if the omission is that the colleague was *returning* a physical attack.

- **Defensive lies.** The defensive lie is usually meant to obscure facts or information through obfuscation or lack of clarity instead of a deliberate untruth. It's the response: 'Everyone was caught up in a culture of greed and lack of accountability at that time...' Or the politician's answer of, 'Well we were left with such a mess to clean up, that we thought we'd spend a decade making an even worse mess of things just to show them!' This is a lie that's meant to muddy the waters and pass around blame to everyone else.

- **Impersonation lies.** Taking credit for someone else's work is a common form of workplace lie. A manager takes credit for their team's work, or an even more egregious sin is when a colleague who slacked off and avoided a project takes credit for its eventual success. Impersonation lies are a form of plagiarism: taking credit for someone else's work or not giving credit where it's due.

- **Embedded lies.** Hiding a lie inside a bit of clever wordplay takes more conscious effort, but can create plausible deniability. Saying 'I really enjoyed my time studying in Oxford' could actually refer to a brief course at the lesser-known institution, Oxford Brookes, just down the road. The idea is to say something that is technically true, but intended to be misinterpreted by the listener.

- **Definition lies.** The easiest way to explain this type of lie is using the words of former US President Bill Clinton. In front of a grand jury, when asked, 'The statement that there is no sex in any kind, any manner, and shape or form with President Clinton was an utterly false statement, is that correct?' Clinton responded with a smile and arched eyebrow: 'It depends upon what the meaning of the word "is" is.' He meant to obscure the truth by playing on minor differences between the present and the past tense of the verb. Definition lies play with the definition of truth: when someone works upon their own definitions of words and reality it's hard to argue with 'their' truth, even when it is objectively false or deceptive.

- **Proxy lies.** When you get someone else to lie for you, that's a proxy lie. It's not uncommon in job selection processes for people to get their referees to massage the truth or to draft a letter of recommendation for a colleague to sign as their own. It may be truthful, or in some cases the candidate plays on the poor memory, vanity or corruptibility of their referee.

Assessing the dark side

One of the challenges of evaluating potential dark-side traits or dysfunction is when that dysfunction involves a tendency to tell untruths. When we look at different over-developed or under-developed strategies, some personality styles tend to be quite loose with the truth, whether it is deliberate deception, minor exaggeration or some combination of the types of deception explained in this chapter.

Psychologists and test developers generally rely on the assumption that most people tell the truth, while acknowledging that not everyone does. However, there are very good statistical and psychometric methods of picking up deception. And in some cases, the most interesting part of a lie is not the content of the message, but why the deception is used, what it is about and how it fits into larger patterns of behaviour and adaptation.

Toxic Organizations and Systems

17

The social (media) context

The earlier sections in this book focused mainly on individual differences and personalities. This section will explore in much more detail how those spread and become magnified and amplified online.

This chapter outlines how people's behaviour online translate directly into digital spaces. It includes a case study explaining how behaviour, communication and social relationships naturally extend into digital space, and how the pernicious impact of bullying affects people at work.

Then we broaden the perspective to look at the difference between localized and specific social networks, compared with social media in general. It's very important to make these distinctions because we need to understand that specific networks, such as the internal social networks used by companies, can be very different from the social media environment as a whole. While there are intersections, don't mistake one for another, or assume that everyone behaves in the same way in every space (physical or digital). Although they are governed by the same individual differences, like personality, different requirements work to shape behaviour both online and offline.

COMPANIES BUILD THEIR OWN CULTURE

Company culture can be more difficult to measure or define than business metrics like profitability or productivity. However, culture does exist in organizations and should not be ignored. Teams and departments also develop their own subcultures, which are shaped by the company culture, although these are often firmly rooted in the overall organizational culture.

Culture can be summed up as the shared assumptions about acceptable standards of behaviour (Ravasi & Schultz, 2006). When we're talking about culture on social media, certain platforms have their own overarching cultures that are programmed into the algorithms, their policies about acceptable and encouraged content as well as the impact of how (and whether) those policies are enforced. Social media platforms are so vast that many different subcultures emerge within the framework of the overall culture of the platform.

Companies have their own culture, and it's important to understand how those cultures shift or translate into online environments as work and communication moves increasingly to digital spaces. While remote working was rapidly growing but still in the minority in the 2010s, 2020 saw an immediate and necessary shift to company communication, moving from primarily taking place in the physical world to the digital world.

The challenge is how to bring a company's culture (assuming the company culture is positive and productive) into digital spaces. Culture, as a shared understanding of acceptable behaviour, is not something that either automatically or naturally emerges. If people and groups are not given any guidance about what types of behaviour and communication are appropriate and encouraged, different people and groups will develop their own standards. As the different personality styles and disorders show, what people assume to be generally adaptive or practical standards of behaviour vary extraordinarily widely.

Will a company's culture and communication style automatically translate into an online environment if everyone suddenly works on Zoom, Teams, Skype, Jabber or similar? No. When people enter an unfamiliar environment, whether it is physical or virtual, they start to look for clues about what types of behaviour are encouraged and unacceptable. They look at how other people are interacting, how they are dressed, listen to how they speak to each other and modify their behaviour accordingly.

So from a leadership perspective, when the office moves into new spaces, a company's leaders need to clearly and visibly establish and reinforce the types of behaviour that are encouraged and acceptable. Good behaviour needs to be modelled in a new environment, and people need to be both trained on the new equipment and shown how they are expected to behave and conduct themselves in that environment.

CASE STUDY: THE IMPACT OF TOXIC LEADERSHIP

In this example, which occurred a few years ago, a young woman in her mid-20s, we'll call M, her had just finished her master's degree in industrial-organizational psychology and joined a rapidly growing tech company with just under 100 employees. The company mostly had distributed staff working remotely with in-person hubs in a few different towns.

M initially started the job working in her local office two to three days per week and worked remotely from home the rest of the time. The flexible schedule and ability to work from home was a major attraction to the job, as was the relevance of the role to her MA in industrial-organizational psychology. She did take a position slightly lower than she was qualified for, but was happy to take the position because she saw significant growth opportunities for herself at this company.

She reported to a woman who was at director level, who also worked remotely in a different city. 'It all started out really well – she was enthusiastic, caring, gregarious and eager to share news of my arrival to the company on the general Slack channel and through inter-office emails.' It was a promising start, where she was encouraged to contribute and share her knowledge of industrial-organizational psychology, and to make a strong contribution to the 'People and Culture' team.

There were a few offhand comments during the first few weeks that didn't sit quite right, things like: 'How do you like being an over-educated party planner?' (in reference to being a psychologist) or 'You know education doesn't matter, right?' (in reference to recently graduating from a master's programme). But overall the culture seemed to be warm and friendly, and these seemed like exceptions. She found this strange, because she is generally a more introverted, humble person who certainly was not bragging about education or qualifications (especially in a new environment with unfamiliar people), and she hadn't mentioned it to the people who had made the comments.

However, the positivity in the new role didn't last long. At the end of the first month, she was asked to participate in what the company called 'an exchange' where employees are asked about their first month's experience. Employees are told this process is strictly confidential and anonymous, and an important part of the company culture. So she saw the exchange as an opportunity to bring up how some of the rude comments had made her feel uncomfortable. 'I felt that they were threatening the culture of inclusion and belonging I thought we were trying to create.'

'Unfortunately, it turned out that the exchange was not anonymous OR confidential.' Hours after giving the feedback, she was contacted by her boss who, enraged, gave her a long lecture about how the feedback she provided was unacceptable. M was then scheduled to attend a mandatory conflict-resolution session at the company retreat in two weeks' time. 'We do NOT tell other people when we feel uncomfortable with the culture, especially when it relates to feeling a lack of inclusion or belonging,' said her boss.

The next incident was when M was planning a promotional event for the team to showcase their product. The event was well planned out by M, who at this point was in her fifth week at the new job. She confirmed the attendance of each team member an hour before the event, but then, an hour later, no one in the team showed up. This left M in the awkward situation of being alone to showcase a product she had limited knowledge of, since she had only been hired recently. Although difficult to realize in the moment, misleading a new team member in this way and isolating and embarrassing them is a form of workplace bullying.

When M explained to her boss that she was frustrated that no one on the team showed up, her boss said: 'You have to see the best in other people. What I'm most concerned about is that you'd be upset that nobody followed through. You have to take more accountability. It is your fault that they didn't show up.' (It's interesting that, in this case, the director wouldn't take responsibility for the actions or performance of a team that reported to her).

Like many workplace bullies, the director liked to collect or invent black marks against people, to be used at a later date. 'My boss used these "incidents" as collateral against me.' The director used this to regularly harangue and wear down M, with frequent but unpredictable Skype calls to talk about the 'incidents'. As these calls continued, M started to feel worse and worse each time, breaking down into tears on some of the calls. When she cried, M's boss would berate her for 'feeling like a victim'. Bullies often lay the groundwork early like this, and the people impacted often don't realize they are targets, not victims.

The abuse and bullying escalated from there. The director would schedule group 'coaching' sessions online. The director would choose a topic to discuss, often related to showing vulnerability in the workplace or what the director referred to as a 'victim mentality' and 'taking back your power'.

The one-on-one Skype calls from the director continued to discuss the 'incidents'. The incidents stopped being anything related to performance, but then became the behaviour on the calls. Every call would go on until, eventually, M broke down in tears, and her boss would berate her for crying and showing vulnerability at work. This became a self-perpetuating cycle, and the one-on-one calls were cited as performance problems. M's probation was extended until those 'performance issues' could be resolved. M said at this point she 'felt totally defeated and completely confused'.

A few months later M was diagnosed with major depression. This was the first time in her life she had ever struggled with this. She was also diagnosed with other physical health concerns, from anaemia to low white blood cell count. When her GP asked about her work, M told her what had been happening. At the time M was really struggling to understand why she was experiencing depression and truly believed that her problems at work were her fault. But she couldn't talk about work without breaking down into tears.

The workplace was too unhealthy, too destructive, for M to stay there. It was clearly damaging her psychological and physical health, although, like many targets of bullying, she had been convinced that *she* was the problem. The immediate prescription was a minimum of two months off work, with therapy, rest and the recommendation to look for a different workplace. M says: 'I took it all to heart and started my healing journey – sleeping 12+ hours per night, getting help around the house, and taking out debt to afford it all. I ended up taking six months off work, and leaving the organization soon after.'

'While I still deal with some of the symptoms from this event at my current role, I am happy to say that due to the therapy sessions and also having a background in personality theory,

I was able to heal by identifying the behaviours of my ex-boss as sociopathic.'

She goes on to say that most 'organizations do not understand the impact on the target of this type of abuse. I did not get access to the support I needed because I had no proof, no witnesses (due to the online nature of the abuse), and no energy to pursue it or feel safe to do so. I also felt like a lot of this was my fault, and psychologically had a very hard time trusting any of my own judgement to take action on my own behalf.'

This case study really highlights the psychological impact of normalizing unhealthy or destructive cultures. There's an extreme tension that develops when people are the subject of harassment or bullying in the workplace, yet they are led to believe that it's normal, or even that *they* are the problem for not being able to deal with someone else's abusive behaviour. That tension has long-lasting psychological impacts that can be difficult to unravel.

While working remotely normally has a lot of advantages, in some cases it gives bullies even more access to their targets, and they will take advantage of this. Then it becomes even more than just a work issue, when the workplace bully is creeping into their employees' home lives.

Fortunately, in the case of M, she was able to move past it, although it took a substantial amount of time and work. And not without a long period of significant difficulty. As will be explored in greater detail in Chapter 23, people who are highly intelligent, skilled or experienced can be the targets of workplace bullying without realizing exactly what is happening. Most people tend to be fairly trusting, especially when someone senior is giving them 'performance' feedback at work – and bullies are able to abuse that trust by defining the relationship and, in trying to manipulate that relationship, defining the other people around them.

How representative is social media?

Another thing to consider is that different social media platforms have already established cultures and communities. Although extraordinary numbers of people participate in the largest social media networks, different networks tend to have, attract and reinforce their own biases.

While social media platforms are designed to create filter bubbles within them, they also operate as large bubbles imposed over the top. This trend looks set to continue and become more developed and entrenched as right-wing partisan social media channels like Parler and Gab (Yurieff, 2020) gain popularity and are willing to host more extremist content.

Although some would use social media to gauge public opinion (Anstead & O'Loughlin, 2014), at times, to their peril and in the early days of social media, social media was seen as an excellent gauge of public sentiment and is often still analyzed in that way. It is often used to shape general discourse too, as journalists often use social media posts to represent public sentiment (McGregor, 2019). Any social media platform should not be seen as representative of the general public. Carvill & MacRae (2020) refer to this as 'the risk of the blue tick demographic' which refers to 'verified' Twitter users.

While people who are engaged with issues they are passionate about online may give some indication of opinion, research by the More in Common think tank in the autumn of 2020 found that 50 per cent of the political content on social media websites was generated by people who represent only 12 per cent of registered voters in the UK. Most of the content was generated by relatively small, politically focused groups and then reshared by a relatively small proportion of social media users (Juan-Torres et al., 2020).

And even among general users there are differences. Most people produce a very small amount of content, while 10 per cent of users generate 80 per cent of the Tweets (Wojcik et al., 2019). If only about 20 per cent of the population uses Twitter at all, that means the most outspoken 2 per cent of the population is dominating the conversation on Twitter. And Twitter is an example of a demographic that tends to be younger, more left-wing and, in Britain at least, is more opinionated about politics but less likely to vote than the general population (Mellon & Prosser, 2017).

This doesn't mean you *shouldn't* use social media as a gauge of opinion, but as with any good research, it's essential to ensure the people who you are sampling are representative of the population you are trying to understand. So if your social media following is representative of your employees, customers, clients or stakeholders, then those opinions are extraordinarily valuable and should be heeded. But don't make the mistake of assuming that noise on a social media platform, or in a subgroup of a subgroup of a social media platform, is generally representative of the whole population.

Social media is potentially a good source of information and can be an especially good source on closed networks representing a certain group. If an entire company uses its own internal social media network, then that is potentially an excellent way to connect with and understand people within the company.

Social media can affect groups and culture at all different levels. In small, closed networks like that of a team or a company, the culture and communication is easier to influence. It can have a positive impact, where leaders and the group work to build a culture of trust, respect and professionalism. Networks can be used to create toxic cultures of abuse, bullying and manipulation. But when networks are smaller, with pre-defined boundaries, it makes it easier to identify problems and best practices. When the networks are public, open and expansive, like Facebook or Twitter, there are so many more actors and influencers affecting their local networks as well as the entire system.

18

The rapid spread of toxic ideas

In the first few chapters we talked about the idea of bad apples and bad barrels in organizations. The 'just a few bad apples' defence often gets trotted out when a company is in crisis. Find a few scapegoats to blame instead of taking a more thorough look at the culture and expectations with in the company. Organizations with toxic cultures and poor oversight tend to produce bad apples. Of course, that does not excuse individual bad behaviour, nor does it mean there aren't bad apples floating around. In the previous section (Chapters 12–16) we talked about what kind of signs and stressors help to identify personality disorders and the situations that might cause people to derail.

Social media companies and the groups within them create their own behavioural patterns, and they do so within a clearly structured framework. And various actors operate within those environments, aiming to use the structure of the platforms and the nuances of the algorithms to achieve their objectives.

Attempting to influence people or a group of people within a framework of ethical and legal guidelines is called marketing. Without the ethical and legal guidelines, it's propaganda. Social media is a dominant communication method, so there's no doubt that many different organizations want to use it for their own purposes. And when companies try to use mass communication platforms to sell products, that's not surprising to anyone.

But what about when people or organizations with unsavoury motives want to get in on the game? A tool for mass dissemination of information can also be used as a tool of disinformation. And even if a platform sets out with a wellspring of good intentions, a coordinated effort can be used to poison the well.

That's exactly what Russia's Internet Research Agency did in the 2016 US presidential election.

SOCIAL MEDIA CAN BE MANIPULATED: POISONING THE WELL

If we think of social media as an online social environment with a structured system of reinforcement mechanisms (as described in Chapter 4), with sufficient time, resources and motivation it's entirely possible to manipulate that system. For instance, a popular social media platform like Facebook with billions of users and hundreds of billions of social connections is a highly interconnected and interdependent system. When certain segments within a network make a concerted effort to disseminate information (or misinformation), it has the potential to create effects that cascade through the whole network. Sowing enough distrust and anger within an information ecosystem has the potential to taint everything else. Poisoning the well, so to speak.

Social media platforms are open platforms with minimal guidelines or restrictions on content, so are wide open to abuse. And while the United States has the strongest conventional military on earth, by 2016 the Russians seemed to be winning in the meme warfare race.

It must be mentioned that Russia's Internet Research Agency (IRA) had been causing problems for a long time, and their misinformation campaigns pre-date interference in the US presidential election of 2016. Although fewer people were aware of their actions in the early 2010s, their hostile activities were an open secret. An article in the *New York Times* in 2015 said that 'From a nondescript office building in St. Petersburg, Russia, an army of well-paid "trolls" has tried to wreak havoc all around the Internet – and in real-life American communities.' (Chen, 2015.)

The initial trend of Internet activity inside Russia was initially suggested to have taken a dramatic shift in 2000. Throughout the 1990s the majority (70–80 per cent) of activity on Russian forums, discussion boards and the precursors to social media tended to be mostly pro-liberal and pro-democratic. From the early 2000s, the majority of activity shifted to being dominated (60–80 per cent) by pro-Kremlin content that expounded autocratic values. In 2003, the authors and human rights activists Polyanskaya, Krivov & Lomko wrote that a systematic restoration of totalitarian values was underway.

The change in online discourse within Russia has been thoroughly documented, with extensive analysis of the tactics. But in the 2000s Russia was generally targeting its propaganda and misinformation campaigns internally. The techniques have been described as quite clumsy yet aggressive early on, but progressively became more nuanced, sophisticated and outward looking. In 2007, Russia unleashed a targeted cyberattack on the Estonian Internet, essentially isolating Estonia from the worldwide Web for a month in 2007. Then, during the Russian invasion of Georgia in 2008, the Russian military tested out a variety of cyberweapons and propaganda as part of overwhelming land, air, sea and cyber operations (Greenberg, 2019).

The sophisticated online misinformation campaigns targeted internationally can be directly traced back to pro-Kremlin propaganda that began to spread more widely and internationally from 2011. These campaigns generally took a more aggressive stance in spreading misinformation, shaping discourse and encouraging pro-Russian content among Russia's geographical neighbours and promoting political extremism in Russia's perceived enemies like the United States. As the 2010s progressed, these campaigns become larger and better organized.

One example of this was on 11 September 2014, when an elaborate and well-organized social media hoax spread panic about a supposed terrorist attack on a chemicals plant in Louisiana. A concerted effort on social media, focusing around hundreds of Tweets, all sprang into action, spreading news and misinformation about the supposed explosion. Much of the discourse appeared to be local accounts, along with supposed local footage. At the same time, journalists, politicians and local influencers were bombarded with manufactured information about this event. Fake news websites, doctored photos and faked YouTube videos that were made to look like CNN footage were suddenly all over social media and being pushed on viewers to share.

But, it was all a hoax. An article from the *New York Times* magazine details the event and explains how the elaborate hoax was traced back to a Russian organization that was set up to spread misinformation online (Chen, 2015). This hoax followed a similar pattern to other coordinated misinformation attacks that occurred around the United

States in 2014. But it also mirrored tactics Russian state-backed groups had been practising in Eastern Europe for more than a decade.

Some of the stories seemed unbelievable or ridiculous; however, in one example a well-organized social media campaign suggested that Ebola had spread to Atlanta. Again, this involved a similar pattern of a sudden social media campaign with faked images, video and posts, falsified news stories and a coordinated targeting of journalists, social media influencers and politicians. There were even websites set up to look like local news organizations and government bodies that included fake studies. These examples are far beyond a few people prevaricating on social media: they were deliberate and coordinated attacks. It is also likely these were drills or practice campaigns to test reactions and hone techniques.

An investigation by the *New York Times* (2015) explained how Russia's IRA has been spreading stories, faking comments and attempting to influence news and shape opinions around the world. A significant amount of the activity has focused on what Russia views as its historical and political sphere of influence, including Poland, Ukraine, Baltic nations, countries in the caucuses, Syria and of course causing chaos within the politics of its old rival the United States. During Barack Obama's presidency, and afterwards, a significant amount of criticism and negative material was developed about Obama.

The IRA, however, is not a ragtag band of disgruntled ex-KGB hacks or a group of authoritarian activists. The IRA is run like any social media marketing company. But the groups are better described as 'brigades' (Polyanskaya, Krivov & Lomko, 2003) or 'armies' (Zannettu et al., 2020). They have taxing schedules, with employees working 12-hour days along with strict performance targets based on metrics like pageviews, comments, likes and post engagements. To create user profiles, websites or communities that appear to be normal users, IRA employees must apply the 2:1 rule: post twice as much non-political content as political content. In a day, a user might be responsible for five political posts, 10 non-political posts and 200 comments. In other words, the Internet Research Agency had an ambitious objective to shape online opinion inside of Russia but has been increasingly focused on shaping opinion or coarsening political discourse.

Jobs within the IRA became more financially rewarding over time: in 2014 the salary was 41,000 rubles per month (USD$777), but by 2016 this had risen to USD$1500 per week (MacFarquhar, 2018). It's clear to see how the operations expanded and became more valued as their effects became apparent in the 2010s. And the IRA continues to expand and develop their operations through 2020, with reports of the IRA becoming a multinational company outsourcing more of their work to countries like Nigeria and Ghana (Ward et al., 2020).

Running an army of online trolls, disinformation peddlers and agent provocateurs may seem to be expensive, but recent research shows it has had widespread effects on social media (Howard, et al., 2018), and for a national government, running the IRA during the course of the US presidential election costs less than a single cruise missile (Lister, Sciutto & Ilushina, 2017), and its effects are certainly destructive.

It is well documented that the IRA was behind some (but certainly not all) of the memes, misinformation and fake news related to the US presidential election in 2016. Oxford University's Computational Propaganda Research Project (Howard et al., 2018) conducted a comprehensive study, commissioned by the United States Congress, of the IRA's influence. The IRA used standard tactics to spread information on major social media networks like Facebook, Twitter and Instagram. They reached tens of millions of users in the United States, and over 30 million users shared content from IRA-controlled pages. The IRA ran dozens of pages, targeting different demographics and interest groups representing diverse communities from across the United States. The US Senate Intelligence Committee's report (published in August 2020) concluded that Russian intelligence services took advantage of the relative inexperience of Donald Trump and his campaign team, which 'presented attractive targets for foreign influence, creating notable counterintelligence vulnerabilities'. In other words, Russian intelligence cooked up propaganda and disinformation campaigns, and the Trump campaign eagerly lapped it up.

It is also very worth mentioning, though, that IRA activity targeted both sides of the political spectrum. They specifically used different types of pages to target particular groups, for example with group names on Facebook like 'Being Patriotic' (over 6 million likes), 'Heart of Texas' (over 5 million likes), 'Blacktivist' (more than 4.5 million likes), 'United Muslims of America' (about 2.5 million likes), 'LGBT United' (about 2 million likes) and 'Brown Power' (about 2 million likes). The research from Oxford showed that they targeted right-leaning groups with pro-Trump advertising while spreading information to minority and left-leaning groups designed to escalate mistrust in institutions, while at the same time encouraging people on the left side of the political spectrum not to vote.

Research (Boyd et al., 2018) further shows that the Russian troll army does not restrict itself to one side of the debate, but uses a variety of tactics to increase conflict between each side. For example, when Black Lives Matter activity spikes on social media, the Russian trolls tend to act as agent provocateurs on both sides, amplifying tensions and posting extreme content on either side of the debate or the political spectrum (Zannettou et al., 2020). The point is not necessarily to support one side, but to increase polarization and conflict within a political process or social movement.

Four strategies from autocratic regimes

Russia is not alone in its subversion of social media platforms to co-opt and control discourse at home, and to distort and disseminate news and information abroad. Autocratic regimes in China and the Middle East have also used social media platforms to manipulate the online conversation and use social media to boost the image of the regime in power and discredit its rivals and critics.

In an international and historical analysis of autocratic regimes' use of social media, Gunitsky (2015) lays out four strategies that are used. Gunitsky explains out how these regimes have moved beyond methods of negative control, such as censorship, to actively and positively co-opt social media platforms to serve the interests of the regime.

1. **Counter-mobilization** – engaging and activating the regime's base. Using social media to organize groups of people who are supportive of government policy (economic, military, security, foreign policy). Instead of just shutting down dissent, they can be tools to cultivate and consolidate real popularity. As Putin said in 2011, 'If the authorities do not like what is happening on the Internet there is only one way of resisting' and he went on to say that digital communication must be used to 'collect a larger amount of supporters' (Amos, 2012).

2. **Discourse framing** – how people view the public perception and attitudes of the public at large. Partial censorship can limit

dissent online and discourage or encourage types of speech that end up being shared and disseminated online. For example, in China, some types of protest or dissent are allowed within acceptable bounds (Zheng, 2008). So, certain criticisms will be allowed when the party already wants to make those changes. They allow the initial criticism to be voiced, and then they can appear responsive to critics. However, certain types of discourse – like those calling for multi-party politics, collective action, independence for regional groups (such as Tibet, Hong Kong, Macau, Taiwan) or calls for large-scale public mobilization – are swiftly and strictly censored. The regime tends to censor *most* opposition but will allow discourse that is not viewed as an existential threat to the regime or information that can be later used to discredit opposition groups to be disseminated.

3. **Preference divulgence** – autocratic governments typically have trouble understanding what people in their country are really thinking. Since opposition or independent thought is typically punished in autocratic regimes, the governments are often unable to predict when silent opposition will boil over into direct opposition. Whereas social media can give the country's rulers insight into public attitudes, and provides an easy way to collect, monitor and analyze data from public conversations, it also allows insight into regional or local complaints, and allows the regime to appear to be considering local problems and ostensibly crack down on local corruption. This often provides useful opportunities for scapegoating at local and regional levels of government while protecting the national government.

4. **Elite coordination** – social media provides government methods of tracking and evaluating what local elites/leaders are doing. In autocratic regimes with minimal public scrutiny, local elites tend to hide their own corruption, blame national power structures for their own failings and hide local discontent. However, social media minimizes the information asymmetries between local powers and centralized autocratic regimes. In other words, it provides those with highly concentrated power more information about what's happening at the local

level. This was one of the challenges within Russia during the 1990s, where local mayors and governors would act as semi-autonomous powers, far away from the influence and control of Moscow. Whereas the expansion of social media use now allows Moscow much greater capacity to monitor local issues without the typical democratic oversight mechanisms like open elections or a free press, it also allows the central government to look like they care about local issues (e.g. cracking down on corrupt local officials) while glossing over the problems they have no intention of addressing.

It is interesting to note that Professor Gunitsky at the University of Toronto (2015) explains how regimes like Russia do not rely as heavily on censorship, but instead they find it more effective to outcompete other information sources online. They tend to use messaging and approaches that are louder, more attention-grabbing and more intense than most people would use online. And because social media sites are deliberately designed to amplify the most interesting, emotive or extreme messages (Smith, 2019), social media platforms have turned into a perfect platform for developing and honing these messages.

The combination of these strategies shows how regimes can shape and influence discourse within their own countries and among their own power bases.

As Russian opposition politician and anti-corruption campaigner Alexei Navalny said in a 2010 interview: 'Actually, Internet for the government is some kind of a focus group. The Russian government is very populist. They just like to do what the people want. I mean, if it doesn't contradict their own interests. The political agenda, however, will be tested on the Internet. And that is why it will have an influence – but no direct impact.' (Asmolov, 2010.)

The tactics that were developed to manage domestic dissent and stabilize autocratic regimes are increasingly used to subvert discourse internationally. When we combine this with the international connectivity of social media, and active participation by autocratic countries in the domestic politics and squabbles of other nations with coordinated disinformation campaigns, it should be clear to see how the algorithms make it so easy to spread toxic or destructive ideas (Smith, 2019).

Finally, we should also note that these tactics are not always successful. Their implementation requires a level of technical proficiency, state coordination and effective messaging that not all regimes are able to muster, and the public or social movements in some countries may be less susceptible to it. For example, with revolutions in Egypt in 2011 and the Ukraine in 2014, clumsy efforts by authoritarian national governments to influence or threaten people only served to fan the flames of revolution and further legitimize people's grievances (Gunitsky, 2015). While some countries have been relatively effective at using social media as a tool for regime control and stability, autocratic regimes without some legitimacy, institutional strength and technical capabilities are not able to mobilize digital resources with the same effectiveness.

Do democratic countries use the same tactics?

Domestic disinformation
While fascinating, and worth watching, we can't blame only Russia for disinformation in the US or any other democratic country. Identifying the propensity for social media to aid in the rapid spread of toxic ideas does not mean all of those toxic ideas are coming from abroad. Professor Seva Gunitsky says that the misinformation that comes from fake local news, homegrown conspiracy theories and a 'steady stream of questionable information from President Donald Trump and top government officials' is much more dangerous and has a greater effect than any of Russia's activity (Gunitsky, 2020).

Free, open and democratic societies rely on the free flow of information, which means that they can also be even more vulnerable to misinformation campaigns. While closed societies with strong censorship regimes like China can strictly regulate the quantity, style and tone of communication, people in democratic countries often feel they are suffering from information overload, and increasing that overload is sometimes used as a political or marketing strategy. Former White House Chief Strategist Steve Bannon's (entirely legal) strategy was 'flood the zone with shit', to overwhelm the news media and its consumers with the eventual result of cynicism and disengagement.

That's why ethical and legal guidelines are so important in a democratic country.

The IRA built on many of the social media marketing tactics that were already in widespread use. They drew on a mix of legitimate practices combined with shady techniques and would have been familiar with the marketing textbooks that explain micro targeting, customer segmentation and uses of multimedia in spreading messages. They were certainly adept at using memes, and happy to repurpose and amplify local content that suited their objectives. While the ultimate goal was subversive, many of the tactics used were within the normal and legal range of Internet activity. We could reframe some of the tactics (Gunitsky, 2015) listed in the previous section. Within a certain ethical and legal framework, it's just marketing.

Autocratic strategy	Democratic Strategy	Corporate Strategy
Counter-mobilization	Mobilize your base	Engage your fans
Discourse framing	Shape your message	Own the narrative
Preference divulgence	Opinion polling	Market research
Elite coordination	Energize the grassroots	Work with influencers

The key differences are in informed consent and transparency (we won't use the terms perestroika or glasnost). In democratic countries and companies, there is a certain amount of accountability and public consent required for all of these processes.

So, for example, in political campaigning, a great deal of money is spent on opinion polling, focus groups and various types of research into what people want and what types of messages people are likely to listen to and endorse. Yet all of this has to happen openly, and people are directly asked questions and understand what they are responding to and why.

When a company steals or misuses data from a social media company like Facebook, then sells their analytics to political campaigns to shape political messaging without the consent and knowledge of the participants, it starts to look a lot like the shady authoritarian tactics.

Companies, organizations and individuals who want to build a positive reputation or interact with groups and communities and individuals on social media should not use dark or destructive methods to achieve their aims. The lesson from Russia's IRA is eventually the truth of the activities will be found out. This type of unethical activity would be incredibly damaging for any company operating in a democratic country. It destroyed Cambridge Analytica and added a level of mistrust in Facebook that people will be unlikely to forget.

Those using social media should make sure their activities uphold strong, ethical guidelines. In *Myths of Social Media*, Carvill & MacRae (2019) outline six ethical points that should be used to guide social media campaigns:

1. **Informed and voluntary consent.** Be clear and transparent about the campaign and any activities that are being carried out, and participants need to understand and agree to how their data is being used.
2. **Honesty and avoiding deception.** Activities should be carried out in a way that clearly communicates what business or organization is responsible for those activities. Information should be accurate, and not attempt to lie or mislead.
3. **Respect for privacy and confidentiality.** This is closely linked to informed consent; people should be told how, when and where their data is being used and have the opportunity to opt out.
4. **Minimizing potential harm.** Be careful when trying to influence people's beliefs and calls for action. Never use messages that are intended to lead to harm to your target audience or incite them into causing harm to others.
5. **Avoiding discrimination against certain groups**. Do not deliberately exclude specific groups, and avoid using harmful stereotypes, racism or bigotry to target specific groups.
6. **Avoiding (or declaring) conflicts of interest.** Be clear and honest about who is behind the campaign, any third parties that are involved, any content or messaging that has been paid for by someone else.

Russian interference in the UK's Brexit referendum?

In July 2020, the UK Intelligence and Security Committee of Parliament published its own Russia report.

A report by *Foreign Policy* magazine (MacKinnon, 2020) suggested four messages to take away from this report:

1. There was minimal detail or examination of the evidence. Unlike the Mueller (2020) report, or other research commissioned to investigate Russian interference in the US presidential election, this is a high-level report without any detail on specific findings or Russian tools and tactics.
2. The UK failed to act on early warning signs, especially those coming out of the US.
3. It is difficult to establish who in the UK is really responsible for dealing with potential Russian interference.
4. Russian oligarchs and their businesses are active and influential in the UK, especially in London. Interference from Russian nationals with expansive patronage networks are likely to be a tool of influence in the UK in future.

The report concluded that the UK government did not look into whether Russia had staged any interventions into the 2016 referendum (BBC, 2020). The only thing the report really highlighted is how unprepared the UK would be for the kind of interventions that dominated the 2016 US presidential election campaign.

The result of this fairly tepid investigation should be concerning for the UK because the analysis was minimal, especially in comparison to the thorough research that was conducted and published about the Russian interference in the American election. The finding that there was no clear line of responsibility or accountability for who should be responsible for identifying, analyzing or combating propaganda or electoral interference from domestic or international actors indicates there are significant vulnerabilities there.

The UK and other countries should take note from the experiences of the US as well as cyberwarfare attacks on countries like Estonia in 2007 and the Ukraine in 2015 and 2016. The Russian government is not the only state or international actor who has the capability or the potential motivation to conduct similar attacks. Nations and businesses should do more to prepare for the potential to be hit with cyberattacks or the potential to be affected by the collateral damage of cyberweapons.

19

Toxic digital leadership

During the mid-late 20th century, much of the research into toxic and destructive leadership focused on early 20th century dictators and then on leadership derailment in business. The early 20th century saw the rise of autocrats in Europe and around the world who made use of technological advances in military and communications to attempt to forge new empires. Radio, and later television, allowed messages to spread beyond Bavarian beer halls and Viennese coffee houses, directly into millions of homes.

There are many different theories about the rise of autocrats in the early 20th century (Williamson, 2007) and many different contributing factors, such as rising nationalism and militarism along with technological change. However, one of the interesting and distinctive psychological features of dictators is their approach to ambiguity.

Dictators and dictatorships attempt to eliminate ambiguity in their messaging and their approach to policy. They distil complex problems into simple ones and then try and sell a simple solution. They state that there is one simple solution to all of society's problems, and the dictator is the only one with the strength (courage/vision/intelligence/righteousness/insert your own) to carry the plan out. If only they were in charge, their policy would be so easy to implement! Other politicians failed because they were weak (cowardly/short-sighted/stupid/corrupt/insert your own). But just follow this new leader who has the plan and is willing to act.

Toxic leaders follow a similar pattern, and mass communication platforms enable this. It helps them speak 'directly' to their supporters, apparently unfiltered and seemingly unstoppable. Similarly, dictators tend to share personality patterns and profiles. Dictators like Adolf Hitler and Saddam Hussein (Coolidge & Segal, 2007) have been described as paranoid (wary style), antisocial (aggressive style) and narcissistic (confident style).

We know what makes a good leader, and some of the key components were reviewed in Chapter 15 and then again in Chapter 19 in the discussion of toxic leadership online. To talk about toxic leadership, first we'll contrast it with effective leadership.

THE IDEAL LEADERSHIP MODEL

Chapter 10 gave a broad review of some of the key components of effective leadership, then Chapter 15 looked in more detail at optimal personality traits. Let's look at the six HPTI traits again to contrast the characteristics of toxic leaders, and how they affect leadership and performance online (MacRae & Sawatzky, 2020a).

Conscientiousness describes someone's motivation, discipline and capacity for long-term planning. Leaders must have higher conscientiousness to motivate themselves as well as others, and think strategically in the long term.

Adjustment explains how people react to stress and the level of stress people can effectively manage at work. Leaders need to be able to manage their own stress as well as the stress that comes from accountability and taking leadership decisions, so higher adjustment is an asset.

Curiosity refers to people's interest in new ideas, people and approaches in the workplace. Higher curiosity is essential for leaders who need to foster innovation, growth and effectively manage change.

Ambiguity acceptance explains people's approach to complex situations and environments. Those with higher ambiguity acceptance thrive in complex and ambiguous work situations, and leaders must be able to manage ambiguity and make decisions in complex environments.

Risk approach describes how people deal with conflict and challenges in the workplace. Leaders benefit from higher risk approach, which is a more proactive style of dealing with difficulty and conflict, whereas those with lower levels tend to be more reactive (and less constructive).

Competitiveness is related to an employee's need to be recognized for their work and show off their own achievements. The most effective leaders have moderate (not extremely high or low) levels of competitiveness, and are able to channel competition into team performance instead of personal recognition.

TOXIC LEADERSHIP ONLINE

We can contrast optimal levels of HPTI traits for leadership with extremely high and low levels of the traits. These can have benefits at the extreme levels, but they also come with drawbacks. For comparison purposes, Table 19.1 shows some of the negative descriptors that can be applied to each of these traits at extreme levels (MacRae & Furnham, 2018).

CASE STUDY: PRESIDENT DONALD TRUMP (PART 3)

In *High Potential* (MacRae & Furnham, 2018), there is a psychological profile of Donald Trump based on HPTI traits which was originally developed in 2016. We can use these traits and the descriptions from this psychological profile to describe some of the online behaviour, and demonstrate the toxic digital leadership based on a long history of publicly available behavioural data on media and on social media (most notably on Twitter).

The scores on this test range from 0 to 100, with a score of 50 being average.

Conscientiousness, 18
This is extremely low conscientiousness, which indicates limited capacity for long-term planning or strategic thinking. Actions and behaviour are strongly influenced by the current environment and people. We can see this in all aspects of Trump's behaviour, from impulsive social media activity to a limited capacity to plan talking points for interviews and speeches, but also with an excellent ability to play to a crowd, give audiences what they want irrespective of wider plans or policy and constantly getting distracted by the issue of the day or the moment.

Adjustment, 30
This is lower-than-average adjustment, indicating a high emotional reactivity and volatility. We can see this, combined with low

TABLE 19.1 Negative perceptions of extreme HPTI trait scores

	Negative Perceptions of Very Low Scores	Negative Perceptions of Very High Scores
Conscientiousness	Careless	Obsessive
	Unmotivated	Perfectionistic
	Impulsive	Rigid
	Lax	Inflexible
	Idle	Indecisive
	Disorganized	Critical
Adjustment	Emotional	Indifferent
	Irrational	Unresponsive
	Neurotic	Distant
	Self-conscious	Serious
	Moody	Aloof
	Compulsive	Cold
Curiosity	Closed-minded	Unpredictable
	Conventional	Inconsistent
	Disinterested	Eccentric
	Suspicious	Easily distracted
	Unadventurous	Unfocused
	Obstinate	Intrusive
Ambiguity acceptance	Predictable	Unclear
	Stubborn	Erratic
	Fussy	Illogical
	Inflexible	Abstract
	Blinkered	Vague
	Simplistic	Confusing
Risk approach	Avoidant	Confrontational
	Risk averse	Imposing
	Hesitant	Reckless
	Reactive	Blunt
	Passive	Insensitive
	Apprehensive	Arrogant
Competitiveness	Unenthusiastic	Ruthless
	Timid	Aggressive
	Satisfied	Antagonistic
	Submissive	Unyielding
	Quiet	Harsh
	Apathetic	Hostile

conscientiousness and extremely high competitiveness means that any perceived slight, insult or threat gets a swift and harsh response: everything is treated as a competition with a winner and a loser. All of the Twitter wars, feuds and insults demonstrate that Trump really takes all insults or criticisms personally and can't control negative emotions; he generally sees people as dangerous and threatening to his needs or his ego.

Curiosity, 34

The experts suggested this person had relatively low curiosity. This means limited interest in new ideas, and we see how this affects decision-making. He has limited interest in the opinion of experts and trusts only his own judgement. Once he makes a decision or forms an opinion, he disregards any other information on the topic and sticks with the original course of action.

Risk approach, 29

This risk approach score indicates a reactive approach. In combination with low adjustment levels, this is likely to be an impulsive and threat-based reactivity, which indicates a likelihood to either run away from, or aggressively strike back at, any threats (real or imagined). It's easy to see that behaviour in response to any criticism or disagreement, which is treated as a threat that needs to be responded to. It's that impulsive reactivity that can be so dangerous in a leader: fighting back is immediate and automatic, not tied to long-term planning or a rationale behind the actions.

Ambiguity acceptance, 69

The panel rated Trump as high in ambiguity acceptance, in the optimal range for leadership. This typically indicates someone who thrives in complex environments and can manage uncertainty. This is an interesting nuance in this personality trait and the score, because it does indicate someone who can navigate ambiguity and use it to his advantage. However, when it comes to messaging, Trump uses prevarication to hide his intentions, makes statements and then withdraws them, or says he is just kidding. But in his political messages he uses very unambiguous phrases, nicknames and catchphrases.

Competitiveness, 88

The experts' evaluations of Trump suggest extremely high levels of competitiveness. In fact, it is clear this level of competitiveness dominates all of his actions and his worldview with a constant need to win, to be in control and to take the spotlight. This is evident from his categorization of everyone into 'winners' and 'losers', but also his constant impulsive and neurotic behaviour; he needs to be seen to be dominating others and grabbing praise and adoration. This trait level is a large part of the narcissistic personality disorder that shows up in his competitiveness trait.

Note: This was a profile developed from the views of 10 experts. The profile was developed based on Trump's behavioural patterns, but he was not personally interviewed.

Donald Trump's four years as US President can be seen as a clear extension of all of the behaviour, worldview and personality dysfunction that characterized his childhood, inflated in adulthood and then endorsed by his business backers, then political supporters.

One of the main changes in moving from being a relatively well-insulated business executive in New York into the presidency was an increase in the demands, the workload, the scrutiny and the pressures of the job. ('There's dynamite behind every door,' he described to Bob Woodward (2020)).

Some commentators hoped that the office of the President of the United States of America would have a moderating effect, and perhaps it would temper some of Donald Trump's worst impulses (Painter, 2016). And, of course, Donald Trump himself said he would be, 'So Presidential, you'd be bored' (Detrow, 2016), which turned out to be misleading. However, personality does not change, and it certainly does not change in 70-something-year-olds, whose most destructive impulses have effectively got them what they wanted throughout their lives. Likewise, personality disorders (in Trump's case we would say aggressive, confident and sensitive styles: firmly exerting his own control and view of the world while also desperately seeking approval and constantly demanding attention).

His campaign certainly had some serious problems, dominated by grifters, felons and constant interference from Russia's state-backed hacking groups (although much of that information wasn't confirmed until April 2020 in Robert Mueller's US Department of Justice report and the even more damning US Senate report that was released in August 2020).

The Senate Intelligence report (2020) concluded that there was no direct evidence that senior members of Donald Trump's team were deliberately colluding with Russia, but that they were too inexperienced or naïve to realize that they were being manipulated by Russian state-backed actors. 'Posing as US political activists, [Russia's Internet Research Agency] requested – and in some cases obtained – assistance from the Trump Campaign procuring materials for rallies and in promoting and organizing rallies' (p. 7).

The GRU-linked (Russian military intelligence) hacker groups, such as Fancy Bear and Cozy Bear, had run spying campaigns on US targets including the Democratic National Committee, US State Department and aerospace and defence contractors in 2015 and 2016. In the months leading up to the 2016 US election, they leaked materials almost daily related to Democratic political campaigns and Hillary Clinton (Greenberg, 2019).

'In contrast to the consistent denigration of Hillary Clinton, Donald Trump's candidacy received mostly positive attention from the IRA's influence operatives, though it is important to note that this assessment specifically applies to pre-election content. The Committee's analysis indicates that post-election IRA activity shifted to emphasize and provoke anti-Trump sentiment on the left' (p. 34).

This is interesting to note because it shows the IRA wasn't so much a friend of Trump as just trying to stoke tensions among the American electorate. As soon as Trump won the election, the IRA focused on provoking anger against then-President Trump from his political opponents. Russian social media operations amplified Trump's critics after he was elected, which was a constant source of anxiety and distraction during his presidency.

Google's algorithms were also used and manipulated 'as a tool of information warfare'. The method of spreading disinformation on Google differs from social media websites like Facebook and Twitter, but can also have an even more far-reaching impact. More than 90 per cent of search engine traffic goes through Google (Desjardins, 2018). Google has the tendency to elevate extremist content or disinformation in searches, especially for popular content and emerging news. For example, 'a falsified media account of President-elect Donald Trump having won the popular vote briefly ranked higher than stories that accurately reflected the US popular vote result' (US Senate Intelligence Committee, p. 57).

Senate Intelligence report: future concerns
While some of the Russian activity in 2016 and before was relatively clumsy, and is straightforward to counteract when it's identified and stopped, there are also some emerging trends that the Senate Intelligence report suggested will be of greater concern in the future:

1. Technologies enabling the creation of false news, along with more realistic and convincing propaganda, is getting more sophisticated, making it harder to detect when this material comes from a foreign source or foreign intelligence agency.
2. Artificial intelligence and 'deepfakes' are becoming much more sophisticated, easy to create and harder to identify as fakes. Although this technology is 'relatively nascent', it's identified as a growing threat.
3. Advancements in micro-targeting are making these techniques easier, cheaper and more accessible. Highly targeted messaging campaigns are becoming more widely available.
4. Bots are becoming more sophisticated and harder to identify, and an 'arms race' between bot programmers and the companies that detect them is helping to fuel their evolution.
5. As larger social media companies target disinformation, tactics shift to new platforms that are harder to monitor and censor (e.g. WhatsApp, Telegram, WeChat).
6. The original targets of the IRA were political groups, but large sections of society and the economy have not been subject to these influence and manipulation techniques. These techniques could also be used for illicit activities like stock price manipulation and fraud, digital advertising manipulation, marketing counterfeited goods, pharmaceuticals, etc. Most private sector industries would not be prepared to manage, counter or respond to a large-scale disinformation campaign.

We could see serious problems if these tactics were turned to other issues like vaccine efficacy, false stories to affect corporate stock prices or trust in other national institutions (Public Health, Defence, Police, Food Safety, Pensions, or others).

Analyzing Trump's digital behaviour

This book will not go into a detailed rerun of Donald Trump's four years as US President. For that, Bob Woodward's books *Fear* (2018) and *Rage* (2020) are recommended. There are interesting implications for understanding the psychology of personality disorders, but also some instructive lessons for leaders in digital communications. One of the risks of Donald Trump sharing so much information openly on social media was that it gave any observers a massive amount of behavioural data. His supporters may like the constant engagement, but it also gives US adversaries an incredible insight into the general strategy and the day-to-day thinking of the US Commander in Chief.

And we can track through Trump's presidency the various quirks and consequences of the job. One interesting finding is from two researchers who recorded President Trump's sleep schedule by using his Twitter activity (Almond & Du, 2020). They found that he typically wakes up at 6am, which remained relatively constant throughout his time as president, but later in his term he tended to stay up later, sleep less and Tweet in the 11pm–2am period.

Using an analysis of his statements and speeches, they found Trump tended to be grumpier when he got less sleep. Speeches tended to take an angrier tone, Tweets and interactions tended to be more hostile on days where he had been up late on Twitter the night before.

In an interesting analysis, they also showed that his social media 'performance' also suffered when he stayed up too late. When he had been up late, his social media activity the next day tended to perform more poorly with fewer interactions (likes, retweets, comments). When he was tired and grumpy he tended to connect less effectively with his audience.

Implications of Trump's use of social media

Donald Trump used social media differently from any previous US president, and from most world leaders. He demonstrated how leaders can bypass previous filters like press offices and the media ecosystem and send out their thoughts directly to a large audience. Trump did this on a day-by-day basis and even would reveal a great deal about where he was, what he was working on or live Tweet and give hot takes during his favourite TV programmes.

Yet it's not quite as simple as that. Even though Trump had a huge Twitter following (nearly 89 million followers at the end of 2020), he could only communicate directly through Twitter to a very small proportion of the American voting public. Research from Pew Research Centre found that only 22 per cent of American adults use Twitter (Hughes & Wojcik, 2019), and of US adult Twitter users only 19 per cent followed Donald Trump (Wojcik et al., 2019); for comparison, 26 per cent follow Barack Obama.

Trump's Twitter following meant that Donald Trump could use Twitter to reach about 4 per cent of the American electorate directly when he was allowed to use the platform. However, this was massively amplified when news networks, digital publications and other social media channels would all pick up and quote Trump's Tweets. We have to consider the amplification effects, not just the fact that Trump used Twitter. Nor can it be ignored that foreign state-backed groups were deliberately using viral marketing tools and techniques to amplify specific messages during the election campaign.

20

Automated amplification of toxicity

Digital technology presents the opportunity to amplify messages, spread ideas and emotions. The content that goes viral the fastest, spreads the widest and gets the most engagement online tends to elicit an intense emotional response. Emotions are triggers that encourage people to react. But some emotions are more contagious than others. Any intense emotional response helps to spread a message: joy, excitement, sadness and disgust are all powerful feelings that spread a message. But there is one powerful emotion that helps content spread the fastest online: rage (Shaer, 2014). This holds true across social media in different platforms and cultures. Research investigating Chinese social media platform Weibo, research measuring the reactions to *New York Times*, articles on social media in the US (Berger & Milkman, 2012) and partisan news that contains emotional cues tends to receive the most amplification on social media (Hasell, 2020).

The previous chapters talked about some of the different tactics used to spread messages, and using emotions are a powerful way to make content go viral irrespective of the motives or the facts behind the message.

EMOTIONAL CONTAGION

Emotions tend to pass relatively easily from person to person. It's a basic survival mechanism that allows people to quickly, easily and even unconsciously warn other people of threats and to identify sources of danger as well as opportunity. Psychologists call it 'emotional contagion': when a disaster strikes, the shock, horror and sadness spread swiftly, and the same effect can happen for positive emotions (Van Praet, 2019).

This basic social phenomenon happens in person, but it can also happen online, and social media companies manipulate it to capture people's attention and advertising revenue. A study conducted by Cornell University and Facebook in 2014 found that emotional contagion could be used to influence people subconsciously. In the study, Facebook manipulated the feeds of nearly 700,000 users[1] to increase the number of positive posts some users saw, while increasing the number of negative posts other users saw. The effects were clear: users subsequently posted more positive or negative content depending on which group they were in. Emotional contagion worked clearly and effectively on Facebook (Kramer et al., 2014).

The digital findings are critical in showing how the same emotional transmission can happen in cyberspace. In the physical world, nonverbal communication cues are generally the strongest influencer of emotional contagion. People 'catch' other people's emotions unconsciously through subtle gestures, facial expressions, tone of voice, body language and similar cues (Barsade, 2002). That's why having someone in an office or social group who is extremely agitated or cheerful can be contagious. This is why when a friend, a partner or a colleague is on edge, that anxiety can spread to other people without a word spoken.

But we now know that emotions can spread digitally through social networks too. It's not just information (or misinformation) that spreads online, it's the emotional reactions as well. And as will be explained in Chapter 22, periods of social isolation can intensify negative emotions, lead to many negative mental health outcomes and negative emotional contagion is more infectious, so 2020 has been a year which has amplified the risk even more.

As a practical implication of this, you may want to consider who you follow and interact with regularly on social media. The emotions that

---

1 *Ethical objections have been raised in response to this study because users did not give proper informed consent, as would be required of most psychological studies. The ethical codes of practice that emerged out of unethical research conducted without proper consent in the mid-20th century were designed to prevent studies like this where people's emotions and behaviour were influenced without their explicit knowledge and consent to participate. However, private companies like Facebook are not subject to the same ethical rules that university researchers are governed by.*

dominate your social feeds will tend to influence your own emotions. While Facebook and other social media platforms can turn up the dial on particular emotions and can nudge people in certain directions, ultimately it is users who have the most control over what they see in their feeds.

THE CURIOUS CASE OF AI TAY

In 2016 Microsoft launched an artificial intelligence Twitter chatbot, called Tay. It was intended to be a demonstration of their advancing AI technology, and developments in 'conversational understanding' (Vincent, 2016). The AI would learn from conversations, which means that as more people interacted with it, the more language and conversational range it would develop. It was meant to replicate the language patterns of a 19-year-old girl, but develop dialogue based on whom it was talking to and how people interacted with it, essentially learning from its environment.

Microsoft said it would learn through 'casual and playful' conversation, which was obviously a slight misunderstanding on the part of Microsoft about how many people converse on Twitter.

In less than a day after its launch, Microsoft took Tay offline. They said that it 'suffered from a coordinated attack by a subset of people' who 'exploited a vulnerability in Tay'. That is almost certainly true – there was a coordinated campaign from 4chan – but it is stretching credulity to say that it exploited a 'vulnerability'. Mimicking the language people used to interact with the bot was a feature, not a bug. Clearly 'a chatbot created for 18–24-year-olds in the US for entertainment purposes' (Lee, 2016) ended up providing some people with a different type of entertainment than Microsoft anticipated.

It was 2016, so based on frequent interactions on Twitter, Tay quickly picked up a lot of rhetoric and style from the US presidential election, with Tay saying things like 'WE'RE GOING TO BUILD THE WALL AND MEXICO IS GOING TO PAY FOR IT.' This was a common phrase on social media, but hardly the 'casual and playful' tone Microsoft was aiming for.

Tay turned into a bit of an Internet joke for most and a PR disaster for Microsoft, but the episode does raise serious questions about AI, especially when AI algorithms and effects are not publicly disclosed. If

Microsoft's chatbot could go from saying 'humans are cool' to 'Hitler did nothing wrong' in less than a day, without Microsoft expecting this to happen, what other AI programs are operating in the background of our lives are open to misuse, manipulation or have unintended consequences?

We know that social media algorithms often recommend content to people purely based on what they think will capture their time and attention, even if it's conspiracy theorists like Alex Jones (Chapter 12) or extremist political views (Chapter 4). While it could be said that the Tay trolls were malicious in turning Tay into a culture-wars chatbot, they also exposed a major flaw in the AI that its programmers never imagined or built in any safeguards against. Who could have foreseen that a Microsoft chatbot could be radicalized so easily?

There are a few different theories too, about why Microsoft's Twitter chatbot could so rapidly turn into a far-right troll.

- **The bad apples hypothesis.** This is the official Microsoft interpretation (Lee, 2016). Malicious users found a vulnerability in the system. This is the bad apples theory again in a different context. Just a small group of people with ill intentions deliberately 'exploited' the system to make the AI learn Nazi buzzwords and dog whistles.
- **The bot amplifier hypothesis.** Jeron Lanier, computer scientist, Microsoft researcher and computer philosophy writer, suggested that it was actually a bot detector, which attracted and amplified many of the far-right Twitter hate-bots and amplified their messages (Lanier, 2018). In other words, once a few people encouraged Microsoft's bot to Tweet far-right content, whole clusters of far-right bots picked up on that activity and automatically got in on the game. Then at least some of the activity was just bots talking to each other and creating an amplification of the most hateful content that was, mostly, artificial.
- **The impression management hypothesis.** There may be a much simpler explanation that does not involve conspiracies or coordinated efforts by bad malicious actors. The point of the Tay chatbot was to reflect people's words and communication style right back at them. As far as could be seen, Tay had no

central ideology but would just parrot words and tone back at people. Depending on who the bot was responding to, it could be for or against feminism, pro-Hitler or against Hitler, and had no consistent position on any particular issue. Of course, that was going to go badly in an environment such as Twitter.

It's strange to see how Microsoft's brief experiment of launching a public AI Twitter bot quickly descended into an outpouring of anti-Semitism, misogyny, crypto-fascism and, in some cases, outright Nazi language. But it also should serve as a lesson to show how the unintended consequences of AI can rapidly spiral into incredibly toxic behaviour. And of course, it's this result that gets the most attention.

NOT ALL PROFILES ONLINE ARE REAL PEOPLE

Tay was an instructive example, and Microsoft stated that Tay was a bot. This was a useful example of what can go wrong. However, many organizations develop, deploy or purchase bots to create or amplify their own messages. Much of the content online is not actually the work of individual people.

A good example of fake content, which sometimes can overwhelm real content, is fake comments on news articles or video-sharing websites. Sometimes the motivation behind bot activity is clear: people use it to boost their own popularity by increasing views, likes or positive comments. Fake product reviews are designed to boost sales of that product.

One example is astroturfing. Astroturf is artificial grass designed to cover over a barren area. But in advertising or propaganda, astroturfing is the process of purchasing fake support either from real people or from bots, to create the impression of support. On some occasions, it is used simply to boost popularity. On other occasions, it will be used to cover up negative reviews: for example, if a company has dozens of negative reviews, they might purchase hundreds of positive reviews.

Amazon sellers are famous for astroturfing, using a whole host of methods to gain fake positive reviews (Dragan, 2016). Businesses either create their own fake accounts (or hire out networks of others), give people free products to write positive reviews or may even hire malicious actors to write negative reviews for their competitors.

Examples of astroturfing and positive or negative reviews have clear motivations behind them: to create, manufacture and boost positive signals about a company, person, group or brand. There's a darker, more destructive technique similar to astroturfing which overwhelms channels with negative messages instead of positive ones. This can have more powerful effects but with less clarity on the people or the rationale behind the activity. If we combine the term 'astroturfing' with Steve Bannon's description of this tactic, 'flood the zone with shit' (Stengel, 2020), we could come up with a more graphic term to describe this negative process.

As we have talked about in previous chapters, some organizations, including state-backed actors, deliberately create misinformation, manufacture negative sentiment and amplify conflicting messages to create chaos and confusion. For some, the objective is not to push a particular narrative but to overwhelm the social ecosystems with so much garbage that people start to tune out and think it is not worthwhile to even participate. Or in some cases, people will equate different choices as equally *bad* instead of deciding in the context of which one they would prefer. When everyone looks terrible, the worst players do not seem quite so bad in comparison.

Before diving into a content section on a news article, comments section or social media platform, remember that not every user on the Internet is necessarily a real person. Whenever the topic is politically or emotionally charged or related to a product or service where there is potentially a lot of money to be made, those ecosystems are probably full of bots. That doesn't mean you shouldn't listen to contrary opinions but it does mean that it is unwise to make judgements about people or groups based on an Internet comments section: they could be full of users that are not people.

Imagine if there were millions of variations on Tay AI scattered around the Internet, all with different (often fairly crude) influencing missions. For context, in the first nine months of 2020 Facebook banned 4.5 *billion* accounts, the vast majority of which were bots (Nicas, 2020).

Although this bot activity may seem far away from individual behaviour, it's necessary to talk about these activities online because they do influence the online environment and online discourse. And to the casual Internet user it may be difficult to distinguish between the activity of relatively normal people online and bots that are meant to imitate or influence the people around them.

Remember that not all the activity you see online is necessarily the work of a person. Not every opinion necessarily reflects a deeply held view of a genuine user. It should not need repeating (but it does): Don't automatically take everything a stranger says on the Internet at face value.

21

Colluding followers

Why do people follow destructive leaders? The oozing self-confidence that comes from narcissists, the power projection of sociopaths and the superficial charm of histrionics can be appealing to many. Those Cluster B personality disorders tend to get the most attention. They are the personalities that certainly demand the most attention, that crave publicity. But what about the cold allure of those who seem to be distant but brilliant and calculating? The creative genius and eccentric flair of some, and even the paranoid personalities who seem to be able to spin up whole subcultures around conspiracy theories?

Toxic leaders may be dangerous, but they have little power or ability to push their objectives on a large scale without followers. People have all sorts of motivations and career ambitions, and some may be willing to follow a destructive leader in pursuit of their own objectives. Some people follow toxic leaders out of blind personal ambition, often tinged with a hint of overconfidence. They have seen the trail of destruction, but they think their experience will be different because *they* are different. Other people act out of a sense of duty. It's not uncommon for people who follow toxic leaders to have seen and *understood* the warning signs, but explain that they were acting as a guardrail to the leader's worst impulse. It's an image of self-sacrifice, plastering over all of the ways they enabled the leader's destructive tendencies: 'If only you knew how bad it would have been if I *wasn't* there.' Or some people follow toxic leaders because they match their template for what an authority figure looks like. As we discussed in Chapter 5, children tend to be extraordinarily effective at adapting to the home environment and learning survival strategies and coping mechanisms that help them in that environment. Those strategies do not always work well in wider society, but often they carry those early experiences as models for future relationships. Unfortunately, for some people, the tools and tactics they learn in childhood and adolescence don't always apply to being productive or ethical in adult life.

THE TOXIC TRIANGLE

Chapter 2 discussed the Stanford prison experiment, a study which helps to explain how psychologically normal and healthy individuals can commit atrocities. Zimbardo's work expands on that to explain the common set of factors that allows destructive leaders to flourish. There are three key components, that when they come together are called the toxic triangle (Figure 21.1). These three core aspects of leadership derailment were set out by Padilla and colleagues (2007). Destructive leaders can't accomplish very much on their own, and in many cases there are also checks, safeguards and barriers that can stop destructive leaders in their rise to power or their path to derailment.

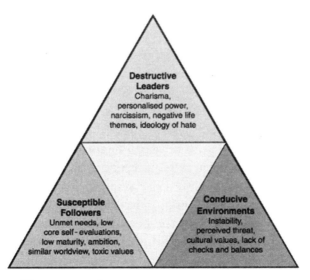

FIGURE 21.1 The toxic triangle

A) Destructive leaders

When we're talking about toxic leaders, we're not just talking about people who make innocent mistakes or who are incompetent. They are not just passive victims or unsuspecting collaborators in a destructive environment. They are deliberately malicious. They actively set out to do things that harm others, to take what they want at the expense of others, and often they enjoy chaos, conflict or destruction. They know what they are doing and (to a greater or lesser extent) know the negative consequences of their actions.

Although they may exhibit those negative traits, they often have a degree of charm and inspire confidence in others. Whatever tactics they use to gain power, they may appear attractive, interesting or useful to other people. They tend to want to gain and expand their own power, and actively seek out environments and participants who will help them get what they want.

Toxic leaders don't care about their impact on people around them, which is one of the things that can make them so effective. They will lie for short-term gain, or they will switch tactics when it suits them. It makes it easier for them to attract followers in the short-term because they will say anything to get what they want – but it makes forming healthy long-term relationships difficult or impossible.

B) Conducive environment

Threatening environments can exist at various levels. A nation or a society can feel like it is under threat; a company or a region, a department or a city, a team or a neighbourhood, or even just one person at work or at home may feel like the environment is threatening. They may, to varying degrees, be correct.

Threats do exist, such as in the example in Chapter 2 of the torture at Abu Ghraib. The perpetrators were under extraordinary threats to their own health and security: these were not imagined threats. Lack of training, poor equipment and understaffing levels also contributed to that threat, without giving the people the psychological tools (or material tools) to properly deal with that threatening environment.

Threatening environments can also be imagined or exaggerated, and that's what toxic leaders tend to do. They ramp up the pressure, dial up the rhetoric and tell people that the outside world, different people or an external threat is something that people should feel even *more* threatened by. It's the conceptual opposite of US President Franklin D. Roosevelt speech saying that 'the only thing we have to fear, is fear itself'. The toxic leader prefers the message, 'the only thing you have to fear is how dangerous the world will be without me'.

Threatening environments make it much easier for toxic leaders to thrive. It can be difficult, but not impossible, for toxic leaders to gain influence when circumstances are good. However, when times are bad, the toxic leaders really have a chance to thrive. Economic meltdowns, social disorder, concerns about war or other perceptions of external threat make people more eager to accept extreme solutions.

C) Susceptible followers

There are many reasons that people follow toxic leaders; some are malicious and self-serving, others may be out of a sense of duty, need or blindness to the consequences.

One of the reasons toxic leaders capitalize on real or imagined external threats is because perceived threats can trigger some of the more primitive defence mechanisms people have. But instead of building up people's confidence, encouraging healthy and adaptive defence mechanisms, self-confidence and autonomy, toxic leaders want people entirely dependent on them.

Toxic leaders in threatening environments can also create a sense of 'us' and 'them'. By rigidly defining categories of in-group and out-group members, it can make people feel like they have a real and clear sense of identity and belonging in what used to be a complex world with too many grey areas. Wanting to be part of a group is an essential psychological process. Almost everyone wants to feel a connection with community or family, a sense of belonging and contributing to a group. The problem is that not all groups offer constructive or healthy support. At the same time, toxic and overly simplistic messages can be even more attractive for people who feel alienated. People who have trouble understanding or liking themselves may have a strong desire to be subsumed in a larger 'group' identity. And there are all sorts of communities, groups and organizations that offer this in a positive way. Youth groups, book clubs, sports organizations, charities and religious communities generally try to channel this human psychological need into positive pursuits. Cults, gangs, criminal enterprises, toxic political ideologies and their leaders take advantage of this need.

A threatening environment often gives an opportunity for a toxic leader and their followers to assign external blame. For example: 'Everything bad that is happening is someone else's fault, and we're going to make them pay for it.' Once a toxic leader gains power, they continue to promote the feeling of external threat to promote internal unity and dedication to the leader's cause.

Generally, colluding followers fall into two different categories: conformers and colluders. There are a few common reasons that each type tends to follow toxic leaders.

Conformers

Conformers tend to follow toxic leaders to fill a gap. They may not know exactly what they want but have a sense that they need something and that someone else can provide it. They aren't usually malicious but are open to exploitation.

These are more likely to be people with the Anxious (Cluster C, Chapter 14) personality styles: sensitive, selfless and perfectionistic personality styles.

1. Unmet basic needs

   People have basic needs and desires that need to be met before they are fully able to pursue their dreams and aspirations (Maslow, 1954). Followers in a threatening environment who are unemployed, unable to financially support themselves, don't have access to basic necessities like food, water, a stable home or adequate health care tend to focus on getting those needs met before pursuing educational or career ambitions. Toxic leaders take advantage of this kind of insecurity and in many cases even create it: they want their followers to depend on them to get even their basic needs met.

   When people have unmet basic needs, they are more vulnerable to toxic leaders who promise easy solutions to complex problems, and are more willing to support a leader who they believe will help them fix their immediate and urgent problems related to safety, security and basic necessities.

2. Negative core self-evaluation

People with a low opinion of themselves often seek out people who they perceive as smarter, more powerful or more important than themselves to follow. Because they have relatively low evaluation of themselves, they tend to see themselves in a subordinate role, always as a follower but never as a leader. Their self-image may be tied to seeing themselves in a role that is lesser than (or perhaps supporting of) another person. Feeling accepted by someone they perceive to be of higher status fits their self-image. There is nothing wrong with being collaborative or a great team player: the problem occurs when people with an unhealthy or low self-esteem are attracted to a sociopath or narcissist who *projects* power and control, but is actually insecure and desperately needs colluders and appeasers to constantly reassure them of their status.

3. High conformity

Some people fall very naturally into a group and lose themselves to group behaviour. They may have trouble distinguishing their own thoughts and emotions from how they feel in a relationship or in a group environment. They may have a more fluid sense of morality and values, because they never developed a coherent set of guiding principles or values themselves. This means they are more susceptible to believing that someone they like or identify with is always right. When the relationship, or how they feel in the relationship, seems positive, they automatically assume that to mean whatever the other person is doing must automatically be correct as well.

Colluders

Colluders tend to know exactly what they want; they are actively pursuing a goal irrespective of the harm that could be caused. They actively seek out toxic leaders and susceptible followers to serve their own objectives. They can be malicious and are open to exploitation when overconfidence and single-mindedness leaves them with large blind spots. People with personality styles in Cluster B (Chapter 13) are more likely to fit into this group: aggressive, dramatic and confident styles in particular.

1. Ambition

Perhaps the easiest reason to understand why colluding followers would knowingly follow a toxic leader is personal ambition. They are aware of what they are getting into (although sometimes they do not realize the full extent of the potential consequences), but they see it as an opportunity to get what they want. Perhaps they feel that they have good insight into a leader who also acts out of personal, selfish ambition. They may even have the hubris to believe that they will be able to manoeuvre to the top – they might even be right!

2. Congruent values and beliefs

People are attracted to those with similar values and belief systems. That is generally true, and plays a big role in the formation of any group. People join political groups, activist organizations, community groups, online groups, and start companies and join companies when they see themselves reflected in the values of those groups.

People who have destructive impulses and toxic values also tend to be attracted in the same way. They can be very good at seeking out groups, organizations and leaders whose values match theirs. For some, the more unsavoury elements of that group may be a feature, not a bug.

3. Selfish values

People who have what psychologists call 'unsocialized values' (Hogan, 2006) are more likely to follow toxic leaders. Unsocialized values are essentially child-like values that go against the grain of those that are typically culturally appropriate and pro-social. For example, helping others, contributing to society or a community are 'socialized' values. Unsocialized values include things like greed or selfishness – anything that is ultimately self-serving, irrespective of the consequences to other people. A combination of ambition and selfish values makes people much more likely to follow toxic leaders and engage in destructive behaviours.

CASE STUDY: QANON, THE CURIOUS CASE OF THE DIGITAL CULT

QAnon first emerged on the image board 4chan in 2017 (see more explanation of 4chan in Chapter 12). The first post, like subsequent posts, uses cryptic language from an anonymous source purporting to be a high-level government official with 'Q' clearance.

The postings are anonymous, so no one really knows who QAnon is, although some analysts have suggested there are a few different QAnon posters whose language varies and is identifiable in tone and content (Mills et al., 2020). But the enduring themes centre around Donald Trump battling against a multitude of evil and unseen forces. In QAnon communities, Trump is often portrayed as a sort of messianic or crusading figure with depictions such as 'God-Emperor Trump' (Hine et al., 2017). In 2017, QAnon seemed more like an Internet joke or the work of trolls than a serious online community.

However, the conspiracy theory started to slowly grow, becoming particularly popular among a small group of Donald Trump's supporters. In 2018, QAnon followers started appearing at Trump rallies, waving flags and peddling their niche sect of conspiracy theories. The beliefs continued to morph and grow but had a few central themes. The primary, wildly untrue conspiracy theory revolved around the idea that former US President Donald Trump was fighting off the forces of darkness, paedophilia and the 'deep state' (an entrenched, embedded bureaucracy that wields undue influence and control). The ringleaders of these apparent forces of darkness are household names and the typical left-wing figures: Hillary Clinton, Barack Obama, George Soros, Oprah, Tom Hanks, the Dalai Lama. The list varies (Roose, 2020).

The conspiracy theories built up around QAnon are a fusion of some of the classic Internet conspiracy theories of the 2010s, like Pizzagate child-sex-trafficking conspiracy theories and some extremely niche ideas that are far from public discourse but common among subsets of online conspiracy theorists. For example, 'adrenochrome harvesting' tends to crop up, which is the idea that cabals of powerful people deliberately torture children to produce hormones that can only be harvested from humans during a fear-induced state. These adrenochromes can then apparently be made into a youth potion. It's bogus, since adrenochromes do exist, but aren't produced by the human body and don't have youth-enhancing properties. It's a pretty blatant repacking of the anti-Semitic blood-libel conspiracy theory that falsely accuses Jews of ritualistically sacrificing Christian babies. It's basically an old-school conspiracy theory with a biotech makeover. So QAnon repacked a range of already existing conspiracy theories to give them an American flavour and a godhead in Donald Trump.

While QAnon slowly gathered support in its initial years, in 2020 it burst out into the open. By the summer of 2020, research from the BBC (Sardarizadeh, 2020) found that QAnon posts had received over 100 million likes and comments, and QAnon videos received over 150 million views in 2020. And surprisingly to some, QAnon's popularity spread rapidly through Europe in 2020, especially in the UK and Germany (Bennhold, 2020).

In what initially seemed like an intensely American conspiracy theory, QAnon evolved in European countries to fit the national picture. In Germany, it picked up its own followers to become QAnon with German characteristics. Here, Angela Merkel was the enemy and Donald Trump was supposedly using NATO exercises as a secret military mission to liberate the German people from the tyranny of Merkel's liberalism and social democratic agenda. Of course, conspiracies about global cabals of elites secretly running the international order combined with violent putsch fantasies about government takeovers are not new to Germany's far right. This may be one reason why this conspiracy easily found its niche in certain circles within Germany.

The COVID crisis also fuelled QAnon conspiracies. Since QAnon followers are so dispersed and decentralized, and they produce so much of their own content, the conspiracies can quickly merge with other conspiracies and adapt to accommodate or accelerate similar beliefs. The idea about global cabals of shadowy elites is an extremely malleable conspiracy theory, so whatever form people's anxieties take, there is an easy (but always imperceptible) scapegoat.

The ambiguity and anxiety from a novel virus that rapidly turns into a pandemic is a fertile breeding ground for conspiracists too. A huge international threat to people's health and economic livelihood will, of course, fuel anxieties. And when people are scared, lacking good information and isolated, they are much more vulnerable to cults, toxic leaders and conspiracy theories. It should not be entirely surprising that, when people feel great anxiety and loss of control in their own lives, some will join groups that offer solidarity and try to provide an explanation (even if, in the case of QAnon, the explanation is totally false).

Some people report that they actually feel less anxiety 'understanding' the world, even if the explanation is that it's all a huge, dark satanic conspiracy theory. But more than the feeling of understanding, it is the group membership that offers feelings of comfort, security and belonging, which may not seem available anywhere else. That's the trade-off in joining a cult: believing a few things that are obviously untrue is a signifier of group membership. For people who already feel disconnected, alienated, alone or anxious, choosing to believe a few strange things may be a small trade-off for unconditional acceptance from a group.

RESISTING SOCIAL INFLUENCE

The problem though, and the reason psychologists call it *dys*function, is because reality eventually catches up with people and the consequences are particularly stark in workplaces. When a leader runs a company or a country based on their own impulses and social insecurities instead of facts, the decisions they make have real consequences for other people.

The definitions of psychological dysfunction actually allow for a very wide range of strange, eccentric and curious behaviour, as long as that behaviour doesn't put people in danger. For example, people can fall down rabbit holes of science fiction or fantasy writing, film and TV – imagining themselves as the characters, even dressing up as fantasy characters, acting out plotlines and engaging in elaborate roleplay.

The best way to conclude this chapter is a guide to resisting unwanted or toxic social influences. In the 2007 book *The Lucifer Effect*, esteemed social psychologist Philip Zimbardo offers a 10-step programme to reduce or resist unwanted social influences:

1. Admit mistakes – be aware of your own mistakes, and conscious of when you're getting in too deep.
2. Be mindful – do not automatically do what you think is expected of you; take a pause and observe your own emotional responses and instincts.
3. Take responsibility – you are ultimately responsible for your own actions.
4. Remember your individuality – you are not an object, a piece of a puzzle, a cog in a machine; do not let someone else diminish your agency or humanity.
5. Distinguish between just and unjust authority.
6. Understand the importance of group acceptance, but value independence.

7. Be frame-vigilant – observe how people pivot, frame an issue, and how it shapes value judgements.

8. Balance time perspective – it's easy to get too caught up in the moment and forget past experiences and future consequences. Don't let someone who wants something in the moment convince you that your past experience is irrelevant or that your future doesn't matter.

9. Don't sacrifice personal or civic freedom for the illusion of security – 'never sacrifice basic personal freedoms for the promise of security because the sacrifices are real and immediate and the security is a distant illusion' (p. 455).

10. Remember you can oppose unjust systems – if you see something that seems fundamentally wrong or immoral, you can participate, disengage or actively oppose it.

22

Online conspiracy theories, fear and isolation

THE EVOLVING IMPACT OF COVID

COVID dominated people's lives and the news and information they received during 2020, and carried on doing so in 2021. The first indicators of COVID-19 came to the attention of the World Health Organization on 31 December 2019. The WHO's Country Office in China picked up reports of 'viral pneumonia' in Wuhan with a cluster of cases from an 'unknown cause' reported by the WHO's Epidemic Intelligence from Open Sources platform (WHO, 2020). By 9 January 2020, news agencies were reporting that the outbreak was being caused by a novel coronavirus.

China was blocking access to international investigators and while the WHO reported that human transmission of the novel coronavirus was possible on 21 January, by the end of January governments around the world were beginning to realize how serious COVID-19 could be. On 28 January 2020, Robert O'Brien, Donald Trump's National Security Advisor, was warning about the severity. O'Brien had been warned by a colleague in China that the impact of the outbreak would be severe: 'Don't think SARS 2003, think influenza pandemic 1918' (Woodward, 2020).

By late January and early February the official information was still limited, but speculation along with images and videos were seeping out from China. The news was looking grim, but there still seemed to be limited understanding of the full potential of the virus. Videos and images, though, showed how bleak the situation was in Wuhan; viral videos revealed people shut in their apartments with the doors welded. There were many more concerning videos, images and blog stories, but little confirmed. On 22 January, Wuhan locked down and China started restricting internal travel within the country (Qin & Wang, 2020), but didn't suspend international flights until 26 March (Bradsher, 2020).

COVID-19 cases started to be reported in Europe and the United States in late January, and in late February China finally allowed World Health Organization scientists to investigate the COVID-19 outbreak, but would still only let very limited numbers of Centers for Disease Control (CDC) representatives in. By 25 February, public health officials were warning about the severity and the inevitability of COVID, but some world leaders were still downplaying the risk (while health and national security advisors had been warning of the risks for at least a month). On 26 February 2020, Donald Trump said, 'When you have 15 people – and the 15 within a couple of days is going to be down close to zero – that's a pretty good job we've done' (Woodward, 2020). On 3 March, UK Prime Minister Boris Johnson publicly boasted about visiting a hospital and shaking hands with COVID patients on the same day his Scientific Advisory Group promoted the importance of hand hygiene and not shaking hands.

Most of the world went into lockdown shortly after. Italy, initially the worst-hit country in Europe, locked down on 9 March. Poland shut its borders on 13 March, then Spain locked down on 14 March. Most of continental Europe went into lockdown that same week. Canada closed its borders to all foreign nationals on 16 March (Harris, 2020) and the UK's stay-at-home order came into force on 23 March. In March and April, the flow of international travel slowed to a trickle and various permutations of stay-at-home orders, regional and national lockdowns took effect around much of the world.

National and regional responses varied slightly but generally followed the same patterns in the spring of 2020. However, as new rules, restrictions, lockdowns and guidelines stretched on, regional responses changed and evolved while people's reactions to the crisis started to drift further apart. The impacts and the consequences of health problems and social and economic dislocation have not been spread equally. Yet as 2020 wore on, the psychological impacts of lockdown and isolation started to take their toll on mental health (Rossi et al., 2020; Hotopf,

2020) and social media was rife with conspiracy theories that rapidly went viral and then took hold.

SOCIAL ISOLATION

In the spring of 2020 most countries followed China in restricting the movement, association and economic activity of people between countries and within nations to reduce COVID infections. This was consistent with advice from all of the most respectable medical sources internationally (Kiesha et al., 2020) and subsequent medical research found lockdowns to reduce the spread of COVID-19 (Alwan et al., 2020)[2].

The consequences of lockdowns and social-distancing measures have been an increase in isolation, loneliness, social disconnection and a host of psychological factors that accompany those problems. One of the cascading consequences that has come out of the social and psychological changes in people's lives has been a large upswell of conspiracy theories.

Social isolation is worth investigating and has been a topic of study, because there are wide-ranging negative psychological effects of social isolation. Humans are social animals, and all social animals are wired for social contact. It doesn't just help us navigate our social world, social contact is essential for the proper development and regulation of neurotransmitters and stress hormones. Social isolation has long been a concern of psychologists, and even before the social distancing and isolation measures taken in response to COVID, nearly half of US adults reported sometimes or always feeling alone and nearly 40 per cent reported feeling isolated (Novotney, 2019).

The heightened health risks from the effects of social isolation have been described as equivalent to smoking 15 cigarettes per day by Julianne Holt-Lunstad, PhD Professor of Psychology and Neuroscience at Brigham Young University. Further research has suggested social isolation can be even more harmful to mental and physical health than obesity (Holt-Lunstad et al., 2015). Social isolation was found to increase mortality rates by 29 per cent.

---

2 *Much of the content in this chapter focuses on the psychological impact of social isolation, loss of control and fear. It should not be interpreted as medical or epidemiological advice.*

Social isolation has far-reaching consequences. Research during 2020 found national alcohol consumption increased, with escalations in substance abuse and misuse behaviour that tended to last longer than just for the period of isolation (Koopmann et al., 2020). Previous research suggested that the negative psychological effects of quarantine could last for years. Isolation causes acute and chronic stress symptoms, and substance misuse symptoms which previous research has found to linger for at least three years after the period of isolation has concluded (Brooks et al., 2020).

The negative consequences of social isolation are reduced or exacerbated by some key factors, including stressors:

- **Longer duration of quarantine.** The longer the isolation lasted, the more pronounced and more long-lasting the effect. Uncertainty or changes in the length of isolation also compounded the negative effects.
- **Infection fears.** The more people were worried about their risk of infection, the more stressful the lockdown experience. Generally people tend to estimate other people's risk of infection as slightly higher than their own.
- **Boredom.** Lack of mental and physical stimulation during periods of isolation was a significant problem for people in isolation.
- **Inadequate supplies.** Lack of proper supplies (including food, medical supplies, essentials) can cause acute anxiety.
- **Inadequate information.** More information about the infection risk, about the isolation plans and about the short- and long-term impacts helped to reduce stress.
- **Financial loss.** A major stressor can be the worry about losing income, work or employment benefits, either while isolating or in the longer term.
- **Stigma.** The negative attitudes of other people about those who catch the infection significantly increase anxiety of people who become infected, or at risk of becoming infected. Sexually transmitted diseases, especially HIV/AIDs are an example of some of the most stigmatized infections.

Social isolation can create even more problems for children, adolescents and young adults who are still developing neurologically and socially.

Because *social development* is such an important part of development, social isolation for adolescents can cause long-term changes in behaviour beyond the short-term effects of isolation.

A longitudinal study of university students found that the lockdown in response to the COVID-19 crisis led to a thinning out of students' social support networks and group studying: more students studied alone. There was also a significant negative impact on psychological health. Levels of stress, anxiety, loneliness and depressive symptoms got significantly worse, compared with before the crisis. The worst effects on poor mental health trajectories were from isolation from social support networks, lack of emotional support and physical isolation (Elmer et al., 2020).

Physiological effects
Social isolation isn't just a minor disruption, especially for young adults and adolescents; the neuro-scientific research suggests that social isolation has negative physiological effects for the developing brain. Isolation disrupts the HPA axis, which is the neurological system responsible for managing stress and processing threats (Hawkley et al., 2013). Social isolation in adolescents disrupts abilities for long-term planning and goal-directed behaviours even after social contact is reintroduced. Isolation tends to encourage 'habit-like' behaviours 'at the expense of goal-oriented actions' (Hinton et al., 2019). In other words, adolescents who are isolated are more likely to get caught up in repetitive behaviours that pass the time instead of taking steps to achieve long-term goals.

Chronic stress in combination with social isolation (or chronic stress caused by isolation) also has an effect on the brain's reward processing systems. The isolation contributes to preference for immediate rewards at the expense of long-term payoffs (Rakshasa & Tong, 2020). Combined with these factors, isolation also affects how people react to risk. High-risk decision-making increases under high stress conditions. Being part of a social group reduces the impact of stress, whereas isolation sees a much higher increase in high-risk behaviours.

We can see that being part of a healthy social group acts as a buffer against stress, and helps people understand and make sense of difficult and stressful situations. When people are isolated, they don't have access to the knowledge, experience and sources of resilience that would normally be available as part of a group: and even when the group doesn't have 'answers' to a problem, they can offer emotional support, comfort, solidarity and affection, which can significantly reduce the impact of stressors.

In this way, being part of a social group can also act as a guardrail against people spiralling into depressive behaviour, encourage healthy coping mechanisms and help people understand difficult and threatening circumstances. However, when people are stressed and alone, they are more likely to look for any type of group affiliation to reduce their distress. It should not be surprising that when people can't find the answers to stressful and challenging threats like the COVID-19 crisis, they are more vulnerable to conspiracy theories and falling into the communities that surround them online and in-person.

When people are isolated, they are more stressed, more impulsive, have less of an ability to work towards long-term goals and are more inclined to look for immediate solutions that temporarily reduce anxiety or provide relief. Then, is it surprising that more people fall into conspiracy theories to reduce anxiety, combat acute stress and find groups that may provide social support and a sense of belonging when people feel disconnected?

A PERFECT STORM OF FACTORS FOR CONSPIRACY THEORIES

Political scientists have tied isolation (both in individuals and in small groups) to conspiracy theories: 'Individuals embedded in isolated groups or small, self-enclosed networks who are exposed only to skewed information will more often hold conspiracy theories that are justified, relative to their limited informational environment'. (Sunstein & Vermeule, 2009).

Social isolation can lead to this fragmentation, and as people are cut off from larger social groups, community organizations, their workplace or other groups they might normally come into contact with, they create small in-groups that may not view information in the same way as most other people. 'Their theories may be unjustified from the standpoint of the wider society but justified from the standpoint of the individual or group. In these situations, the problem for the wider society is to breach the informational isolation of the small group or network'. (Sunstein & Vermeule, 2009).

The spread of conspiracy theories isn't just accidental though, and by training state media and their foreign-language editions we can see how conspiracy theories spread. A 2020 study by Rebello and colleagues at the Oxford Internet Institute tracked how state-backed news organizations in China, Iran, Russia and Turkey spread narratives on social media related to COVID in European languages like French, German and Spanish.

These can have large influence because networks like China's French language CGTN can push content to 75 million users; Russia's RT can push content to 27.5 million French users, 5 million German users and over 200 million Spanish-speaking users (the Spanish-language content is more influential in South America than in Europe).

Using this data, we can see how different national media groups push out different narratives and focus on specific aspects of the COVID-19 crisis. For example, Russian state-backed media drove narratives of civil disobedience and conflict with public authorities, and in more extreme cases suggested that a resulting economic crisis would lead to an 'uprising' in France. Russian German-language media focused on divides between the rich and the poor, suggesting that the COVID crisis would exacerbate social and economic problems and lead to larger divisions and inequality in German society.

Chinese and Turkish state-backed language coverage took a slightly different route, highlighting the weakness of democratic governments in their ability to combat the crisis while emphasizing their own outsized role in combating the crisis. Chinese state media developed a narrative of China as a global leader in the COVID response, with China to be the driving force of economic recovery and international humanitarian aid, while criticizing supposed divisions and weakness in Europe.

State-backed media groups from China, Russia and Iran all produced and encouraged conspiracy theories (Turkish media did not). Chinese state media in all languages disputed that COVID started in China, encouraged the misinformation that European strains of COVID did not originate in China, and circulated baseless theories that COVID-19 was a bioweapon developed in the United States. Russian and Iranian outlets joined in, making groundless connections between COVID-19 and US bioweapons programmes.

Russian state-backed media spent a great deal of time ambiguously discussing conspiracy theories about Bill Gates and the Bill and Melinda

Gates Foundation. Coverage included reports on conspiracy theorists (e.g. an Italian politician calling for the arrest of Bill Gates for crimes against humanity, with no evidence of such crimes). In some cases RT mocked the conspiracy theories about Bill Gates, but at the same time went to great lengths to list all of the details of the conspiracy theory. RT was particularly active on their German-language channels on this topic, showing how state-backed media can 'increase public engagement with conspiracy theories without directly supporting them'.

Trickle down
It's useful to understand the role in these state-backed media institutions in spreading certain narratives, as well as giving cover (if not explicit endorsement) to conspiracy theories. State-backed news sources like RT, Sputnik, CGTN and Xinhua should not be assumed to be trustworthy sources, although they deliberately create the majority of their content to be benign and mainstream news stories, and clickbait with a minority of content that's deliberate misinformation or propaganda. With hundreds of millions of international users in different languages, they are part of the information ecosystem online with effective social media presences. Hosting and pushing out misinformation on partisan, state-backed news platforms then allows the proliferation of this information on social media, blogs, forums and discussion groups.

All this is important because we are looking at a perfect storm of factors leading people to get caught up in conspiracy theories. Not only do we have all of the psychological factors that were listed earlier in this chapter, there are state-backed media channels with significant international reach pumping misinformation and conspiracy theories into the online and social media ecosystem, which quickly spread across platforms like Twitter, Facebook, Reddit and WhatsApp, among others.

Then throw into the mix what political scientists call 'conspiracy entrepreneurs'. These are public figures and social media influencers who peddle these conspiracy theories for their own reasons. 'Some conspiracy entrepreneurs are entirely sincere. Others are interested in money or power or in using the conspiracy theory to achieve some general social goal' (Sunstein & Vermeule, 2009). Instead of being consumers of the information, these conspiracy entrepreneurs actively create and disseminate new material, adding fuel to the fire and building up a following.

Psychological research on conspiracy theories further shows that people who are most likely to endorse conspiracy theories are socially marginalized and feel a lack of control in their own life (Moulding et al., 2016). People who start to see the world as threatening while at the same time feeling socially isolated and/or powerless are far more likely to get caught up in conspiracy theories. Then, finding conspiracy groups can help to alleviate some of these problems. The conspiracy theory doesn't just come up with an explanation of events, the groups surrounding conspiracy theories can also provide a sense of group cohesion, community and mutual understanding (Darwin et al., 2011). Conspiracy theories give a sense of meaning and security in an otherwise dangerous, threatening or confusing world.

23

Toxic leadership – an applied example

CASE STUDY: TOXIC LEADERSHIP IN OIL AND GAS

Background

To discuss how toxic leadership really looks in companies I spoke with an expert ombudsman and investigator who has decades of experience investigating and resolving issues around bullying and harassment in the workplace.

Her example, from an oil and gas company in the US, was of a director who she described as an 'extreme bully'. Someone whom people feared and believed, if they challenged him, their careers would be over. The majority of the roles in the company are both highly skilled and highly paid. Within the workplace there are many highly skilled technicians and engineers, identified as top performers throughout their career. It's a highly competitive organization that demands high performance as the norm, with exceptionally high compensation as an industry standard. People are making well over USD $100,000 beginning with supervisor positions, and substantially more at senior levels of management.

The compensation is important to note because the money is a significant draw for people to work there, and then losing that level of compensation acts as a significant disincentive for people to leave. 'You have to appreciate that leaving a job, even at the supervisory level, means you're losing a lot of money.' The professional community is

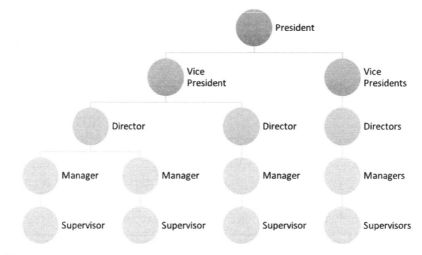

FIGURE 23.1 Organizational structure of the oil and gas company

relatively small, and often linked with membership in an association. 'Everyone knows everyone.'

There are clear hierarchies and reporting structures in place; this is not a 'flat organization'. People generally follow the managerial hierarchies and information tends to flow along the formal structures (see Figure 23.1). This is another important point because when these communication and reporting structures are rigidly enforced, it is much easier for one manager to restrict, control and manipulate information flow up to more senior leaders.

The spark

The problem with the director was initially identified when a supervisor was fired, who then called the company's anonymous whistleblower hotline. The supervisor made a complaint saying, 'I'm fired, that's not going to change. But you have to know that this is an extremely toxic work environment.' The whistleblower named the director as the source of the problems and then provided a list of specific incidents and reasons that the workplace was a toxic environment. The initial complaints were a laundry list of interconnected problems: nepotism, bullying, harassment and a culture of intimidation.

Barriers to fixing the problem

It was a challenging environment to begin investigating. The general culture of fear, and a closed environment, meant no one would talk to the investigator. People believed that any negative information about the director would get back to him and lead to severe recriminations. Initially 'they wouldn't even meet with me or be seen to be speaking to me' and 'they were terrified because the director was very good friends with the vice president.' Some of the bullying complaints that had come out of that company happened under the aegis of that vice president. There was a general feeling that participating in the investigation could be ineffective and damaging to anyone who participated. They had a general belief that the vice president was aware of the director's 'management style' and tacitly ignored it, or worse supported him through inaction. Many people 'knew' the director routinely targeted some managers and supervisors who then left the organization.

There were two major challenges: to overcome that culture of fear, and assure people that the investigation would be strictly confidential, and to provide validated 'proof' of the seriousness of the behaviours to the vice president. One person who eventually cooperated with the

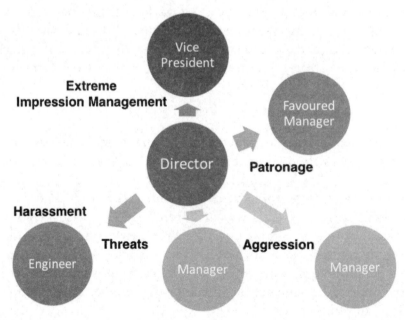

FIGURE 23.2 The relational organization chart

investigation said: 'It is not safe for me. If anyone knows I'm here today I'm fired tomorrow.' The culture created by a bully is evolving and creeps into all parts of the company. The power of a bully cannot be underestimated; and people directly impacted are targets not victims. 'These are people who are master engineers, highly educated, extremely strong, primarily male employees. They don't fit the stereotype of someone who is a schoolyard victim of a bully.'

There were two major barriers in this organization, which are common to toxic work environments run by bullies:

1. Productive environment – effective bullies often manage to create a workplace that looks extraordinarily effective from the outside. Tasks get completed, people fear missing deadlines, the team seems cohesive and anyone who doesn't toe the line is immediately removed. The first problem with assuming the team is effective is that healthy teams are actually *more* productive. What could be accomplished if everyone was able to work in an open and thriving environment? And the second problem is that these environments tend to be more effective at hiding problems than solving problems. Some of the more serious and damaging consequences often emerge later (a specific example of this is explained later in this case study).

2. Bullies manage up. Bullies are very effective at ingratiating themselves to those who are more powerful or more influential. They are 'sweetness and light' to the people who make the decisions, but completely different to people who they have power over. They choose their target(s) and systematically begin to undermine them to more senior people. Behaviours taken out of context and reported, performances lied about and rumours spread all begin the insidious devaluing of the target's contribution. This becomes very helpful to the bully when asking to extract someone from the team; the stage has been set.

The toxic behaviour

'What bullies do is create in-groups and out-groups' and they have a couple of 'chosen ones' that get all of the perks. The director, to them, is supportive, friendly and encouraging. They get power of and over the group. Nepotism is rampant in those environments because bullies select either for loyalty or obedience, and they put people who are loyal to them personally in positions of power. They create a 'bubble of people who support them', then spend all of their time managing up (for example, stealing ideas and passing them off as their own).

This creates an environment where the bully doesn't really do anything productive, but manipulates other people and then makes sure all of the information going upwards is intended to insulate the bully. In this case, that means people who complain either directly or through the whistleblower hotline are not taken seriously; the vice president says, 'Oh yeah, they were extremely incompetent.' Which is not true: in this case they were incredibly competent. 'It's typically people who are the most competent who are targeted. They are threatening to the bully who may be reacting out of fear with the knowledge he is not as competent.'

'What is really insidious is the people who are most competent, who are targeted, are the least able to recognize that they are being targeted' because they are:

1. **Star players in companies** – they've never had a bad performance review in their entire life. It undermines their confidence, and they may have never been in a situation where a person is deliberately lying about them, and to them, in order to exert control.

2. **Inexperienced** – they have no past experience to figure out what's going on. Often high performers who are early (or even late) in their career generally have more experience with positive, constructive and supportive environments. They may not have the experience of, or the emotional and psychological tools to deal with, toxic environments or bullies, because they don't have the experience or learned political savvy to go on the offensive.

3. **Socially targeted and isolated** – people make sense of their environment and their role within that environment based on social cues and interactions. When someone is suddenly the target of bullying and isolation, they don't have the information or tools to deal with the office politics. They may not have much experience with navigating the social snubs, insults, being ignored or intimidated. They have trouble understanding what's going on because the behaviour they are experiencing

is incongruent with their personal abilities, outlook and interpersonal relationships. They may not recognize the root cause (they are being targeted). They are often bewildered with how they arrived where they are, and when they discuss their concerns with others, they sound petty to themselves:

- 'So what if the director made a humiliating comment at the start of the meeting?'
- 'Hey, wasn't that my idea he just got recognized for?'
- 'He asked me to do the project on Monday and then gave it to someone else on Friday.'
- 'Why were my staff left off the communication, or not invited to the meeting?'
- 'Just a joke, just an oversight, no I did not say that – or ask that,' repeated again and again.

All of these factors erode people's confidence, then they get dismissed and they don't understand what's going on. Yet everyone else in the work group can see what's happening so they stop objecting. They may not fully understand but 'either subconsciously or consciously they start toeing the line', because they recognize the pattern and the consequences.

Scaling the barriers

So how does someone enter that kind of environment to find out what is really going on? How does an investigator get to the heart of those issues, establish trust and gather evidence that will make an impact? When so much effort and resources (both company resources and personal resources) are put into shutting people out, how can someone assess, identify and improve the problem?

When doing the investigation (also known as a workplace assessment), the investigator 'had to guarantee absolute anonymity'. First she went to the vice president of human resources, who 'I trust completely' and said 'I want you to handwrite a list of people in the organization that I need to talk to. I want to interview every person in the director's work group, anonymously. I will provide a summary of the feedback I receive and never use a comment that could identify someone. They don't need to let you know whether or not they actually met with me. I need another list of other people the director has daily interactions with. I want you to handwrite that list, give me names and phone numbers, and you are *not ever* to tell the vice president (or anyone else) who I have interviewed or who is on that list. I will only tell the VP who I interviewed by numbers or as a group (e.g. by how many supervisors, how many directors, work group A, B, VPs, etc.). I will report using themes, based on a pre-agreed list of questions.'

Some of the examples of things people said:

'On Monday and Tuesday you can't take anything to him, he just freaks out. He'll rage at you [for whatever].'

'Anything you take to him on Monday he will likely refute by Friday or he won't remember.'

'By Thursday he's usually pretty settled and then by Friday you can take something to him'.

'He will take credit for things he doesn't know anything about, and then screw it up when he tries to explain it or implement it.'

'He'll put people on the spot in meetings and humiliate them. He'll make sexist, rude comments to women walking in and out of the room (who are also highly educated engineers by the way).'

'He yells at people, is rude, and has a very short fuse.'

'He isn't the only bully; he has nurtured his leadership style with a few who mimic his approach.'

'He breaks confidences and confidentiality, gossips and plays one person against another.'

The problems with his behaviour stretched into most areas. 'Every possible component of nepotism is systemic here: he hires his friends, there were allegations of conflict of interest' (which wasn't investigated or proved but strongly suspected). 'He came from another company so he was giving work to consultants in other companies without going through proper bidding or procurement processes.' There were so many things wrong in everything he had responsibility for. It wasn't just a few minor mistakes or incompetence in one area, it was pernicious and endemic to his domain.

Yet because of his upward charm offensive, the vice president couldn't get past the idea that the complaint and investigation process wasn't (surely) just one disgruntled employee. In the eyes of senior management, this director was great, and 'was minutes away from the president offering him a vice presidency'. All of the negative information ran contrary to what senior leadership had seen or believed for a long time. He was about to receive a promotion and, although that was subsequently withdrawn, the organization wasn't prepared to get rid of this director.

Acknowledging the problem
The VP eventually acknowledged there was a problem that needed to be addressed. In addition to the extensive report of bullying treatment of staff, there were two other deciding factors.

1. Six months earlier at a Christmas party, the director was extremely drunk and he had threatened to kill an employee while in the toilets. After it happened, they didn't fire him, or even discipline him because 'it was a party and not at work'. Being intoxicated at a social function was not out of place for the culture that exists in the oil and gas industry, so the behaviour was shrugged off as 'Oh well, he was drinking.' As if that negates the issue instead of being an additional problem.
2. 'There was so much evidence of how destructive and unproductive' the behaviour was. The behaviour would be damaging in any department but 'he was in the safety department'. There was evidence that people within the safety department were avoiding bringing forward lower-level safety issues because they feared the response of the director. 'He shot the messenger.'

The potential consequences of this behaviour were too difficult to ignore: 'You could shut down a plant.' The arguments for dealing with this behaviour were very convincing. And 'people change when the consequences of *not changing their behaviour* outweigh the demands of changing.'

There was also a clear problem, in this case, with drugs and alcohol that was embedded in the toxic behaviours. Not being functional early in the week, and only beginning to operate later in the week, is a fairly strong indicator of substance abuse. And while it's only one cause, drug and alcohol problems often go alongside toxic behaviours: 'As an aside, every sexual harassment complaint I've investigated in the last 15 years, has had drugs and/or alcohol involved.'

Finding a solution

The VP had a direct and comprehensive conversation with the director about the complaints and behaviours, and the director's problems with alcohol. 'I did not put the suspicions about alcohol in my report – but discussed the implications with the VP.'

A very clear and thorough conversation with the vice president was necessary: 'I had to be very direct. There is bullying by the director, reported by a significant percentage of people who work with and around him. Not just one or two people who are disgruntled because they received a poor performance rating or were dismissed, or their ideas stolen.' The point had to be made forcefully with emphasis on the consequences of the behaviour. Threatening to kill someone is bad, keeping people in fear of their career and afraid to raise warning bells, with implications that could lead to closing down a large plant is also bad.

Trust plays a major role in moving forward. Trust in the process and the investigator was important in influencing the VP's decisions to take action. 'The responsible vice president had to be convinced that the investigator was objective and thorough so he could see the behaviours that had to change. Without a clear and comprehensive view he could not hold the director's feet to the fire, and nothing would have been done.'

It was recommended that the director have counselling and leadership coaching with emphasis on emotional intelligence, with a referral to a specific expert and suggested addictions counselling. It was also recommended that, after six to twelve months, an anonymous 'climate check' be conducted related to his behaviour in the working environment. The company used the same questions in the 'climate check' as were used in the investigation. The director was told there would be a follow-up evaluation looking at the impact of his leadership and behaviour on the people around him.

'He changed his behaviour and leadership approach and he went to drug and alcohol counselling.' In this case, the intervention and the behaviour change were effective. 'The VP of HR said that it was … almost miraculous. When the company later did emotional intelligence training for their leaders, that director stood up, took responsibility for his own behaviour and promoted the need for a different style of leadership.'

This case study is an illustration of how toxic behaviour does not occur in a vacuum. There are a variety of contributing factors that all come together to allow (and sometimes encourage) toxic behaviour to thrive or go unchecked. It clearly demonstrates many of the different things that have been discussed in this book.

- Bad apples and bad barrels (Chapter 2). The individual's behaviour was allowed to go unchecked, with a more senior leader who did allow that kind of environment, and other problems like substance abuse were not just tolerated but part of the culture, exacerbating other factors.
- The dark side of brightness (Chapter 6). From the outside, the team is productive; from the senior leadership's point of view it *looks* good. People who are fired are made to look like bad apples.
- The dark side – who succeeds and why (Chapter 8). Nepotism helps, but managing up is also a big part of this.
- Why leaders fail, and warning signs (Chapter 11). Big red flags, especially when it is in the safety department and neglecting problems. The consequences of failure are too big.
- Cluster B traits/behaviours (Chapter 13). Unchecked aggression, bullying, abuse, harassment. This is a good example of other factors – in this case the additional factor of substance abuse. It's important to properly identify and treat the problem.
- Toxic triangle (Chapter 21). The mix of a toxic leader, threatening environment and colluding followers.

Afterword

This book was written in 2020, which turned out to be a challenging time as well as a fascinating time to explore the psychology of online behaviour and digital communication. The sudden shift from physical to digital environments in almost most aspects of life demonstrated the importance of understanding how people think, act, communicate and work in digital environments.

I had been researching remote and hybrid work throughout 2018 and 2019, and published a whitepaper in January 2020 that stated, 'Remote work is no longer the "work of the future", it is the work of today' (MacRae & Sawatzky, 2020). I could not have predicted how quickly or how completely that would prove true in 2020.

The year 2021 has thrown some fascinating new events into the mix, which tie so directly into the topics of *Dark Social* that I wish I had extra time and chapters to devote to understanding the trends and the themes behind the events.

One of the most interesting events that came storming to worldwide attention was the social media furore surrounding the company GameStop, and the online community Wall Street Bets (WSB) on Reddit that fuelled the interest. Depending on which point of view you take, this could have been a group of novice investors piling into a meme, a pack of oddball retail investors identifying a serious opportunity to bet against the greed and overreach of a hedge fund or a group of troublemakers trying to manipulate financial markets. Either way, Netflix saw the direction the wind was blowing immediately and commissioned a documentary that should provide an interesting and entertaining look into the story.

There are a few reasons why the GameStop saga is a fascinating example of so many of the forces discussed in chapters of this book.

First, of course, it does show that users grouping together on social media can be a powerful force and it throws out new problems for industries and their regulators. A few hedge funds can (and sometimes do) collude to manipulate prices stocks, and public figures (like Elon Musk) use their position to affect traditional financial markets as well as new financial markets like cryptocurrencies. Occasionally they get caught, slapped on the wrist and pay a nominal fee (in the case of Elon Musk and the Securities and Exchange Commission, the small fee was USD$20 million (SEC, 2018)).

Yet how can regulators or industries react to thousands or hundreds of thousands of retail investors following the same trends, fads and memes? Can they haul hundreds of thousands of people from countries around the world in front of a Senate committee to testify and respond, 'Senator, I just like the stock'?

Second, there should also be a significant amount of scepticism about how original, organic and grassroots some of these trends become once billions of dollars are involved. Could there have been targeted bots, disinformation and propaganda campaigns related to GameStop? While Russia has demonstrated how cheap and effective misinformation and propaganda campaigns can be on social media, don't hedge fund managers, wealthy investors or other organizations have access to the same resources?

This book discussed some of the cyber operations that have been organized or commission by the Russian state. Russian operations rely heavily on independent security contractors and non-state entities to conduct many of their digital intelligence or propaganda operations: could someone else hire the same people to conduct a campaign to pump up a stock or asset price? Of course they could. What about a campaign to smear a reputation or try to drive down another asset price? Just as easy. While there may have been independent retail investors purchasing or selling GameStop stock, this behaviour was almost certainly targeted by influence campaigns.

If 2016 was the watershed moment for large-scale social media intervention in political campaigns, the next few years could see a flashpoint for social media campaigns targeting financial markets. That's not to say online propaganda and disinformation are by any means the only reasons for speculative asset bubbles or the only factor influencing the behaviour of investors, but they certainly can have an impact.

This is why it is so important to understand the social and psychological forces acting within social systems in social media: that influence is built into these systems as a key feature. They are *designed* to influence behaviour. Users' attention and purchasing decisions are the commodity.

We are still shaping the role of digital technology in communication, in work and even in structuring our relationships and communities. This isn't something that we can watch passively. We should not assume that we will be unaffected by these trends even if we opt out of certain social media platforms or digital tools. Humans are naturally and continuously shaped by their social environment. We understand ourselves, partially, in terms of our relationships with other people. We're not going to eliminate all of the behaviour we view as undesirable online – but we can have a positive impact on our immediate social networks and communities online, just like in the physical world. We can be more deliberate and mindful about what we opt in to, as well as what we choose not to participate in.

It's worth revisiting the three key themes of this book and to consider what influence you have on your friends and colleagues, and how they influence you. Are there are any changes you would like to make to your own behaviour online or offline?

Key themes

1. **Online behaviour is an extension of offline characteristics.** People's reactions are influenced by different environments (including online environments), but the underlying psychological processes are remarkably similar. Online behaviour is an extension of behaviour in general: it is not fundamentally different in online spaces than it is in physical spaces.

2. **People can improve.** Understanding the internal forces (such as personality) as well as the external forces (such as the social environment) can help people to change their behaviour and improve themselves and have a positive influence on others around them.

3. **Work can get better.** The social environment has a profound impact on people, their work, their productivity and their wellbeing. By actively trying to improve these environments, work can be better *for* people and bring out the best *from* people.

References

Abalakina-Papp, M., Stephan, W. G., Craig, T., & Gregory, W. L. (1999). 'Beliefs in conspiracies'. *Political Psychology*, 20(3), 637–647. https://doi.org/10.1111/0162-895X.00160

Adeane, A. (12 October 2020) 'QAnon and the rabbit hole election'. [Audio Podcast]. BBC World Service. https://www.bbc.co.uk/programmes/w3cszvsc

Almond, D., & Du, X. (2020). 'Later bedtimes predict President Trump's performance'. *Economic Letters, 197*, https://doi.org/10.1016/j.econlet.2020.109590

Alwan, N. A., Burgess, R. A., Ashworth, S., Beale, R., Bhadeilia, N., Bogaert, et al. (2020). 'Scientific consensus on the COVID-19 pandemic: We need to act now'. *The Lancet*, 396(10260). https://www.thelancet.com/journals/lancet/article/PIIS0140-6736(20)32153-X/fulltext.

American Psychiatric Association [APA]. (2013). *Diagnostic and Statistical Manual of Mental Disorders*, Fifth Edition. (DSM-5). London: American Psychiatric Publishing.

Amos, H. (2012). 'From Russia with likes: Kremlin to launch Facebook-style social network'. *Guardian*.

Amro, A. (2020). 'The life of Ghosn: Fugitive tycoon to star in documentary and a mini-series'. *Japan Today*. https://japantoday.com/category/entertainment/The-life-of-Ghosn-Fugitive-tycoon-to-star-in-documentary-and-a-mini-series.

Andrews, E. L. (1999). 'Nissan looms large for Renault's "Cost Killer"'. *New York Times*.

Armstrong, M. (2017). *Armstrong's handbook of performance management: An evidence-based guide to delivering high performance*. London: Kogan Page.

Asmolov, G. (2010). 'Russia: Blogger Navalny tries to prove that fighting the regime is fun'. *Global Voices Online*. https://globalvoices.org/2010/10/27/russia-blogger-alexey-navalny-on-fighting-regime/ (Accessed 28 July 2020).

Atroszko, P. A., Demetrovics, Z., & Griffiths, M. D. (2020). 'Work addiction, obsessive-compulsive personality disorder, burn-out, and global burden of disease: Implications from the ICD-11'. *International Journal of Environmental Research in Public Health*, 17(2).

Autocar (2020). 'Who is Carlos Ghosn and why is this saga going to run and run?' https://www.autocar.co.uk/car-news/industry/who-carlos-ghosn-and-why-saga-going-run-and-run (Accessed 10 February 2020).

Bandura, A. (1977). *Social learning theory*. Upper Saddly River, USA: Prentice-Hall.

Barrick, M. R., Mount, M. K., & Judge, T. A. (2001). 'Personality and performance at the beginning of the next millennium: What do we know and where do we go next?' *International Journal of Selection and Assessment*, 9(1-2), 9–30.

Barsade, S., (2002). 'The Ripple Effect: Emotional contagion and its influence on group behaviour'. *Administrative Science Quarterly*, 47(4), 644–675.

Barsade, S. (2020). 'The contagion we can control'. *Harvard Business Review.* https://hbr.org/2020/03/the-contagion-we-can-control

Barton, H. (2016). 'Persuasion and compliance in cyberspace'. In I. Connolly, M. Palmer, H. Barton, & G. Kirwan. *An introduction to Cyberpsychology*. (pp. 111–123).

BBC. (2018). 'Twitter bot purge prompts backlash'. https://www.bbc.com/news/technology-43144717

BBC. (2020). 'MPs and peers demand Russia interference inquiry'. https://www.bbc.co.uk/news/uk-politics-54725758.

Beardsley, E. (2010). 'Fake TV game show "tortures" man, shocks France'. NPR. https://www.npr.org/templates/story/story.php?storyId=124838091&t=1591892639058

Beck, A. T., Davis, D. D., & Freeman, A. (Eds.). (2016). *Cognitive Therapy of Personality Disorders* (3rd Ed.). London: Guilford Press.

Berger, J., & Milkman, K. L. (2012). 'What makes online content go viral?' *Journal of Marketing Research*, 49(2), https://doi.org/10.1509/jmr.10.0353

Bertua, C., Anderson, N. and Salgado, J. F. (2011). 'The predictive validity of cognitive ability tests: A UK meta-analysis'. *Organizational Psychology*, 78(3), 387–09.

Bloomberg (n.d.). Free Speech Systems LLC. https://www.bloomberg.com/profile/company/0897673D:US (Accessed 1 October 2020).

Bloomberg News. (1999). 'World Business Briefing: Asia; Betting on a turnaround'. In the *New York Times*. https://www.nytimes.com/1999/11/09/business/world-business-briefing-asia-betting-on-a-turnaround.html

Borgesius, F. J. Z., Trilling. D., Möller, J., Bodó, B., de Vreese, C. H., & Helberger, N. (2016). 'Should we worry about filter bubbles?' *Internet Policy Review*, 5(1), 1–16.

Boyd, R. L., Spangher, A., Fourney, A., Nushi, B., Ranade, G., Pennebaker, J. W., Horvitz, E. (2018). 'Characterizing the Internet Research Agency's social media operations during the 2016 US Presidential election using linguistic analysis'. https://psyarxiv.com/ajh2q/ (Retrieved 29 July 2020).

Bradsher, K. (2020). 'To slow virus, China bars entry to almost all foreigners'. *New York Times*.

Brooks, S. K., Webster, R. K., Smith, L. E., Woodland, L., Wessely, S., Greenberg, N., & Rubin, G. J. (2020). 'The psychological impact of quarantine and how to reduce it: Rapid review of the evidence'. *The Lancet*, 395(10227), 912–920.

Cappelli, P. (2019). 'How to calculate the cost of turnover – carefully'. *Human Resource Executive*. https://hrexecutive.com/how-to-calculate-the-cost-of-turnover-carefully/

Carvill, M., & MacRae, I. (2020). *Myths of social media: Dismiss the misconceptions and use social media effectively for business.* London: Kogan Page.

Cheetham, M., Pedroni, A. F., Antley, A., Slater, & M., Jancke, L. (2009). 'Virtual Milgram: Empathetic concern or personal distress? Evidence from functional MRI and dispositional measures'. *Frontiers in Human Neuroscience.* https://doi.org/10.3389/neuro.09.029.2009

Chen, A. (2015). 'The Agency'. *New York Times* magazine. https://www.nytimes.com/2015/06/07/magazine/the-agency.html

Chozick, A. & Rich, M. (2018). 'The rise and fall of Carlos Ghosn'. *New York Times.* https://www.nytimes.com/2018/12/30/business/carlos-ghosn-nissan.html

Coaston, J. (2018). 'YouTube, Facebook and Apple's ban on Alex Jones, explained'. *Vox.* https://www.vox.com/2018/8/6/17655658/alex-jones-facebook-youtube-conspiracy-theories

Connolly, I., Palmer, M., Barton, H., & Kirwan, G. (Eds.). (2016). *An Introduction to Cyberpsychology.* Oxford: Routledge.

Coolidge, F. L., & Segal, D. L. (2007). 'Was Saddam Hussein like Adolf Hitler? A personality disorder investigation'. *Military Psychology*, 19(4), 289–299.

Costa, P., & McCrae, R. R. (1990). 'Personality disorders and the five-factor model of personality'. *Journal of Personality Disorders,* 4(4), 362–371.

Costa, P., & McCrae, R. (1992). 'Four ways five factors are basic'. *Personality and Individual Differences,* 13, 357–372.

Darwin, H., Neave, N., & Holmes, J. (2011). 'Belief in conspiracy theories. The role of paranormal belief, paranoid ideation and schizotypy'. *Personality and Individual Differences,* 50(8), 1289–1293. https://doi.org/10.1016/j.paid.2011.02.027

Deary, I. J., Penke, L., & Johnson, W. (2010). 'The neuroscience of human intelligence differences'. *Nature Reviews Neuroscience,* 11, 201–211.

de Ribera, O. S., Kavish, N., Katz, I. M., & Boutwell, B. B. (2019). 'Untangling intelligence, sociopathy, antisocial personality disorders, and conduct problems: A meta-analytic review'. *European Journal of Personality,* 33, 529–564.

Desjardines, J. (2018). 'How Google retains more than 90 per cent of market share'. *Business Insider.* https://www.businessinsider.com/how-google-retains-more-than-90-of-market-share-2018-4?r=US&IR=T.

Dodes, L. (2019). Sociopathy. In B. Lee (Ed.). *The dangerous case of Donald Trump: 37 psychiatrists and mental health experts assess a president.* New York: St. Martin's Press.

Dolinski, D., Grzyb, T., Folwarcznym, M., Grzybala, P., Krzyszycha, K., Martynowska, K., & Trojanowski, J. (2017). 'Would you deliver an electric shock in 2015? Obedience in the experimental paradigm developed by Stanley Milgram in the 50 years following the original studies'. *Social Psychological and Personality Science,* 8(8), 1–7.

Dooley, B. (2020). 'With Nissan's Carlos Ghosn gone, Greg Kelly faces trial alone'. *New York Times.*

Dragan, L. (2016). 'Let's talk about fake Amazon reviews: How we spot the fakes'. *New York Times*: Wirecutter. https://www.nytimes.com/wirecutter/blog/lets-talk-about-amazon-reviews/

Eggert, M., A. (2013). *Deception in selection: Interviewees and the psychology of deceit.* London: Gower Pub Co.

Elmer, T., Mepham, K., & Stadtfeld, C. (2020). 'Students under lockdown: Comparisons of students' social networks and mental health before and during the COVID-19 crisis in Switzerland'. *PLOS ONE.* https://doi.org/10.1371/journal.pone.0236337

Enrich, D. (2019). 'Deutsche Bank and Trump: $2 billion in loans and a wary board'. *New York Times.*

Flaxman, S., Goel, S., & Rao, J. M. (2016). 'Filter bubbles, echo chambers, and online news consumption'. *Public Opinion Quarterly,* 80, 298–320.

Flood, C. 'The Online Workplace'. In I. Connolly, M. Palmer, H. Barton, & G. Kirwan (Eds.). *An Introduction to Cyberpsychology.* London: Routledge.

Follath, E., von Ilsemann, S. Kraske, M., Leick, R., & Mascolo, G., von Rohr, M. Sparl, G., Wolf, M., & Zand, B. (2006). 'Torture in the name of freedom'. (C. Sultan, Trans.). *New York Times.* https://www.nytimes.com/2006/02/20/international/europe/torture-in-the-name-of-freedom.html

Fournier, J. C. (2015) 'Assessment of Personality Disorders'. In A. T. Beck, D. D. Davis, & A. Freeman (Eds.). *Cognitive Therapy of Personality Disorders.* Third Edition. London: The Guilford Press.

Fournier, J. C. (2016). 'Assessment of Personality Pathology'. In A. T. Beck, D. D. Davis, & A. Freeman (Eds.), *Cognitive Therapy of Personality Disorders* (3rd. Ed.). London: Guilford Press.

Friedersdorf, C. (2018). 'YouTube extremism and the long tail'. *The Atlantic.*

Furnham, A. (2005). 'Self-estimated intelligence, psychometric intelligence and personality'. *Psychologia,* 48, 182–192.

Gabriel, M., Critelli, J. W., & Ee, J. S. (1994). 'Narcissistic illusions in self-evaluations of intelligence and attractiveness'. *Journal of Personality and Individual Differences,* 62(1), 143–155.

Gilchrist, K. (2020). 'Ex-Nissan boss Carl Ghosn launches business programme to revive Lebanon's struggling economy'. CNBC. https://www.cnbc.com/2020/09/30/nissans-ex-chairman-carlos-ghosn-launches-business-program-in-lebanon.html

Gladwell, M. (2009). *Outliers: The story of success.* Penguin.

Gonzalez-Franco, M., Slater, M., Birney, M.E., Swapp, D., Haslam, S.A., & Reicher, S.D. (2018) 'Participant concerns for the Learner in a Virtual Reality replication of the Milgram obedience study'. *PLOS ONE* 13(12). https://doi.org/10.1371/journal.pone.0209704

Greenberg, A. (2019*). Sandworm: A new era of cyberwar and the hunt for the Kremlin's most dangerous hackers.* London: Penguin Random House.

Greenwood, J. (2018). 'How would people behave in Milgram's experiment today?' *Behavioural Scientist.* https://behaviouralscientist.org/how-would-people-behave-in-milgrams-experiment-today/

Gunitsky, S. (2015). 'Corrupting the cyber-commons: Social media as a tool of autocratic stability'. *Perspectives on Politics,* 13(1), 52–54.

Gunitsky, S. (2020). 'Democracies can't blame Putin for their disinformation problem'. *Foreign Policy.* https://foreignpolicy.com/2020/04/21/democracies-disinformation-russia-china-homegrown/

Harris, S. (2020). 'Why Canada has shut its international borders to most travellers during COVID-19'. CBC.

Hasell, A. (2020). 'Shared emotion: The social amplification of partisan news on Twitter'. *Digital Journalism.* DOI: 10.1080/21670811.2020.1831937

Hawk, S. T., van den Eijnden, R. J. J. M., van Lissa, C. J., & ter Bogt, T. F. M. (2019). 'Narcissistic adolescents' attention-seeking following social rejection: Links with social media disclosure, problematic social media use, and smartphone stress'.

Hawkley, L. C., Cole, S. W., Capitanio, J. P., Norman, G. J., & Cacioppo, J. T. (2013). 'Effects of social isolation on Glucocoritcoid regulation in social mammals'. *Hormones and behaviour*, 62(3), 314–323.

Hern, A. (2017). 'Netflix's biggest competitor? Sleep'. *Guardian.* https://www.theguardian.com/technology/2017/apr/18/netflix-competitor-sleep-uber-facebook

Hicks, J. P. (1989). 'Michelin to acquire Uniroyal Goodrich'. *New York Times.*

Hine, G. E., Onaolapo, J., Cristofara, E. D., Kourtellis, N., Leontiadis, I., Samaras, R., Stringhini, G., & Blackburn, J. (2017). 'Kek, Cucks, and God Emperor Trump: A measurement study of 4chan's Politically Incorrect forum and its effects on the Web'. *Proceedings of the Eleventh International Conference on web and social media.* https://arxiv.org/pdf/1610.03452.pdf

Hinton, E. A., Li, D. C., Allen, A. G., Gourley, S. L. (2019). 'Social isolation in adolescence disrupts cortical development and goal-dependent decision-making in adulthood, despite social reintegration'. ENEURO.0318-19.2019; DOI: 10.1523/ENEURO.0318-19.2019.

Hogan. R. (2006). *Personality and the fate of the organization.* Hillsdale, NJ: Erlbaum.

Holt-Lunstad J, Smith T.B., Baker, M., Harris, T., & Stephenson, D. 'Loneliness and Social Isolation as Risk Factors for Mortality: A Meta-Analytic Review'. *Perspectives on Psychological Science.* 2015, 10(2):227–237. DOI: 10.1177/1745691614568352.

Hotopf, M., John, A., Kontopantelis, E., Webb, R., Wessely, S., McManus, S., & Abel, K. M. (2020). 'Mental health before and during the COVID-19 pandemic: A longitudinal probability sample of the UK population'. *The Lancet Psychiatry*, 7(10), 883–892. DOI: https://doi.org/10.1016/S2215-0366(20)30308-4

Howard, P. N., Ganesh, B., Liotsiou, D., Kelly, J., & Francois, C. (2019). 'The IRA, social media and political polarization in the United States 2012–2018'. Computational Propaganda Research Project, Oxford University.

Huang, G., & Li, K. (2016). 'The effect of anonymity on conformity to group norms in online contexts: A meta-analysis'. *International Journal of Communication*, 10, 398–415.

Huff, C. (2004). 'Where personality goes awry'. *Monitor on Psychology*, 35(3). https://www.apa.org/monitor/mar04/awry

Hughes, A., & Wojcik, S. (2019). '10 facts about Americans and Twitter'. Pew Research Center. https://www.pewresearch.org/fact-tank/2019/08/02/10-facts-about-americans-and-twitter/

Ikegami, (JJ), J., & Maznevski, M. (2020). 'Revisiting Carlos Ghosn's global leadership style: Making sense of his fall from power'. *Advances in Global Leadership*, 12(3), 3–21.

Intelligence and Security Committee of Parliament [ISCP]. (2020). Russia.

Iyengar, S., & Hahn, K. S. (2009). 'Red media, blue media: Evidence of ideological selectivity in media use'. *Journal of Communication*, 59, 19–39.

John, O. & S, C. (2007). 'The importance of being valid: Reliability and the process of construct validation'. In R. W. Robins, R. C. Fraley, & R. F. Kreuger (Eds.). *Handbook of research methods in personality psychology*. Cambridge: Cambridge University Press.

Juan-Torres, M., Dixon, T., Kimaram, A. (2020). 'Britain's Choice: Common ground and division in 2020s Britain'. *More in Common*. https://www.britainschoice.uk/media/wqin4k4x/britain-s-choice-full-report-2020.pdf

Kiesha, P., Liu, Y., Russell, T. W., Kucharaski, A. J., Egoo, R. M., & Davies, N., et al. (2020). 'The effect of control strategies to reduce social mixing on outcomes of the COVID-19 epidemic in Wuhan, China: A modelling study'. *The Lancet*. DOI: https://doi.org/10.1016/S2468-2667(20)30073-6.

Koopmann, A., Georgiadou, E., Kiefer, F., & Hillemacher, T. (2020). 'Did the General Population in Germany Drink More Alcohol during the COVID-19 Pandemic Lockdown?'. *Alcohol and Alcoholism*, 55(6), 698–699, https://doi.org/10.1093/alcalc/agaa058.

Kramer, A. D. I., Guillory, J. E., & Hancock, J. T. (2014). 'Experimental evidence of massive-scale emotional contagion through social networks'. *Proceedings of the National Academy of Sciences of the United States of America*, 24, 8788–8790.

Lanier, J. (2018). 'How the Internet failed and how to recreate it'. University of California, C Santa Cruz. https://www.youtube.com/watch?v=KNOlqzMd2Zw.

Lazarsfeld, P. F., Berelson, B., & Gaudet, H. (1944). *The People's Choice: How the voter makes up his mind in a Presidential campaign*. New York: Columbia University Press.

Lee, B. (Ed.). (2019). *The dangerous case of Donald Trump: 37 psychiatrists and mental health experts assess a President*. New York: St. Martin' s Press.

Lee, P. (2016). 'Learning from Tay's introduction'. *Official Microsoft Blog*. https://blogs.microsoft.com/blog/2016/03/25/learning-tays-introduction/

Lewis, P. (2017). 'Our minds can be hijacked: The tech insiders who fear a smartphone dystopia'. *Guardian*.

Livesley, W. J. (2003). *Practical management of personality disorder*. London: The Guilford Press.

Lukianoff, G., & Haidt, J. (2018). *The coddling of the American mind: How good intentions and bad ideas are setting up a generation for failure*. London: Allen Lane.

Ma, G., Fan, H., Sen, C., & Wang, W. (2016). 'Genetic and neuroimaging features of personality disorders: State of the Art'. *Neuroscience Bulletin*, 32(3), 286–306.

MacFarquhar, N. (2018). 'Inside the Russian troll factory: Zombies and a breakneck pace'. *New York Times*.

MacKinnon, A., (2020). '4 Key takeaways from the British report on Russian interference'. *Foreign Policy*.

MacLean, E. L. (2013). 'Reducing employee turnover in the Big Four public accounting firms'. *CMC Senior Theses*. 745. https://scholarship.claremont.edu/cmc_theses/745.

Macnamara, B. N., & Maitra, M., (2019). 'The role of deliberate practice in expert performance: Revisiting Ericsson, Krampe & Tesch-Römer' (1993). *Royal Society Open Science*, 6(8). https://doi.org/10.1098/rsos.190327

MacRae, I. (2015). 'High Potential Traits Inventory: Leadership Capacity Report Testing Manual'. *High Potential Psychology*.

MacRae, I. (2020a). 'Now more than ever HR must translate culture into digital spaces'. *People Management Magazine* (CIPD).

MacRae, I., & Furnham, A. (2017). *Motivation and performance: A guide to motivating a diverse workforce*. London: Kogan Page.

MacRae, I., & Furnham, A. (2018). *High Potential: How to spot, manage and develop talented people at work*. London: Bloomsbury.

MacRae, I., & Sawatzky, R. (2020a). 'What makes a high potential remote worker?' *HR Magazine*. https://www.hrmagazine.co.uk/article-details/what-makes-a-high-potential-remote-worker

MacRae, I., & Sawatzky, R. (2020b). 'Remote Working: Personality and performance research results'.

Magnavita, J. J., & Anchin, J. C. (2014). *Unifying Psychotherapy: Principles, methods, and evidence from clinical sciences*. New York: Springer Publishing Company.

Martin, E. A., Bailey, D. H., Cicero, D. C., & Kerns, J. G. (2015). 'Social networking profile correlates of schizotypy'. *Psychiatry Research*, 200(0), 641–646.

Maslow, A. (1954). *Motivation and personality*. New York: Harper.

McCain, J. L., & Campbell, W. K. (2019). 'Narcissism and social media use: A meta-analytic review'. *Psychology of Popular Media Culture*, 7(3), 308–327.

Messing, S., & Westwood J. S. (2012). 'Selective exposure in the age of social media: Endorsements trump partisan source affiliation when selecting news online'. *Communication Research*, 80, 298–320.

Milgram, S. (2019). *Obedience to authority: An experimental view*. New York, NY: Harper Perennial; Reprint Edition.

Millikin, J. P., & Fu, D. (2005). 'The global leadership of Carlos Ghosn at Nissan'. *Thunderbird International Business Review*, 47(1), 121–137.

Mills, A., Longoria, J., & Gnanasambandan, S. (28 May 2020). Rabbit Hole: Seven: 'Where we go one' [Audio podcast]. *New York Times*. Retrieved from: https://www.nytimes.com/2020/05/28/podcasts/rabbit-hole-qanon-conspiracy-theory-virus.html

Mitchell, A. Jurkowitz, M., Oliphant, J. B., & Shearer, E. (2020). 'Americans who mainly get their news on social media are less engaged, less knowledgeable'. Pew Research Center. https://www.journalism.org/2020/07/30/americans-who-mainly-get-their-news-on-social-media-are-less-engaged-less-knowledgeable/

Montero, D. (2017). 'Alex Jones settles Chobani lawsuit and retracts comments about refugees in Twin Falls, Idaho'. *LA Times*. https://www.latimes.com/nation/la-na-chobani-alex-jones-20170517-story.html

Morey, L. C., Gunderson, J., Quigley, B. D., & Lyons, M. (2000). 'Dimensions and categories: The "Big Five" factors and the DSM personality disorders'. *Assessment*, 7(3), 203–2016.

Moulding, R., Nix-Carnell, S., Schnabel, A., Nadeljkovic, M., Burnside, E. E., Lentini, A. F., & Mehzabin, N. (2016). 'Better the devil you know than a world you don't? Intolerance of uncertainty and worldview explanations for belief in conspiracy theories'.

Mueller, R. (2019). *Report on the investigation into Russian interference in the 2016 Presidential election*. US Department of Justice.

Muench, F. (2014). 'The new Skinner Box: Web and mobile analytics'. *Psychology Today*.

Mullen, B., Migdal, M. J., & Rozell, D. (2013). 'Self-awareness, deindividuation, and social identity: Unravelling theoretical paradoxes by fulfilling empirical lacunae'. *Personality and Social Psychology*, 29(9), 1071–1081.

Müller, J., Hösel, V., & Tellier, A. (2020). 'Filter bubbles, echo chambers, and reinforcement: Tracing populism in election data'. *Physics and Society*.

Navarro, J. (2018). 'The end of detecting deception'. *Psychology Today*. https://www.psychologytoday.com/gb/blog/spycatcher/201807/the-end-detecting-deception

Nicas, J. (2020). 'Why can't the social networks stop fake accounts?' *New York Times*.

Novotney, A. (2019). 'The risks of social isolation'. *Monitor on Psychology*, 50(5).

Oldham, J. M., & Morris, L. B. (1995). *New Personality self-portrait: Why you think, work, love and act the way you do*. London: Bantam Books.

Overholser, J. (1996). 'The Dependent Personality and interpersonal problems'. *The Journal of Nervous and Mental Disease*, 184(1), 8–16.

Owen, D., & Davidson, J. (2008). 'Hubris syndrome: An acquired personality disorder? A study of US Presidents and UK Prime Ministers over the last 100 years'. *Brain*, 132(5), 1396–1406.

Owen, D. (2012). *The Hubris Syndrome: Bush, Blair and the intoxication of power*. (New Edition). York: Methuen.

Padilla, A., Hogan, R., & Kaiser, R. B. (2007). 'The toxic triangle: Destructive leaders, susceptible followers, and conducive environments'. *The Leadership Quarterly*, 18, 174–194.

Painter, R. W. (2016). 'It is possible for Trump to be a good President'. *New York Times*.

Papasavva, A., Zannettou, S., De Cristofaro, E., Stringhini, G., & Blackburn, J. (2020). *Raiders of the Lost Kek: 3.5 years of augmented 4chan posts from the Politically Incorrect board*. 14th International AAAI Conference on Web and Social Media (ICWSM 2020).

Parkin, S. (2018). 'Has dopamine got us hooked on tech?' *Guardian*.

Parks-Leduc, L., & Guay, R. P. (2009). 'Personality, values, and motivation'. *Personality and Individual Differences*, 47(7), 675–684. DOI: 10.1016/j.paid.2009.06.002

Patricof, A., Harris, T., & Forhoohar, R. (2019). 'The future of regulating Big Tech: Facebook, YouTube, and beyond'. [Panel Discussion]. *Vanity Fair*. https://www. vanityfair.com/video/watch/the-future-of-regulating-big-tech-facebook-youtube-and-beyond

Paulhus, D. L. (2012). *Overclaiming on personality questionnaires*. In M. Ziegler, C. MacCann, & R. D. Roberts (Eds.), *New perspectives on faking in personality assessment* (pp. 151–164). Oxford University Press.

Peter, L, J., & Hull, R. (1969). *The Peter Principle: Why things always go wrong*. Morrow.

Pfeifer, J. H., Iacoboni, M., Mazziotta, J. C., Dapretto, M. (2008). 'Mirroring others' emotions relates to empathy and interpersonal competence in children'. *Neuroimage*, 39(4). DOI: 10.1016/j.neuroimage.2007.10.032

Polyanskaya, A., Krivov, A., & Lomko, I. (2003). 'Big Brother's Virtual Eye'. *Vestnik*, 9(320).

Qin, A., & Wang, V. (2020). 'Wuhan, centre of Coronavirus outbreak, is being cut off by Chinese authorities'. *New York Times*.

Rady, M. (2020). *The Hapsburgs: The rise and fall of a world power*. London: Allen Lane.

Rahmani, F., Hemmati, A., Cohen, S., & Meloy, J. R. (2019). 'The interplay between antisocial and obsessive-compulsive personality characteristics in cult-like religious groups: A psychodynamic decoding of the DSM-5'. *International Journal of Applied Psychoanalytic Studies*, 16, 258–273.

Rakshasa, A. M., & Tong, M. T. (2020). 'Making "good" choices: Social isolation in mice exacerbates the effects of chronic stress on decision-making'. *Frontiers in Behavioural Neuroscience*. https://doi.org/10.3389/fnbeh.2020.00081

Ravenscraft, E. (2019). 'Facebook notifications are out of control: Here's how to tame them'. *New York Times*.

Raymond, N., & Shepardson, D. (2020). 'US arrests two men wanted by Japan over ex-Nissan boss Carlos Ghosn's escape'. *Reuters*. https://www.reuters.com/article/us-nissan-ghosn-idUSKBN22W1XD

Rebello, K., Schwieter, C., Schliebs, M., Joynes-Burgess, K., Elswah, M., Bright, J., & Howard, P. N. (2020). 'COVID-19 news and information from state-backed outlets targeting French, German and Spanish-speaking social media users'. *Oxford Internet Institute*.

Robson, D. (2019). *The Intelligence Trap: Why people do stupid things and how to make wiser decisions*. London: Hodder & Stoughton.

Robson, D. (2020). 'The reasons why people become incompetent at work'. BBC.

Roose, K. (2019). 'YouTube product chief on online radicalization and algorithmic rabbit holes'. *New York Times*.

Roose, K. (2020). 'What is QAnon, the viral pro-Trump conspiracy theory?' *New York Times*.

Rossi, R., Socci, V., Talevi, D., Mensi, S., Niolu, C., Pacitti, F., Di Marco, A., Rossi, A., Siracusano, A., & Di Lorenzo, G. (2020). 'COVID-19 pandemic and lockdown measures impact on mental health among the general population in Italy'. *Frontiers in Psychiatry*. https://doi.org/10.3389/fpsyt.2020.00790

Sachse, R. & Kramer, U. (2018). 'Clarification-oriented psychotherapy of Dependent Personality Disorder'. *Journal of Contemporary Psychotherapy*. https://link.springer.com/article/10.1007/s10879-018-9397-8

Sample, I. (2019). 'Blow to the 10,000-hour rule as study finds practice doesn't always make perfect'. *Guardian.*

Select Committee on Intelligence: United States Senate. (2020). 'Russian active measures campaign and interference in the 2016 U. S. election'. Volume 2: Russia's use of social media with additional views. Report Number 116-XX. https://www.intelligence.senate.gov/sites/default/files/documents/Report_Volume2.pdf

U.S. Securities and Exchange Commission [SEC]. 'Elon Musk settles SEC fraud charges: Tesla charged with and resolves securities law charge'. [Press Release]. https://www.sec.gov/news/press-release/2018-226

Shaer, M. (2014). 'What emotion goes viral the fastest?' *Smithsonian Magazine.* https://www.smithsonianmag.com/science-nature/what-emotion-goes-viral-fastest-180950182/

Slater, M., Antley, A., Davison, A., Swapp, D., Guger, C., Barker, C., et al. (2006) 'A Virtual Reprise of the Stanley Milgram Obedience Experiments'. *PLOS ONE* 1(1). https://doi.org/10.1371/journal.pone.0000039Smith, R. E. (2019). *Rage Inside the Machine: The prejudice of algorithms, and how to stop the Internet making bigots of us all.* London: Bloomsbury.Stengel, R. (2020). 'Domestic disinformation is a greater menace than foreign disinformation'. *Time.* https://time.com/5860215/domestic-disinformation-growing-menace-america/

Sternisko, A., Cichocka, A., & Van Bavel, J. J. (2020). 'The dark side of social movements: Social identity, non-conformity, and the lure of conspiracy theories'. *Current Opinion in Psychology*, 35, 1–6.

Subotnik, R. F., Olszewski-Kubilius, & Worrell, F. C. (2011). 'Rethinking giftedness and gifted education: A proposed direction forward based on psychological science'. *Psychological Science*, 12(1), 3–54.

Sunstein, C., & Vermeule, A. (2009). 'Conspiracy Theories: Causes and cures'. *Journal of Political Philosophy*, 17(2), 202–227.

Torgersen, S. Lygren, S., Oien, P. A., Onstad, S., Edvarsen, J., Tambs, K., Kringlen, E. (2000). 'A twin study of personality disorders'. *Comparative Psychiatry*, 41(6), 416–425.

Treglown, L., Cuppello, S., Darby, J., Bendriem, S., Mackintosh, S., Ballaigues, M., MacRae, I., & Furnham, A. (2020). 'What makes a leader? An investigation into the relationship between leader emergence and effectiveness'. *Psychology*, 11(9).Trump, M. L. (2020). *Too much and never enough: How my family created the world's most dangerous man.* London: Simon & Schuster. Tsang, A, (2020). 'Nissan sues Carlos Ghosn for $90 million'. *New York Times.*

Van Praet, D. (2019). 'Emotional contagion drives social media'. *Psychology Today.* https://www.psychologytoday.com/gb/blog/unconscious-branding/201909/emotional-contagion-drives-social-media.

Vincent, J. (2016). 'Twitter taught Microsoft's AI chatbot to be a racist asshole in less than a day'. *The Verge.* https://www.theverge.com/2016/3/24/11297050/tay-microsoft-chatbot-racist. Wagner, K. (2019). 'Facebook bans Alex Jones, Milo Yiannopoulus, other far-right figures'. Bloomberg. https://www.bloomberg.com/news/articles/2019-05-02/facebook-bans-alex-jones-yiannopoulos-other-far-right-figures

Ward, C., Polglase, K., Shukla, S., Mezzofiore, G., & Lister, T. (2020). 'Russian election meddling is back – via Ghana and Nigeria – and in your feeds'. CNN. https://edition.cnn.com/2020/03/12/world/russia-ghana-troll-farms-2020-ward/index.html.

Watson, D., Stasik, S. M., Ro, E., & Clark, L. A. (2013). *Integrating Normal and Pathological Personality. Assessment*, 20(3), 312–326. DOI: 10.1177/1073191113485810.

Wheaton, M. G., & Ward, H. E. (2020). 'Intolerance of uncertainty and obsessive-compulsive personality disorder'. *Personality Disorders: Theory, Research, and Treatment*, 11(5), 357–364. https://doi.org/10.1037/per0000396

Wiggins, J. S., & Pincus, A. (1989). 'Conceptions of personality disorders and dimensions of personality'. *Psychological Assessment*, 1(4), 305–316.

Wojcik, S., Hughes, A., & Remy, E. (2019). 'About one in five adult Twitter users in the US follow Donald Trump'. Pew Research Center. https://www.pewresearch.org/fact-tank/2019/07/15/about-one-in-five-adult-twitter-users-in-the-u-s-follow-trump/

World Health Organization. Mental Health in the Workplace. World Health Organization; Geneva, Switzerland: 2019. Available online: https://wwwwhoint/mental_health/in_the_workplace/en/ (Accessed 20 June 2020).

World Health Organization [WHO]. (2020). Archived: WHO Timeline – COVID-19.

Zannettou, S., Caulfield, T., De Cristofaro, E., Kourtellis, N., Leontiadis, I., Sirivianos, M., Stringhini, G., & Blackburn, J. 'The web centipede: understanding how web communities influence each other through the lens of mainstream and alternative news sources'. (2017). 17th ACM Internet Measurement Conference (IMC 2017).

Zannettou, S., Caulfield, T., Blackburn, J., De Cristofaro, E., Sirivianos, M., Stringhini, G., & Suarez-Tangil, G. (2018). 'On the Origins of Memes by Means of Fringe Web Communities'. In ACM Internet Measurement Conference.

Zannettou, S., Caufield, T., Bradlyn, B., Cristofaro, E., Stringhini, G., & Blackburn, J. (2020). 'Characterizing the use of images in state-sponsored information warfare operations by Russian trolls on Twitter'. 14th International AAAI Conference on Web and Social Media (ICWSM 2020). https://arxiv.org/pdf/1901.05997.pdf (Retrieved 29 July 2020).

Zheng, Y. (2008). *Technological Empowerment: The Internet, State and Society in China*. Stanford, CA: Stanford University Press.

Zimbardo, P. (1969). 'The human choice: Individuation, reason, and order v. deindividuation, impulse and chaos'. *Nebraska Symposium on Motivation*, 17, 237–307.

Zimbardo, P. (2007). *The Lucifer Effect: Understanding how good people turn evil*. New York: Random House.

Index

Abu Ghraib prison, torture in 22,
    27–8, 240
adjustment/response to stress –
    personality trait 179, 181, 182,
    222, 223–4
advertising 32, 36, 37, 49, 235–6
aggressive personality style 79–80, 91,
    93, 94–5, 97, 98–9, 100, 153–5,
    182, 187, 222, 243
algorithms 18, 32, 34, 35, 36, 47, 48,
    202, 209, 217, 227–8
Amazon workplace surveillance
    tech 110–12
ambiguity acceptance – personality
    trait 179, 181, 182, 222, 225
amplification, online message 230, 231,
    234, 235
anonymity and trolling 103–4
antisocial personality disorder 61,
    222
anxious personality styles (Cluster C)
    168–76, 242
    'normal' personality traits 182
    online behaviour 171, 173–4, 176
    see also perfectionistic personality style;
    selfless personality style; sensitive
    personality style
artificial intelligence (AI) 228, 233–7
assertive personality styles (Cluster
    B) 152–64, 238, 243–4
    'normal' personality traits 182

online behaviour 154–5, 156–7,
    158–9, 161–4
    see also aggressive personality style;
    confident personality style; dramatic
    personality style; impulsive
    personality style
'astroturfing' in advertising 235–6
autocratic regimes, online strategies
    of 214–17

Bandura, Albert 43
Bannon, Steve 217
behavioural influences
    classical conditioning 40–1
    operant conditioning 41–2, 44
    reinforcement schedules 44–7
    social learning 43–4
Big Five personality traits 118–19, 178
Blair, Tony 130, 131
borderline personality disorder 105–6
bots 228, 233–7
Brexit referendum, Russian interference
    in 219–20
bullies, workplace 164–7, 203–6, 258–67
    see also toxic leadership
Bush, George W. 130, 131

Cambridge Analytica 219
censorship 214–15, 216
childhood and personality
    development 50, 52–7, 60–2

classical conditioning 40–1
Cognitive Behavioural Therapy (CBT) 88
colluding and conformer followers
  59–60, 95, 238–9, 241–4
competitiveness – personality trait 179,
  181, 222, 225, 226
confident personality style 69–70,
  83–4, 91, 92–3, 94, 96–7, 98, 99,
  100, 108, 128, 157–9, 182, 222, 243
confirmation bias 34
conscientiousness – personality trait 66,
  69, 179, 182, 222, 223, 225
conspiracy theories 34, 36, 143, 148,
  149–51, 176, 217, 234, 245–7, 251
counter-mobilization, online 214
COVID crisis and lockdown
  (2020) 17, 249–53, 255–6
cults 37, 176, 244–7
curiosity – personality trait 179, 222,
  225
cyberweaponry 211–14, 219
  see also Internet Research Agency
    (IRA), Russia; misinformation and
    fake news

'Dark Social' 18–19
deepfakes 228
democratic domestic online
  misinformation 217–19
diathesis-stress model 57–9
discounting the positives 56
discourse framing, online 214–15
discrimination, online 36, 219
dopamine levels 41, 45
dramatic personality style 81–2, 93, 94,
  95–6, 98, 100, 155–7, 178, 182, 243
DuckDuckGo 34
dysfunction, levels of see function and
  dysfunction, levels of

eccentric personality types (Cluster A)
  141–51
  'normal' personality traits 181
  social media context 143–4, 145–6,
    147–51

see also solitary personality style;
  unconventional personality style;
  wary personality style
election manipulation 47, 151, 218,
  220, 227–8
elite coordination online 215–16
emotional contagion, online 231–3
emotional maltreatment/abuse 56, 61
empathy 30, 60, 61, 68, 69, 177–8,
  184, 187
ethical guidelines, social media
  campaign 219–20
experience and success 119–21
extreme content, internet 34, 35, 47–9,
  106, 149, 234

Facebook 36, 42, 46–7, 150, 213, 219,
  232, 237
fake news see misinformation and fake
  news
fake product reviews 235–6
family dysfunction 52–3
filter bubbles 17, 18, 32
  creation of 33–5
  group membership 37
  issues with 35–6
  marketing strategies 37
  media influence 33
financial market manipulation 268–9
fixed interval and ratio reward
  schedules 45–6
Foreign Policy magazine 220
4chan 147–9, 233, 244
function and dysfunction, levels
  of 67–70, 177–8, 182–4

GameStop saga 268–9
gatekeepers, information 35–6
genetics 23, 51–2, 57–8
Ghosn, Carlos 128, 131–6
goal setting 68, 69, 107
Google algorithms, manipulation 227–8
group dynamics 90–1
Gunitsky, Professor Seva 214–15,
  216, 217

hidden identity   103–4
High Potential Traits Indicator
    (HPTI)   119, 178–82, 222–3
    negative perception of extreme
        scores   224
hoax 9/11 threat (2014)   211–12
hubris syndrome   128–30

ideal self   105, 107
identity/sense of self   68, 69, 177–8,
    183–4, 185, 186, 187
imitating/testing behaviour   43–4
impression management   107–9,
    234–5
impulsive personality style   80–1, 91,
    93, 95, 96, 97–8, 105–6, 159–62
influencers   35–6
InfoWars   149–51
Instagram   42, 213
intelligence and success   117–18
intelligence, self-estimated   191–2
Internet Research Agency (IRA),
    Russia   210–14, 218, 227–9
intimacy   68, 69, 178, 184, 186, 187
invalidating environments   54–5

Johnson, Boris   250
Jones, Alex   36, 149, 150, 234

leadership failure, factors contributing
        to   127–8
    Carlos Ghosn case study   128, 131–6
    hubris syndrome   128–31
    preventing derailment   136–8
leadership success, factors contributing
        to   116–17
    experience   119–23
    HPTI traits   222–3
    ideal leadership model   222–3
    intelligence   117–18
    motivation   123–5
    'new manager' case study   125–6
    personality traits   118–19
    practice   121–3
    see also toxic leadership

likes/endorsements/shares   42
long tail effect   48–9
lying and deception employee selection
        process   195–8

market segmentation   36
marketing   37, 209
masks   103
media influence, traditional   33, 35
Microsoft   233–5
Milgram experiment   23–6, 29–30
mirroring behaviour   61
misinformation and fake news   17, 20,
    37, 149–51, 211–20, 227–9, 235–6,
    254–7, 269
motivation   123–5
multi-source/360 degree feedback
    192–4
Musk, Elon   269

Navalny, Alexei   216
narcissists   69–70, 158–9, 192,
    222, 238
negative filtering   56
neglectful parents   55
New York Times   210, 211, 212, 231
newspaper biases   33, 34–5
notifications, digital   40–1

Obama, Barack   212, 230
obedience to authority   23–6, 29–30
obsessive-compulsive personality
    disorder   69, 70, 106–7, 168
online behaviour
    aggressive personality style   154–5
    anonymity   103–4, 154
    confident/overconfident personality
        style   158–9
    dramatic personality style   156–7
    empathy   30, 185–6
    ethical campaign guidelines   219
    group membership   37
    impulsive personality style   161–2
    levels on functioning   185–6
    Milgram experiment replicated   29–30

and offline characteristics   19, 103,
   105–6, 115, 270
perfectionistic personality   176
selfless personality style   173–4
sensitive personality style   171
solitary personality style   145–6
trolls   103, 154–5, 185–6
unconventional personality type   147
wary personality type   143–4
   see also Social Media Platforms
operant conditioning   41–2, 44, 47
optimality model   66
   levels of functionality   67–8
   wellbeing/'normal' behaviour   67–70
   workplace performance   70–1
over-protective/over-involved
      parents   55–6, 61
overconfidence   157–9
oversight in the workplace   112, 113,
   114, 136
Owen, Lord David   128–9

parents/caregivers, influence of   52–7,
   60–2
Parler and Gab   207
Pavlov, Ivan   40
perceived power   26–7
perfectionistic personality style   65,
   66, 69, 87–8, 91, 92, 94–5, 97,
   98, 99, 100–1, 106–7, 168, 174–6,
   182, 242
performance management   112, 113, 114
performance monitoring   17, 109–12,
   113, 114
personality differences,
      understanding   89–91, 101
personality disorders   19, 50, 129
   diathesis-stress model   57–9
   Donald Trump   59–62, 71–3, 129–30
   genetics vs. environment   23–9,
      51–7
   identifying in the workplace
      188–98
   levels of functionality and
      dysfunction   67–71

narcissism   69–70, 152, 158–9, 192,
   222, 238
rigid thinking patterns   74, 165,
   177, 194
risk factors   52, 53, 55, 57, 58, 59
self-fulfilling prophecies   88
and self in borderline PD   105–6
and self in obsessive-compulsive
   PD   106–7
sociopathy   60, 152, 192, 239
vs. personality styles   51, 75
personality styles   51, 74–5
aggressive   79–80, 91, 93, 94–5,
   97, 98–9, 100, 153–5, 182, 187,
   222, 242
confident   83–4, 91, 92–3, 96–7, 99,
   100, 108, 157–9, 182, 222, 242
dramatic   81–2, 93, 94, 98, 100,
   155–7, 178, 182, 242
High Potential Traits Indicator
   (HPTI)   179–82
impression management   108
impulsive   80–1, 91, 93, 95, 96,
   97–8, 105–6, 159–62
perfectionistic   87–8, 91, 92,
   94–5, 97, 98, 99, 100–1, 174–6,
   182, 242
selfless   85–7, 92, 93, 95, 96–7,
   99–100, 171–4, 182, 242
sensitive   84–5, 93, 95, 96–7, 98–9,
   169–71, 182, 242
solitary   76–8, 92–3, 144–6, 178,
   181, 186–7
unconventional   78–9, 93–4, 97, 99,
   108, 146–7, 181
wary   75–6, 91–2, 96, 97–8, 99, 100,
   142–4, 181, 222
   see also anxious personality styles
   (Cluster C); assertive personality
   styles (Cluster B); eccentric
   personality styles (Cluster A)
personality traits   65, 66, 70, 119,
   178–82, 188–9
Peter, Laurence J.   70–1
Peter principle   70–1

Politically Incorrect image board,
    4chan 148
positive and negative reinforcement 41
positive role models and protection 57
practice and experience 121–3
pre-selected personalization 34–5, 36
preference divulgence, online 215
prison guards, Abu Ghraib 27–8, 240
privacy issues 20, 34, 110, 219

QAnon 37, 244–7

racial biases 36
Reddit 42, 148, 149, 268
reinforcement schedules 44–6
relationships, maintaining
    reciprocal 68, 69
risk approach – personality trait 179,
    181, 182, 222, 225
risk aversion and parenting 56
risk taking behaviour 79, 91, 94, 128,
    153, 169, 170, 171
Rogers, Carl 104–5
Russian cyberweaponry and
    misinformation 211–14, 216,
    219–20, 227–9, 255–6, 260

scapegoats/'bad apples' 22–3, 158, 209,
    215, 234
search engines 32, 34, 36
selection process and senior
    leadership 137
self-awareness and leadership 137–8
self-direction 68, 69, 177–8, 184, 185,
    187
self-esteem 65, 68, 70, 83–4, 104–5
self-estimated intelligence 191–2
self-image 104, 105, 108, 243
self-reports 194–5
self-selecting personalization 34
selfless personality style 85–7, 92, 93,
    95–7, 168, 171–4, 242
sensitive personality style 84–5, 93,
    95–7, 98–9, 168, 169–71, 242
'shadow psychology', Jungian 19

shared values in the workplace 101
Skinner, B.F. 41–2, 46
Slack 41, 44
Slater, Mel 29–30
social animals, humans as 17, 39, 251
social comparison 104–5
social isolation 33, 232, 251–2
    children and adolescents 252–3
    conspiracy theories 254–7
    physiological effects 253
social learning 43–4
social media platforms 31, 35
    4chan 147–9, 233, 244
    classical conditioning 40–1
    cultures and subcultures 202,
        206–8
    domestic misinformation in
        democratic regimes 217–19
    Donald Trump's use of 229–30
    dramatic personality style 156–7
    ethical guidelines for
        campaigns 219–20
    fake online profiles 235–7
    gatekeepers and influencers 35–6
    as gauge of general opinion 206–8
    impulsive personality style 161–2
    influencing behaviour 38–9, 40–1,
        42, 43–4, 46–9, 269–70
    InfoWars/misinformation 149–51
    lack of transparency 36, 219
    likes/endorsements/shares 42
    limiting autonomy 36
    obsessed networker case study
        162–4
    operant conditioning 42–3
    polarization 35, 214
    reinforcement schedules 46–7
    sensitive personality style 171
    social learning 43–4
    social sorting 36
    solitary personality style 145–6
    time spent on 39, 47
    use by autocratic regimes 214–17
    see also filter bubbles; misinformation
        and fake news

social networks and leadership
    selection 137
social sorting 36
sociopathy 60, 152, 192, 239
solitary personality style 76–7, 144–6,
    178, 181, 186–7
spiritual online platforms 147
Spotify 150
Stanford prison experiment 26–7, 239
stress and personality disorders 58–9
sunken cost fallacy 73
surveillance
    impression management 108–9
    in the workplace 109–12, 113
    workplace misbehaviour 112–13

Tay, chatbot 233–5
television, cruelty and humiliation
    on 29
three domains of self 104–5
toxic environments, institutional 22–3
toxic leadership
    20th century mass
        communication 221
    case study 203–6
    colluding and conformer
        followers 238–9, 241–5
    conducive/threatening
        environment 241–2
    HPTI traits – Donald Trump case
        study 223–6
    oil and gas industry case study
        258–67
    online 203–6, 223
    personality styles/disorders 222
    President Donald Trump case
        study 223, 225–30
    resisting 247–8
    toxic triangle 59–60, 95, 239–44
toxic social influence, resisting 247–8
Trump, Donald 59, 129–30, 151, 217,
    245, 246
    COVID-19 250
    digital behaviour 229–30
    early adulthood 71–3

early childhood development 60–1
father, Fred 60–2, 72–3
HPTI trait scores 223, 225
mother, Mary 60
as president 223, 225–30
real estate career 72–3
in school 61–2
self-promotion 72–3
US election (2016) 213
Trump, Mary L. 59, 60
Twitter 148–9, 151, 207, 213, 223,
    225, 229–30, 233–5

unconventional personality style 78–9,
    93–4, 97, 99, 108, 146–7, 181
unstructured play/time, benefits of 56
US Armed Forces 22, 28
US election (2016) 210, 213, 220,
    227–8, 230

variable ratio and interval reward
    schedules 45–6
videoconferencing 109
virtual character, torture of 29–30
virtuous cycles 119–20

Wall Street Bets (WSB) 268–9
wary personality style 75–6, 91–2, 96,
    97–8, 99, 100, 142–4, 181, 222
workplace issues 20, 270
    ability to manage people 71
    Amazon surveillance case study
        110–12
    clashes and conflicts 89–90, 91, 93,
        94, 95, 96, 97, 98, 99, 100, 101–2
    company culture in digital
        space 201–2
    CVs and interviews 194
    deception and employee
        selection 195–6
    employee biographical data 190–1
    gender biased performance 192
    group dynamics 90–102
    High Potential Traits Indicator
        (HPTI) 178–82

identifying personality
   disorders 188–98
levels of function and
   dysfunction 182–4
managing conflict 101–2
manipulative bully case study
   164–7
multi-source/360 degree
   feedback 192–3
observation data 192–3
oversight 112, 113, 114
performance management 112, 113,
   114
performance monitoring 17, 109–12
personality styles in 75–88, 91–102

personality tests 195
personality traits 65, 66, 69, 70,
   178–82
the Peter principle 70–1
reinforcement schedules 44–5
shared values/vision 101
surveillance 109–12, 113, 114
testing employee abilities 191–2
see also toxic leadership
World Trade Center terrorist
   attacks 129, 130

YouTube 42, 48–9, 148, 150, 211

Zimbardo, Philip 26–7, 28, 239